STUDIES IN RUSSIA AND EAST E

formerly Studies in Russian and East E

This series includes books on general, po... social and cultural themes relating to Russia and East Europe ... edited by members of the School of Slavonic and East European Studies in the University of London, or by authors working in association with the School. Titles already published are listed below. Further titles are in preparation.

Phyllis Auty and Richard Clogg (*editors*)
BRITISH POLICY TOWARDS WARTIME RESISTANCE IN YUGOSLAVIA AND GREECE

Elisabeth Barker
BRITISH POLICY IN SOUTH-EAST EUROPE IN THE SECOND WORLD WAR

Richard Clogg (*editor*)
THE MOVEMENT FOR GREEK INDEPENDENCE, 1770–1821: A COLLECTION OF DOCUMENTS

Olga Crisp
STUDIES IN THE RUSSIAN ECONOMY BEFORE 1914

John C. K. Daly
RUSSIAN SEAPOWER AND 'THE EASTERN QUESTION', 1827–41

Dennis Delatant and Harry Hanak (*editors*)
HISTORIANS AS NATION BUILDERS: CENTRAL AND SOUTH-EAST EUROPE

Jane Grayson and Faith Wiyzell (*editors*)
NIKOLAY GOGUL: TEXT AND CONTEXT

D. G. Kirby (*editor*)
FINLAND AND RUSSIA, 1808–1920: DOCUMENTS

Martin McCauley
THE RUSSIAN REVOLUTION AND THE SOVIET STATE, 1917–1921: DOCUMENTS (*editor*)

KHRUSHCHEV AND KHRUSHCHEVISM (*editor*)
KHRUSHCHEV AND THE DEVELOPMENT OF SOVIET AGRICULTURE

COMMUNIST POWER IN EUROPE, 1944–1949 (*editor*)

MARXISM–LENINISM IN THE GERMAN DEMOCRATIC REPUBLIC: THE SOCIALIST UNITY PARTY (SED)

THE GERMAN DEMOCRATIC REPUBLIC SINCE 1945

THE SOVIET UNION UNDER GORBACHEV (*editor*)

Martin McCauley and Stephen Carter (*editors*)
LEADERSHIP AND SUCCESSION IN THE SOVIET UNION, EASTERN EUROPE AND CHINA

Martin McCauley and Peter Waldron
THE EMERGENCE OF THE MODERN RUSSIAN STATE, 1855–8

Evan Mawdsley
THE RUSSIAN REVOLUTION AND THE BALTIC FLEET

Laszló Péter and Robert B. Pynsent
INTELLECTUALS AND THE FUTURE IN THE HABSBURG MONARCHY 1890–1914

J. J. Tomiak (*editor*)
WESTERN PERSPECTIVES ON SOVIET EDUCATION IN THE 1980s

Stephen White and Alex Pravda (*editors*)
IDEOLOGY AND SOVIET POLITICS

IDEOLOGY AND SOVIET POLITICS

Edited by

Stephen White

Department of Politics and Institute of Soviet and East European Studies, University of Glasgow

and

Alex Pravda

Royal Institute of International Affairs and Department of Politics, University of Reading

MACMILLAN PRESS

in association with the School of Slavonic and East European Studies University of London

First published 1988

Published by
THE MACMILLAN PRESS LTD
Houndmills, Basingstoke, Hampshire RG21 2XS
and London
Companies and representatives
throughout the world

Filmsetting by Vantage Photosetting Co. Ltd
Eastleigh and London

Printed in Hong Kong

British Library Cataloguing in Publication Data
Ideology and Soviet politics. – (Studies in
Russia and East Europe).
1. Ideology—History 2. Communism—
Soviet Union—History—20th century
3. Soviet Union—Politics and government
—1917- I. White, Stephen, *1945*– II. Pravda
III. Series
320.947 JN6581
ISBN 0–333–43449–8 (hardcover)
ISBN 0–333–43910–4 (paperback)

Contents

List of the Contributors

Mary Buckley, Department of Politics, University of Edinburgh.

Peter Duncan, Royal Institute of International Affairs, London.

David A. Dyker, School of European Studies, University of Sussex.

Alfred B. Evans, Department of Political Science, California State University.

Graeme Gill, Department of Government, University of Sydney.

Alfred G. Meyer, Department of Political Science, University of Michigan.

Alex Pravda, Department of Politics, University of Reading.

Stephen Shenfield, Centre for Russian and East European Studies, University of Birmingham.

Michael E. Urban, Department of Political Science, Auburn University, Alabama.

Michael Waller, Department of Government, University of Manchester.

Stephen White, Department of Politics, University of Glasgow.

Preface

Ideology is defined in this volume as the official doctrine of Marxism–Leninism to which the Soviet leadership, party and state are all formally committed. There has never been much doubt that ideology, defined in this manner, is among the most important elements of political life in the USSR. Far too often, however, the official ideology of Marxism–Leninism has been taken as a 'given' in discussions of this kind, and little detailed attention has been given to the changes that have been taking place in official doctrine over the years or to the changing functions that the ideology has been called upon to perform. The last sustained discussion of the role of ideology in Soviet politics, indeed, occurred some twenty years ago, prompted by an article in *Soviet Studies* by one of the contributors to this volume, Alfred Meyer, whose chapter serves to link that earlier discussion with our own.

In the pages that follow, we have tried to do three things: first of all, to review some more recent approaches to the study of ideology and Soviet politics; secondly, to examine the changes that have taken place in the official ideology from the Lenin, Stalin and Khrushchev periods up to Brezhnev's concept of 'developed socialism' and the modification of that doctrine by the current General Secretary, Mikhail Gorbachev, particularly in the new version of the Party Programme adopted by the 27th Party Congress in 1986; and thirdly, to consider in some detail the evolution and impact of official doctrine in a variety of major policy areas. The extent to which the official ideology has been debated, and even modified, over the years will, we believe, surprise many readers; it should, we hope, at least make clear that the official ideology is not simply a determinant of the Soviet political process, but rather a political construct whose changing nature reflects the varying impact of groups, institutions and individuals within the Soviet system over the years.

This volume was first conceived at a panel on political ideology and communist politics which took place at the annual conference of the UK Political Studies Association, and was prompted particularly by a paper to that panel by Rachel Walker of the University of Southampton, on ideology and politics in the USSR. A more sustained discussion took place at a conference on ideology and Soviet politics which was held at the School of Slavonic and East European Studies, University of London, in May 1985, with the financial assistance of the Nuffield Foundation and of the Ford Foundation sub-grant administered by the British University Association of Slavists and the National Association of Soviet and East European Studies. Earlier versions of the papers included in this volume were presented at the conference and discussed extensively, together with a number of other papers whose inclusion in this volume did not prove feasible, and all have been revised or rewritten specially for this publication. We would like to record our thanks to those, other than the present authors, who made a contribution to the success of the conference either as paper-givers, discussants or in some other capacity, particularly Ron Amann, Archie Brown, Michael Gibson, Jeff Gleisner, Neil Harding, Ron Hill, Geoffrey Hosking, Mary McAuley, Neil Malcolm, Robert Porter, Susan Saunders, Bob Service, Alex Shtromas and Rachel Walker, whose important work on the subject will be appearing elsewhere. We wish also to thank Professor Michael Branch, Bob Service and the staff of the School of Slavonic and East European Studies, University of London, for their efficient administration of the conference and of the production of this volume. We ourselves will be satisfied if the pages that follow help to revive discussion of an aspect of Soviet politics which has been too long neglected.

STEPHEN WHITE
ALEX PRAVDA

1 Ideology and Soviet Politics

STEPHEN WHITE

There has been general agreement that the official ideology of Marxism–Leninism plays a central role in Soviet politics. To at least some Western scholars, the importance of the official ideology is such that we are justified in regarding the Soviet political system as an 'ideology' or even 'utopia in power', with the official ideology functioning as a kind of blueprint which determines, or at least prescribes, the course of that society's development.[1] To the Soviet authorities themselves, there is equally no doubt that (in the words of the current Constitution) the October Revolution has given rise to a 'new type of state', a 'basic instrument for defending the gains of the revolution and for building socialism and communism', which in turn is part of a world-wide transition from capitalism to socialism.[2] Yet, at least in Western scholarly circles, the nature of the ideology itself has tended to be taken as a 'given' in discussions of this kind.

Relatively little detailed consideration, for instance, has been given to the complex changes that the official ideology has undergone over the years, or to the social role that the ideology has performed over the same period. Perhaps still more important, there has been hardly any discussion of the detailed operation of the ideology in specific policy areas, examining the interaction between theory and practice and the complex negotiation of an operational version of the ideology in each case. In this volume we seek to redress the balance, dealing first of all with the evolution of the official ideology from the revolution to the present day, and then secondly with the development of the ideology in a series of important policy areas. This introductory chapter is intended to set the other contributions in some kind of context by dealing in turn with three distinct but related topics: first of all, with some of the more notable contributions of earlier years to the study of ideology and Soviet politics; secondly, with some of the main developments in the official ideology over recent decades; and then, finally, with some of the debates and discussions that have taken place on ideological matters in the USSR in recent years with a view to indicating, at least in general terms, some of the scope that now exists for the reconsideration and even revision of particular aspects of official doctrine.

1.1 IDEOLOGY AND SOVIET POLITICS: SOME EARLIER APPROACHES

One of the earliest treatments of ideology and Soviet politics that still repays attention is Barrington Moore's *Soviet Politics – The Dilemma of Power*, which was first published in 1950.[3] Moore's book reflected the advances that had taken place in Western social science under the influence of Freudian psychology, anthropology, studies of mass communications, and the powerful recent example of the Nazi experience in Germany. It also reflected the more generous climate for the support of Soviet studies that developed after the USSR had attained superpower status in the immediate aftermath of the Second World War. Moore's concern was not with ideology as such, but with the 'role of ideas in the shaping of human behavior'. More particularly, Moore sought to establish which Marxist–Leninist doctrines had been put into effect in the Soviet Union, which had been set aside, and why. His interests centred particularly upon the organisation of political authority and economic institutions. What had been the Bolshevik attitude, for instance, towards authority, discipline and the respective roles of leaders and led? How had the Soviet leaders reacted to the impact of political responsibility after the revolution, in domestic affairs (over which they had some measure of control) and in foreign affairs (over which they had much less)? What difficulties and social tensions had arisen, if any, as a result of the contrast between promise and fulfilment? And did any of the lessons that might be drawn from the Soviet experience suggest more general conclusions about the organisation of modern industrial societies, or about the role of ideas in relation to political action, or about social and political movements?[4]

Moore attempted to answer these and other questions in the main body of his book, which examined the interplay between ideology and behaviour from the emergence of pre-revolutionary Bolshevism up to the late Stalin period. In certain areas, Moore found, the Bolshevik theoretical inheritance had made a major contribution to Soviet political behaviour. One of these was the strong emphasis upon the need for authority and discipline, which by the 1950s had become a justification for sharp inequalities in the distribution of political power. The

Bolshevik ideal of equality of rewards, however, had been abandoned under the pressure of the attempt to build an industrial society, and was replaced by a system of bonuses and incentives related directly to output (it was denied that equality in matters of this kind had in fact ever formed a part of Marxist doctrine). In foreign affairs, early revolutionary theories continued to play an important role, but the failure of attempts to extend the October Revolution internationally had led the authorities to fall back increasingly on traditional balance of power techniques. Since the Soviet regime was itself the revolution's only lasting territorial gain, however, the defence of that regime could be rationalised as a defence of the October Revolution itself; and during and after the Second World War, Soviet action suggested that they had not lost all of their commitment to the international extension of socialist rule. The original goals in this respect were no longer openly proclaimed, but they remained 'latent influences' in Soviet policy and 'could recur in a modified form under favourable conditions'. In many of the areas he considered Moore concluded that the response of the Soviet government was not simply an adaptation to the social and political realities it faced but a reflection of the much more general requirements of modern industrial society, and on the whole he was much more impressed by the flexibility of Soviet doctrine than by its rigidity.[5]

Several other contributions to the study of ideology and Soviet politics in these early years focused rather more closely upon the doctrine itself. Rudolf Schlesinger's *The Spirit of Post-War Russia*, which appeared in 1947, examined Soviet theory and practice under a variety of headings, including the social structure, constitution and law, art and literature, and philosophy.[6] Henri Chambre, in his *Le Marxisme en Union Soviétique* (1955), devoted particular attention to legal theory and practice, moral and religious questions, and economics.[7] Gustav Wetter, a professor at the Papal Oriental Institute in Rome, contributed a massive study of *Dialectical Materialism* in 1952, which appeared in a revised English version in 1958. It remains the fullest and most rigorous account of its kind.[8] Wetter published another study, *Soviet Ideology Today*, in 1962, which concentrated upon the philosophical basis of Soviet ideology in the post-Stalin period.[9] A parallel study by Wolfgang Leonhard of the political doctrines of Soviet ideology in the early Khrushchev period appeared in the same year.[10] Studies of the philosophical basis of Soviet ideology have continued up to the present, particularly in *Studies in Soviet Thought* (quarterly since 1961) and other publications of the East European Institute of the University of Freiburg in Switzerland. Richard T. de George, in *Patterns of Soviet Thought* (1966) and other work, dealt with many of the same issues in a more Anglo-American idiom.[11] David Joravsky, in his *Soviet Marxism and Natural Science 1917–1932* (1961), contributed an important study, still not superseded, of the relationship between Soviet scientists, their doctrines and regime policies over the first decade or so of Soviet rule.[12] Herbert Marcuse's *Soviet Marxism*, essentially a study of the political doctrines of the late Stalin period, appeared in 1958;[13] and there were several other contributions of some note.[14]

Despite the existence of studies of this kind, there was none the less a ready response when Alfred Meyer published his essay 'The functions of ideology in the Soviet political system' in *Soviet Studies* in January 1966.[15] Subtitled 'A speculative essay designed to provoke discussion', it led, in the columns of the same journal, to perhaps the most serious and sustained discussion of Soviet ideology and its functions that has taken place up to the present day. Meyer defined ideology ('the body of doctrine which the Communist Party teaches all Soviet citizens, from school children to the higher party leadership') as consisting of five elements: '(1) a philosophy called Dialectical Materialism; (2) generalisations about man and society, past and present, called Historical Materialism; (3) an economic doctrine called Political Economy, which seeks to explain the economies of capitalism and imperialism on the one hand, and of socialist construction on the other; (4) a body of political thought, or guidelines, now called Scientific Communism, which deals, first, with the strategy and tactics of communist revolution, and, second, with political problems of socialist states; and (5) the official history of the CPSU'.[16] Pointing to the difficulty of deciding whether a particular policy was determined either by the ideology or a *post hoc* rationalisation of it, Meyer suggested a reorientation of the study of the official ideology in terms of the functions it performed within the political system. Those functions included providing the language of politics in the USSR, and also a code of communications; the ideology served additionally as a legitimising device, and as a means of socialisation. Social and other changes, however, suggested to Meyer that these functions, already difficult to perform effectively and to reconcile with each other, might become increasingly routinised and emptied of content over the years to come.[17]

The discussion was taken further in a variety of other contributions over subsequent months. Alec Nove and Peter Reddaway joined the debate in the next issue.[18] David Joravsky, in a complex but rewarding contribution in the July 1966 issue, took issue with Meyer's definition of Soviet ideology and suggested a reformulation in terms of 'unacknowledged dogma that serves social functions'. Even this definition, however, produced difficulties for the outside investigator, lacking access to many of the sources that might be relevant to such an approach and precluded from the genuine understanding of a society's norms and assumptions that came from living one's daily life within it.[19] Further contributions to the discussion were made by Frederick Barghoorn, Robert V. Daniels, Morris Bornstein, Nigel Harris and Henri Chambre,[20] and also by Roy Laird (who suggested that Marxist–Leninist ideology in the strict sense had long ago been superseded in the Soviet Union by a combination of traditional Russian nationalism, some elements of the Marxist heritage and axioms derived from the pragmatic lessons of Soviet successes in various fields).[21] The discussion rumbled on over several more issues, with contributions by Rudolf Schlesinger, Kurt Marko and Robert G. Wesson, before coming to a somewhat indeterminate conclusion.[22]

The discussion in *Soviet Studies* provided a range and variety of reflections upon the role of ideology in Soviet politics upon which it is still difficult to improve. Relatively little attention, however, was devoted to the content of Soviet official ideology, as at least one of the participants, Robert V. Daniels, pointed out at the time.[23] The question, as Daniels noted, was not often asked, because the answer seemed so obviously to have been provided by the corpus of Marxism–Leninism. The ideology, however, had not survived the successive phases of the revolutionary process as a factor of constant value; in particular, the pressure of events had forced the Soviet leaders (mainly Lenin and Stalin) to make important reinterpretations of the meaning of the doctrine which they had then imposed upon their followers. The operational meaning of the doctrine – to sustain the Soviet system – had by now very little in common with the Marxist–Leninist scriptures as originally formulated. So far from predicting a communist utopia, and thereby exposing a gap between that ideal and everyday realities, successive leaders had so redefined the notion of Utopia (as in the 1961 Party Programme) that it now represented 'nothing more than the present system plus the material fruits of a couple of further five-year plans'.[24] Further changes in the official ideology in recent years, including the elaboration of the notion of 'developed socialism', have powerfully reinforced this point and emphasised the inadequacy of regarding Soviet official ideology as a 'given', to be either implemented or ignored, rather than as a changing body of doctrine whose specific content as well as role and function requires the closest scholarly attention.

1.2 FROM STALINISM TO DEVELOPED SOCIALISM

Soviet Marxism–Leninism finds its origins in the teachings of Marx and Engels, as developed by Lenin, Stalin and their successors. The founders of 'scientific socialism', however, had relatively little to say about the nature of a fully communist society, and in any case their legacy has been drawn upon to a varying extent and in different ways over the Soviet period. The doctrine of the 'negation of the negation', for instance, all but disappeared under Stalin, and the notion of alienation, together with Marx's early and more humanistic writings, received very little attention in Soviet sources (indeed the texts themselves were often not available) until the Khrushchev period.[25] The decisive contribution of Lenin and Stalin to the further elaboration and systematisation of this varied, ambiguous and fragmentary body of doctrine is the subject of Graeme Gill's contribution to this symposium; Alfred Evans then considers the evolution of official doctrine from the Stalin period through the innovations of the Khrushchev years up to the Brezhnev doctrine of 'developed socialism' in its current interpretation. Throughout the period as a whole, almost all elements of the official ideology, as identified by Meyer, have been subject to continuous revision and change: in itself good reason for regarding the official ideology as an adaptable body of doctrine, negotiated and renegotiated through a recognisably political process, rather than as a fixed set of precepts with clear and binding implications of every area of Soviet life.

Although his own contributions to the subject were soon discounted, it was in fact Khrushchev who initiated the revival of Soviet Marxism–Leninism as something more than the stultifying, catechetic dogma which it had become by the late Stalin period. Khrushchev's assault on Stalinism began at the 20th Party Congress in 1956, particularly in his 'secret speech' in which he openly attacked the violations of Leninist norms of party life and of socialist legality which had taken place under Stalin and with his direct participation. Steps were taken under Khrushchev's leadership to eliminate the harmful consquences of Stalinism in all walks of Soviet life: prisoners were released and rehabilitated, a new criminal code was introduced in 1958, and the CPSU began both to expand its own membership and to restore some measure of 'inner-party democracy' to its decision-making procedures. More positively, Khrushchev began to revive the notion of the possibility of a direct transition to full communism within the historically foreseeable future. The current period of Soviet development was defined at the 21st Party Congress in 1959 as one of the 'full-scale construction of communist society' (*razvernutoe stroitel'stvo kommunisticheskogo obshchestva*), rather than its earlier and more modest designation as one of the 'gradual transition to communism'.[26] It was now held that the dictatorship of the proletariat had come to an end with the victory of socialism in 1936; since then an 'all-people's state' had come into existence, an 'organ expressing the interests and will of the people as a whole', which would itself wither away with the further development of socialist democracy.[27] The doctrine of 'communist social self-management' was also proclaimed, and a variety of public functions, such as sport and law enforcement, were transferred to non-state bodies within a general framework of party guidance.[28] Two new authoritative volumes were produced, *Fundamentals of Marxist Philosophy* in 1958 and *Fundamentals of Marxism–Leninism* in 1959, which together set out the main elements of post-Stalinist political philosophy and theory.[29]

The most remarkable of Khrushchev's ideological innovations was the new Party Programme, which was adopted in its final form at the 22nd Party Congress in October 1961.[30] The Programme, the first the party had adopted since 1919, boldly set out a strategy for the transition from capitalism to communism in the West, and from socialism to full communism in the USSR itself. The Programme is perhaps best known for having incautiously predicted the dates by which this transformation would take place. By the end of the 1960s, the Programme promised, the strongest and richest capitalist country, the USA, would be overtaken in absolute and per capita production, and living and cultural standards would improve substantially. By the year 1980, the Programme went on, an abundance of material and cultural values for the whole population would have been created, and a communist society would 'in the main' have been constructed. These dates proved hopelessly optimistic, and have been unmentionable in print in the USSR since shortly after Khrushchev's fall from power. In other respects, however, the Programme provided a more reliable guide to future developments, and many of its detailed provisions have remained among the party's priorities. The Programme envisaged, for instance, electrification and widespread automation throughout the USSR, the reduction of differences between town and country, greater attention to the special needs of women, and an enhanced role for public and social organisations such as trade unions and the cooperatives. Relations with the non-communist countries, equally, continue to be based upon the principle of peaceful coexistence, by which the class struggle between capitalism and socialism was to continue, but military (and particularly thermonuclear) conflict between them was so far as possible to be avoided.[31]

The 1961 Programme had solemnly concluded with the words: 'The present generation of Soviet people shall live under communism!' By the late 1960s, however, the notion of communism had begun to be referred to much less often, and official ideologists made it increasingly clear that Khrushchev's assumptions of a rapid transition from socialism to communism were unrealistic if not, indeed, un-Marxist.[32] In its place, and explicitly from the 24th Party Congress (1971) onwards, official theory asserted that the USSR had become a society of 'mature' (*zrelyi*) or 'developed socialism' (*razvitoi sotsializm*). This stage of development was held to have been reached in the late 1950s or early 1960s, and it was held to be a relatively extended period, with its own laws and dynamics, whose further transformation into full communism was a matter for an unspecified point in the fairly remote future.[33] References to 'developed socialism' had appeared in print as early as 1960, and Brezhnev used the term in passing in speeches in 1967 and 1970. In his report to the 24th Party Congress the following year, however, the concept of developed socialism was held up for formal approval as a distinct phase of the Soviet Union's development towards the ultimate communist goal. Speaking of the 'specific features' of the present stage of Soviet economic development, Brezhnev noted that the Soviet economy had attained a qualitatively new level of development as compared with the late 1930s, when socialism in a formal sense had been established. Much higher levels of production had been reached, and there had been major changes in social relations, in culture, and in mass consciousness. The 'developed socialist society', of which Lenin had spoken in 1918 as the future of Soviet society, Brezhnev went on, had now been built; this in turn placed qualitatively new tasks before the party in economic and other terms.[34] The same emphases were repeated in his speeches to the 25th and 26th Party Congresses in 1976 and 1981 respectively.[35]

Official theory of the Brezhnev period, as set out in the 1977 Constitution and in authoritative commentaries, posited that a socialist society had 'in the main' been constructed in the USSR by the second half of the 1930s, and confirmed by the adoption of the 1936 Constitution and the decisions of the 18th Party Congress of 1939. It had been based on socialist reconstruction of the entire economy, the complete liquidation of exploiting classes and far-reaching cultural changes. Over subsequent years the USSR was held to have advanced to a much higher level of economic, social and cultural development and the influence of socialism to have increased internationally, such that socialism could be regarded as not just fully, but finally and irreversibly confirmed by about the time of the 21st Party Congress in 1959. This transition, completed over the late 1950s and early 1960s, was supposed in turn to have made possible the establishment of a developed socialist society in the USSR. In the development of a fully communist society in the USSR, accordingly, three main stages could be distinguished: (1) a transitional period, which had ended with the victory of socialism; (2) a period which had begun with the establishment of the bases of socialism and had led to the formation of a developed socialist society; and (3) a period of developed socialism and of further evolution (*pererastanie*) into full communism. Developed socialism was located within the first or lower phase of communist society, as Marx and Lenin had originally described it; the second or higher phase of communist society would be capable of development within the framework of developed socialism, although this would be a 'long and gradual process' and would depend upon the construction of the appropriate material-technical prerequisites.[36]

Even before the death of Brezhnev, official spokesmen had made it clear that the notion of developed socialism (itself a postponement of the communist future) was based upon a complacent and over-optimistic assessment of Soviet developmental perspectives. Andropov, writing as general secretary in 1983 on 'The teaching of Karl Marx and some questions of communist construction in the USSR', emphasised that there must be a proper understanding of the stage of development that Soviet society had reached. Any attempt to run ahead of that level, he warned, would simply raise unrealisable tasks. The Soviet Union was only at the 'beginning' of the long historical stage of developed socialism; there should be no exaggeration of the country's closeness to the higher phase of communism, and there should be a frank acknowledgement of the contradictions and difficulties that still remained.[37] Chernenko's speech at a meeting of the commission to prepare a new edition of the party programme in April 1984 took the same practical and unheroic approach. Developed socialism, he reminded his audience, would be an historically protracted period, and there was a need to focus on the problems that still remained rather than dwelling on what Lenin had called the 'relatively distant, beautiful and rosy future'. He repeated the warning that the perfection of socialism would require a 'whole historical epoch' in an article in the theoretical journal *Kommunist* at the end of 1984.[38] Chernenko's successor, Mikhail Gorbachev, carried the reassessment even further by avoiding all but occasional references to developed socialism and emphasising rather the need for an 'acceleration' (*uskorenie*) of socio-economic development as the key to future advance.[39]

The new Party Programme, adopted by the 27th Party Congress on Gorbachev's recommendation in March 1986, is discussed further in several contributions to this volume. Perhaps its central feature is the abandonment of the optimistic perspectives of its predecessor of 1961. Whereas the 1961 Programme had declared itself to be a 'programme for the building of communist society', the revised text of 1986 describes itself as no more than a programme for the 'planned and all-round perfection of socialism'. The dates and stages by which full communism was to be reached, which were present in the 1961 Programme, disappear entirely; the 1986 version notes rather that the party 'does not attempt to foresee in detail the features of complete communism' and warns that any attempt to advance too rapidly was 'doomed to failure and might cause both economic and political damage'. The collectivist emphases of the 1961 Programme – more and more services such as transport and housing to be provided free of charge, more public catering and collective upbringing of children – find no place in the new text, nor does the promise of a minimum one-month paid holiday for all citizens. The 1986 Programme contains no provision for the regular renewal of party and state bodies, and makes no reference to the development of public self-government or to the historic goal of the withering away of the state. Perhaps not surprisingly, many of the six million citizens who wrote in to comment on the draft of the Programme suggested it be designated a new, fourth Programme, rather than a revision of the existing third Programme of 1961.[40] The practical, unromantic perspectives of the new Party Programme are likely in turn to set the parameters of official ideology for many years to come.

1.3 IDEOLOGY AND POLICY-MAKING

Three different levels of communist ideology have usefully been distinguished by A. Ross Johnson, basing himself upon the work of Brzezinski and Huntington on political power in the USA and USSR. These three levels are, first of all, general philosophical assumptions – for example, dialectical materialism; secondly, doctrinal elements, indicating the general direction of political action in a given historical period – for example, the dictatorship of the proletariat; and thirdly, 'action programmes', or programmes of political action specifically tied to particular historical and socio-economic conditions – for instance, Stalin's 'socialism in one country' or Mao Zedong's 'modern revisionism'. 'Action programmes' are always subject to revision by the political leaderships, and such revision is considered to be both necessary and desirable; they represent the communist equivalent of what in a Western liberal-democratic system would be called 'policies', and differ from such policies in that they are continuously and consciously derived from and justified in terms of the doctrinal and also the philosophical elements of the ideology. 'Doctrine is thus the politically crucial link between dogmatic assumptions and pragmatic action'; or expressed in different language, this is the 'unity of theory and practice'.[41]

It would be difficult to argue that the Soviet period has seen any fundamental reconsideration of the general philosophical assumptions of the ideology, as great as that of the Chinese, for instance, who have been willing to state publicly that Marx and Engels did not provide answers to all (not as originally reported, any) of their country's present-day problems.[42] Even here, however, as already noted, different aspects of the philosophical bases of the ideology have been given different emphases at different periods; and at the second level, that of doctrine, there have been considerable changes, from classic Stalinist formulations to Khrushchev's 'full-scale development of communism' and on to 'developed socialism' in its various interpretations. It is at the level of 'action programmes' (or policies), however, that changes have been most readily apparent, not only because of reconsiderations in other areas of the official ideology, but also because of the impact of external circumstances and of domestic politics. It would probably be fair to say, in almost every field, that the general tendency of development since at least the 1960s has been for official prescriptions to become increasingly qualified and amorphous, less distinctively 'Soviet' or 'socialist', and more like policies than action programmes as Brzezinski and Huntington originally conceived of them.

In the field of literature, for instance, the period since the 1960s has seen the gradual erosion of the Stalinist orthodoxy in terms of which writers were supposed to be 'engineers of human souls' working to a doctrine of 'socialist realism', which in turn prescribed a positive hero, a production location, a clear struggle between progressive and reactionary forces which was invariably won by the former, and a straightforward, accessible and optimistic style. More recent years have seen the gradual disappearance of the positive hero and other features of this tradition, and their replacement, even in officially published Soviet work, by a body of literature which much more readily accommodates (for instance) reservations about collectivisation and contemporary rural life, 'negative phenomena' such as bribery and corruption, the *de facto* inequality of women, juvenile delinquency and promiscuity, and spiritual, ethical or even religious issues which have always bulked large in Russian literature but which are difficult to reconcile with official materialist values.[43] In history, similarly, the post-Stalin years have seen a greater emphasis upon the complexity and many-sidedness of events, and upon access to and publication of archival sources which at least as effectively erode the position of official custodians of historical truth. Since about 1962, when an important all-union conference deplored the 'harmful consequences of the cult of personality' in historical research and resolved to eliminate them, there have been attacks upon 'schematic' and 'unilinear' interpretations of the historical past and much more emphasis has been placed upon other aspects of the Soviet experience such as the pre-revolutionary bourgeoisie, non-proletarian parties, and the post-revolutionary emigration.[44]

In economic policy (which is dealt with by David Dyker in his contribution to this volume) there has been a largely parallel process of reconsideration of earlier orthodoxies. The most important single date is probably again 1962, the year in which Evgeny Liberman first published his reformist proposals in *Pravda*. Since then, there has been an open and relatively undogmatic discussion of the role of prices and of a market mechanism, of different forms of labour organisation in industry and agriculture, of profits and incentives, of decentralisation of decision-making, and even (in guarded terms) of unemployment. It is likely that practical considerations such as the country's great size and diversity, the priority requirements of defence and the political influence of central ministries represent at least as significant an obstacle to further reform as do the Marxist scriptures (which anyway have almost nothing to say about the management of a post-capitalist economy).[45] In international affairs, over which the Soviet authorities have even less control, the post-Stalin and even post-Krushchev periods have seen significant modifications of official positions. Conceptualisations of developments in the Third World, for instance, have had to accommodate a series of reverses for Soviet policy as well as a proliferation of (often military) regimes claiming to adhere to Marxism–Leninism, and apparently anomalous phenomena such as militant Islam. Relations between communist parties and even communist governments have proved far from harmonious; and the major capitalist countries have expressed misgivings about détente and shown few signs of electing communist governments to power. The existence of nuclear weapons has proved particularly difficult to reconcile with earlier and more optimistic scenarios.[46]

Perhaps the most remarkable of all reconsiderations has taken place in the field of philosophy, one with considerable implications for the basic assumptions of the ideology as well as for particular programmes of political action. Following Marx and Lenin, the traditional assumption of Soviet official theory has been that socialism, as a society in which the means of production belongs to the people as a whole rather than to an exploiting class, provides no basis for antagonistic contradictions between groups of individuals, although non-antagonistic contradictions will continue to exist at least until the establishment of full communism. As an authoritative source has put it, 'in the process of development of socialism some aspects and forms of socialist relations become outdated, cease to answer to the growing needs of the society. As a consequence of this contradictions arise, the solution of which becomes a necessary prerequisite for further progress'. Although relations between the different parts of socialist society are held 'objectively' not to provide any basis for social conflicts, non-antagonistic contradictions may none the less arise in a variety of circumstances. The contradiction between the continuation of 'extensive' economic growth and the objective requirement for a greater emphasis upon 'intensive' growth is cited as one example of a contradiction of this kind; and the gradual evolution of socialist society towards communism is held to take place precisely through the progressive resolution of contradictions of this kind.[47]

These traditional, somewhat complacent formulations have been challenged since the early 1980s by a far-reaching debate which has exposed the inadequacy of the concept of non-antagonistic contradictions and suggested a reconceptualisation which lays much more emphasis upon the connection between antagonisms under socialism and the different interests of different social groups, and which draws much of its inspiration from the Polish crisis of 1980–82.[48] The debate began in earnest in the columns of *Voprosy filosofii*, the Soviet Union's main philosophical journal, in 1982, and continued up to 1984 and beyond. Opening the discussion in the July 1982 number, V.S. Semenov, the journal's main editor, suggested that the basic contradiction of socialist society was that between its productive forces and productive relations. Under socialism, it was generally agreed, this contradiction was of a non-antagonistic character; and yet there were very different views about the manner in which such antagonisms arose, and about the form that they assumed. Semenov himself suggested that contradictions of this kind, in contemporary Soviet society, might be of three distinct types: 'horizontal' contradictions, such as those which occurred when productive forces developed in advance of productive relations; 'vertical' contradictions, such as those between different branches of the economy; and finally a more complex form of contradictions between production and exchange and between production and management.[49] In a further contribution to the journal, Semenov pointed out that contradictions could be of varying degrees of intensity; in the most serious cases, as in Poland, they could lead to a crisis situation. It might even be possible to find antagonistic contradictions under socialism. These, however, were the result either of external factors, or of temporary and subjectively-determined deviations from the real nature of socialism. Socialism and contradictions, properly speaking, were mutually exclusive.[50]

These general propositions did not satisfy Anatoly Butenko, a department head at the Institute of the Economics of the World Socialist System of the USSR Academy of Sciences, who joined the discussion in October 1982. Drawing extensively upon the Polish experience, Butenko refused to accept that contradictions under socialism were necessarily non-antagonistic. Much more controversially, he located the main contradiction of socialism in the relationship between the growth of productive forces and such aspects of productive relations as the forms of production, distribution and exchange, methods of planning and management, and the political system of the society as a whole. Contradictions of this kind were to be avoided, in Butenko's view, not simply by a better-judged choice of policies by the leaderships concerned, but by an improvement of the economic and political system so that individual, group and societal interests might so far as possible be allowed to establish an accommodation with each other. This in turn required mechanisms which encouraged political and industrial activism and an attitude which regarded the state and economy as 'one's own' and not 'alien'. In the absence of such mechanisms the accumulation of discontent could lead to labour indiscipline, a deterioration in economic performance and even (as in Poland) open political conflict. The renewal of outmoded forms of economic and political organisation, in order to avoid such crises, was the task of the ruling party. Butenko went on to identify contradictions between production and consumption, even under socialism, which could lead to 'collisions' between personal and societal needs and interests, especially where short-term and long-term interests were concerned. Further contradictions arose in the political sphere between the respective claims of broader mass participation in government and more high-qualified central control.[51]

Butenko's views were in turn subject to criticism by Richard Kosolapov, at this time editor in chief of *Kommunist*. Writing in *Pravda* in March 1983 on the 'wholeness' of developed socialism, Kosolapov stressed the convergence that was occurring in the property base, in the work process and in social relations in the contemporary Soviet Union. This, in his view, excluded antagonisms based on social group membership, nationality or any other grounds. Kosolapov was particularly dismissive of those who had suggested a 'new reading' of Lenin's dictum that antagonisms and contradictions were not identical, and that the former would disappear, but the latter remain, under socialism.[52] Circumstances in Poland were highly specific, Kosolapov maintained; the socialist transition had not yet been completed, there had been several decades of private farming, and there were 'influential anti-socialist ideological currents'. The same conditions did not apply in the Soviet Union or in the other socialist countries which had nationalised their industry and had a collective and mechanised agriculture, although both conflicts and clashes would continue to occur, based on differences between individuals or between individuals and the society as a whole.[53] Kosolapov reinforced these points in a further article in *Pravda* and in a contribution to *Literaturnaya gazeta*.[54]

Butenko and Semenov replied to the debate in *Voprosy filosofii* in February 1984, following a wide-ranging discussion in academic and other circles. Butenko, unrepentant, noted that the problem of contradictions within the world socialist system as a whole had been almost entirely ignored, and took the opportunity to advance his argument still further. It was generally agreed, he noted, that socialism knew not only more or less easily resolvable non-antagonistic contradictions but also sharp conflicts and clashes and even 'serious collisions'. Here two positions had identified themselves. One, of long standing, was that contradictions of this kind derived from 'survivals of capitalism'. But could such explanations account, for instance, for the outbreak of the Polish crisis, or for its occurrence in that particular country at that particular time? Another position was that such phenomena arose from the inept resolution of those antagonisms that were inherent in socialism by the local party and state leaderships. Both these positions, Butenko pointed out, in practice tended to encourage a political response which made it all the more likely that such collisions would recur, and diverted attention from the unresolved problems of socialism itself. It was essential, Butenko continued, in speaking of contradictions of this kind to make clear their association with the particular interests of particular individuals and social groups. Managers, for instance, might seek to make use of their position in order to advance their own selfish and sectional interests at the expense of the society as a whole, or of those whom they had been placed in authority. The interests of the groups concerned would, in this case, be in conflict, and the contradiction would be an antagonistic one. This had nothing to do with survivals of capitalism; and yet experience had shown that a 'regressive evolution' of this kind was not only possible but had in fact occurred under socialist conditions. The whole problem, Butenko concluded, required a great deal of further study.[55]

Butenko himself was subsequently persuaded to reconsider his position, and *Voprosy filosofii* was sharply criticised for having allowed an exchange of this kind to take place.[56] The debate on contradictions under socialism has none the less continued, not in *Voprosy filosofii* but in the monthly economics journal *Voprosy ekonomiki*,[57] and the issues are obviously ones to which official theory has as yet no adequate or convincing answer. The Party Programme approved by the 27th Congress made at least two direct references to the matter: 'prompt identification and resolution of non-antagonistic contradictions', it noted, were among the 'vital prerequisites for the acceleration of socio-economic progress', and social scientists urged as a matter of urgency to provide a 'scientific analysis of the objective contradictions in socialist society' and the means by which they might be overcome.[58] Gorbachev himself, in his speech to the Congress, complained that the 'sharpness of the contradictions in life' had been too frequently ignored and that there had been a lack of 'realism' in assessing the actual state of affairs in Soviet society.[59] The debate – like several others[60] – has at least made clear the importance of examining the continuous interplay between official theory and those responsible for its formulation and implementation within particular policy areas. As other contributions to this volume will help to demonstrate, the ideology should not be seen in every case as the determining, or even as a constant factor; at least as important is the continuing process of negotiation and conceptualisation, in general as well as policy-specific terms, which in turn reflects the particular interests and objectives of the various institutions, groups and individuals of which the wider society is composed. This process – the politics of ideology-making – should surely receive as much of our attention in future years as the influence of ideology on policy-making has done over the recent past.

NOTES

1. For these terms, see respectively Bertram Wolfe, *An Ideology in Power: Reflections on the Russian Revolution* (London: Allen and Unwin, 1969), and Mikhail Geller and Aleksander Nekrich, *Utopiya u vlasti*, 2 vols. (London: Overseas Publications Interchange, 1982).
2. *Konstitutsiya (Osnovnoi Zakon) Soyuza Sovetskikh Sotsialisticheskikh Respublik* (Moscow: Politizdat, 1977), pp. 3–5.
3. Barrington Moore, Jr., *Soviet Politics – The Dilemma of Power* (Camb. Mass.: Harvard University Press, 1950).
4. Ibid., pp. 1, 9–10.
5. Ibid., pp. 402–5, 416.
6. Rudolf Schlesinger, *The Spirit of Post-War Russia. Soviet Ideology 1917–1946* (London: Dennis Dobson, 1947).
7. Henri Chambre, *Le Marxisme en Union Soviétique* (Paris: Seuil, 1955).
8. Gustav A. Wetter, *Dialectical Materialism* (London: Routledge, 1958). See also James P. Scanlan's recent and important book, *Marxism in the USSR* (Ithaca, NY: Cornell University Press, 1985).
9. Gustav A. Wetter, *Soviet Ideology Today* (New York: Praeger, 1962).
10. Wolfgang Leonhard, *Die politischen Lehren* (Frankfurt: Fischer, 1962).
11. Richard T. de George, *Patterns of Soviet Thought* (Ann Arbor: University of Michigan Press, 1966).
12. David Joravsky, *Soviet Marxism and Natural Science 1917–1932* (London: Routledge, 1961).
13. Herbert Marcuse, *Soviet Marxism. A Critical Analysis* (New York: Columbia University Press, 1958).
14. See for instance Ivo Lapenna, *State and Law: Soviet and Yugoslav Theory* (London: Athlone Press, 1964) and Nigel Harris, *Beliefs in Society* (London: Watts, 1968).
15. Alfred G. Meyer, 'The functions of ideology in the Soviet political system', *Soviet Studies*, vol. 17, no. 3 (January 1966), pp. 273–85.
16. Ibid., p. 273. Meyer noted that some shorter-range party pronouncements might also be included.
17. Ibid., pp. 275, 276, 276–80, 284–5.
18. Alec Nove, 'Ideology and agriculture', *Soviet Studies*, vol. 17, no. 4 (April 1966), pp. 397–407; Peter B. Reddaway, 'Aspects of ideological belief in the Soviet Union', ibid., pp. 473–83.
19. David Joravsky, 'Soviet ideology', *Soviet Studies*, vol. 18, no. 1 (July 1966), pp. 2–19, at pp. 4, 18–19.
20. Frederick Barghoorn, 'Observations on contemporary Soviet political attitudes', *Soviet Studies*, vol. 18, no. 1 (July 1966), pp. 66–70; Robert V. Daniels, 'The ideological vector', ibid., pp. 71–3; Morris Bornstein, 'Ideology and the Soviet economy', ibid., pp. 74–80; Nigel Harris, 'The owl of Minerva', ibid., vol. 18, no. 3 (January 1967), pp. 328–39; Henri Chambre, 'Soviet ideology', ibid., pp. 314–27.
21. Roy Laird, 'The new Soviet myth: Marx is dead, long live communism', *Soviet Studies*, vol. 18, no. 4 (April 1967), pp. 511–18.
22. Rudolf Schlesinger, 'More observations on ideology', *Soviet Studies*, vol. 19, no. 1 (July 1967), pp. 87–99; Kurt Marko, 'Soviet ideology and

Sovietology', ibid., no. 4 (April 1968), pp. 465–81; and Robert G. Wesson, 'The Soviet state, ideology and patterns of autocracy', ibid., vol. 20, no. 2 (October 1969), pp. 179–86. A related contribution which appeared elsewhere was Daniel Bell, 'Ideology and Soviet politics', *Slavic Review*, vol. 24, no. 4 (December 1965), pp. 591–621.

23. Daniels, 'Ideological vector', p. 71.
24. Ibid., pp. 71–2.
25. De George, *Patterns*, pp. 193, 210, 213. The first substantial Soviet collection of Marx's early works was Karl Marx and Fridrikh Engel's, *Iz rannikh proizvedenii* (Moscow: Politizdat, 1956).
26. *KPSS v rezolyutsiyakh i resheniyakh s"ezdov, konferentsii i plenumov TsK*, 8th edn, 14 vols. (Moscow: Politizdat, 1970–82), vol. 7, p. 373. A helpful source on this period is Jerome M. Gilison, *The Soviet Image of Utopia* (Baltimore, Md: Johns Hopkins University Press, 1975).
27. *KPSS v rez*., vol. 8, p. 273. On this point see particularly Roger E. Kanet, 'The rise and fall of the "all-people's state"', *Soviet Studies*, vol. 20, no. 1 (July 1968), pp. 81–93.
28. *KPSS v rez*., vol. 7, p. 381.
29. F. V. Konstantinov, ed., *Osnovy marksistskoi filosofii* (Moscow: Nauka, 1958); O. V. Kuusinen (ed.), *Osnovy Marksizma–Leninizma* (Moscow: Politizdat, 1959).
30. The Programme is reprinted in *KPSS v rez*., vol. 8, pp. 196–305, and in English translation with extensive commentaries in Leonard Schapiro, ed., *The USSR and the Future* (New York: Praeger, 1963).
31. Ibid. On the changes in foreign policy, see particularly William Zimmerman, *Soviet Perspectives on International Relations 1956–1967* (Princeton University Press, 1969).
32. Gilison, *Soviet Image of Utopia*, p. 182.
33. On 'developed socialism', see particularly Alfred B. Evans, 'Developed socialism in Soviet ideology', *Soviet Studies*, vol. 29, no. 3 (July 1977), pp. 409–28. See also Marie Lavigne, 'Advanced socialist society', *Economy and Society*, vol. 7, no. 4 (November 1978), pp. 367–94; Ronald J. Hill, 'The "all-people's state" and "developed socialism"', in Neil Harding (ed.), *The State in Socialist Society* (London: Macmillan, 1984); and, for a recent Soviet view, V. P. Dmitrenko, 'Stanovlenie kontseptsii razvitogo sotsializma v SSSR', *Voprosy istorii*, 1984, no. 8, pp. 3–22.
34. L. I. Brezhnev, *Leninskim kursom*, vol. 3 (Moscow: Politizdat, 1972), pp. 234–5.
35. Ibid., vol. 5 (1976), pp. 450–550, and vol. 8 (1981), pp. 633–728.
36. G. E. Glezerman et al., *Razvitoe sotsialisticheskoe obshchestvo: sushchnost', kriterii zrelosti, kritika revizionistskikh kontseptsii*, 3rd ed. (Moscow: Mysl', 1979), pp. 20–3.
37. Yu. V. Andropov, *Izbrannye rechi i stat'i*, 2nd edn (Moscow: Politizdat, 1983), pp. 245–6.
38. K. U. Chernenko, *Narod i partiya ediny. Izbrannye rechi i stat'i* (Moscow: Politizdat, 1984), p. 456; Chernenko, 'Na uroven' trebovanii razvitogo sotsializma', *Kommunist*, 1984, no. 18, pp. 3–21, at pp. 4, 8.
39. See further in Alfred Evans's contribution to this volume.
40. *Programma Kommunisticheskoi partii Sovetskogo Soyuza. Novaya redakt-*

siya (Moscow: Politizdat, 1986), various pages; *Pravda*, 26 February 1986, p. 10.

41. A. Ross Johnson, *The Transformation of Communist Ideology: the Yugoslav Case, 1945–1953* (Camb. Mass.: MIT Press, 1972), p. 2; Zbigniew Brzezinski and Samuel P. Huntington, *Political Power: USA/USSR* (New York: Viking, 1964), pp. 21–22.
42. *Guardian*, 29 December 1984, p. 5.
43. See Martin Crouch and Robert Porter, *Understanding Soviet Politics through Literature* (London: Allen and Unwin, 1984); Geoffrey Hosking, *Beyond Socialist Realism* (London: Elek, 1980); and Mary Seton-Watson, 'Myth and reality in recent Soviet fiction', *Coexistence*, vol. 19, no. 2 (October 1982), pp. 206–35.
44. See for instance Nancy Whittier Heer, *Politics and History in the Soviet Union* (Cambridge, Mass.: MIT Press, 1971); Samuel H. Baron and Heer, eds, *Windows on the Russian Past: Essays on Recent Soviet Historiography* (Columbus, Ohio: AAASS, 1977).
45. See Aron Katsenelinboigen, *Soviet Economic Theory and Political Power in the USSR* (New York: Praeger, 1980); and Erik P. Hoffman and Robbin F. Laird, *The Politics of Economic Modernization in the Soviet Union* (Ithaca: Cornell University Press, 1982). On a related issue, see Joan DeBardeleben, *The Environment and Marxism–Leninism* (Boulder, Col.: Westview Press, 1985).
46. See Stephen Shenfield's contribution to this volume, and also R. Judson Mitchell, *Ideology of a Superpower, Contemporary Soviet Doctrine on International Relations* (Stanford, Calif.: Hoover Institution Press, 1982), and Jerry F. Hough, *The Struggle for the Third World* (Washington, DC: Brookings Institution, 1986).
47. Glezerman et al., *Razvitoe sotsialisticheskoe obshchestvo*, pp. 48–9.
48. Good surveys of this debate are available in Ernst Kux, 'Contradictions in Soviet socialism', *Problems of Communism*, vol. 33, no. 6 (November – December 1984), pp. 1–27; and Rene Ahlberg, 'Konflikttheorie und Konflikterfahrung in der UdSSR', *Osteuropa*, vol. 35, no. 4 (April 1985), pp. 233–55.
49. V. S. Semenov, 'Problema protivorechii v usloviyakh sotsializma. Stat'ya pervaya', *Voprosy filosofii*, 1982, no. 7, pp. 17–32.
50. V. S. Semenov, 'Problema protivorechii v usloviyakh sotsializma. Stat'ya vtoraya', ibid., no. 9, pp. 3–21.
51. A. P. Butenko, 'Protivorechiya razvitiya sotsializma kak obshchestvennogo stroya', ibid., no. 10, pp. 16–29.
52. *Leninskii sbornik*, vol. 11 (Moscow: Gosizdat, 1929), p. 357.
53. *Pravda*, 4 March 1983, pp. 2–3.
54. *Pravda*, 14 June 1984, p. 2–3, and *Literaturnaya gazeta*, 1 February 1984 (I am grateful to David Wedgwood Benn for drawing my attention to these items).
55. A. P. Butenko, 'Eshche raz o protivorechiyakh sotsializma', *Voprosy filosofii*, 1984, no. 2, pp. 116–23 (Semenov's reply appeared in ibid., pp. 130–40).
56. See Helmut Dahm, *Die Ideologie als Chriffre der Politik* (Bonn: Berichte des Bundesinstituts für ostwissenschaftliche und internationale Studien no. 25,

1985), p. 149; *Voprosy filosofii*, 1984, no. 10, pp. 3–9.
57. See V. Kulikov, 'Protivorechiya ekonomicheskoi sistemy sotsializma kak istochnik ee razvitiya', *Voprosy ekonomiki*, 1986, no. 1, pp. 117–28.
58. *Pravda*, 7 March 1986, pp. 5, 6.
59. *Pravda*, 26 February 1986, p. 9.
60. See, for instance, the discussion of conceptions of 'interests' under socialism in Ronald J. Hill, *Soviet Politics, Political Science and Reform* (Oxford: Martin Robertson, 1980), ch. 5, and of the influence of political scientists on the formation of official theory in Archie Brown, 'Political science in the Soviet Union: a new stage of development', *Soviet Studies*, vol. 36, no. 3 (July 1984), pp. 317–44.

2 What is to Count as Ideology in Soviet Politics?

MICHAEL WALLER

The vigorous debate about Soviet ideology that took place in the 1960s was followed by a reaction in which many of the participants who were not Marxists abandoned a discussion in terms of ideology for one in terms of political culture. The impulse was given not so much by the difficulties of pinning down a highly volatile concept: this was a time when people were beginning to seek explanations for the evident differences between societies ruled by communist parties. Accustomed to a discourse in which ideology as presented as one of the factors that linked those societies, commentators on the communist scene, not unnaturally, looked to culture as a factor of differentation.

This chapter, by contrast, presents some of the reasons for retaining a concept of ideology in analysing the Soviet political system. It will be argued that the discussion on two central aspects of Soviet politics is very much the poorer without a concept of ideology. The first is the historical impact of the revolution on the pre-revolutionary culture. The second is quite simply the structure of power in the Soviet Union.

It is true that ideology is conceived in many, often conflicting ways. This is not necessarily, however, a good reason for throwing out the baby with the bathwater and abandoning the term altogether. The problem with ideology, in any case, stems not so much from this diversity of meaning, as from attempts to adopt too restrictive a use of the term to the exclusion of all others. In this chapter three broad and overlapping senses of the term will be encountered:

1. Ideology as a general and comprehensive set of ideas about the world and man's place in it (Arendt's 'key to history, or the solution for all the "riddles of the Universe"');[1]
2. Ideology as mythos, or memory – in our case that of Soviet society, as

shaped to a considerable extent by the Communist Party of the Soviet Union (CPSU);
3. Ideology as doctrine and as programmes of political education.

If it be asked why these three senses are being privileged for treatment out of the very many that the term 'ideology' can be given, the answer is that reflection on Soviet history and on the Soviet political system today suggests *ex hypothesi* that they have a particular salience. The aim in this chapter is to demonstrate this salience, by focusing on the relationship between ideology and culture and on the political use of ideology in the Soviet Union.

2.1 APPROACHES TO SOVIET IDEOLOGY

The question of the relationship between the various senses of ideology has provided some of the most perceptive and valuable discussions on the politics of communism.[2] There has been no problem in accommodating differing interpretations within the general discourse on ideology, nor need there be. But there are certain points that must be made clear at the outset, if the senses in which the terms being used in any particular discussion are to be reconciled in a way that aids an understanding both of that concept and of the nature of the Soviet political system.

First, although an ideology comprises abstract ideas, those ideas are generated and transmitted by *people*. Secondly, ideology is not only about ideas but also about power, and about the political use that can be made of ideas. Thirdly, and above all, the safest treatments of ideology are those that start with the group, organisation or movement and seek its ideology; it can be very misleading to start with the ideology and to explain a group's actions in terms of it. There is, of course, a perfectly valid discussion to be had on what properly constitutes Marxism, and many participants in it would regard the CPSU as a Marxist party. But that discussion can leave out of account other elements of the CPSU's ideology that are at least equally important; it can also lead us to forget that Russian Marxism was made by Russian Marxists, and that Soviet ideology today may differ in essential respects from Soviet ideology yesterday. Such problems as the notion of a dead Marx teleguiding the Soviet Union of today and the assumption that Marxism alone provides the ideology of the CPSU can be diminished (though it is doubtful if they will ever be resolved) by taking as one's starting-point the organisation and not the ideology.

It might be argued that the case is different with Marxism–*Leninism*.

Lenin was one of the Russian Marxists who created Russian Marxism. The Leninism of Marxism–Leninism can be held to encompass those elements of the CPSU's ideology that go beyond what Marx said and thus constitute a full inventory of the CPSU's ideology today. But once again, the CPSU's ideology comprises more than can be attributed to a canon enlarged by adding Lenin's ideas to Marx's; and few would deny that there have been fundamental shifts in power relations within the CPSU since Lenin was active on the political stage. The appearance over the years of works with titles such as 'What Lenin Really Said' should put us on our guard.

It is, therefore, reasonable to ask whether the essential clues to understanding ideology in the context of Soviet politics might not lie less in examining what Marx said than in seeing how the CPSU has interpreted Marx's ideas and what it has done with them, and indeed continues to do with them in the routine functioning of the political system. It is reasonable also, if the enquiry is to be taken further, to analyse the changing circumstances of the CPSU through time and the power relations between individuals and groups within it, and to examine in detail the sources of the ideology that has emanated from the party over this period.

The same basic considerations suggest that the useful questions about ideology in the Soviet Union should be posed in terms of the CPSU itself and its role, and of its functionaries and their roles. Further, these questions should be put in an open-ended way that avoids unnecessary assumptions. Instead of assuming that the ideas of Marx provide the ideology of the CPSU, it should be asked what the actual components of the CPSU's ideology are. The appropriate question is not 'In what ways does ideology influence policy-making in the Soviet Union?', but rather 'What are the factors that influence policy-making in the Soviet Union?' or, with Jerry Hough, 'What things might a regional party first secretary be expected to take for granted?'.[3] Finally, instead of asking how successful is the CPSU's vast propaganda exercise, we should seek to discover why the CPSU employs, and continues to employ, so vast an establishment devoted to propaganda.

The first question in each of these cases can make assumptions that often go unchallenged or even unnoticed. The question whether ideology influences policy-making in the Soviet Union often assumes that the answer must be given in terms of the Marxist canon. Yet nationalism – as we shall see – is just as clearly a component of the CPSU's ideology as are the ideas of Marx on, say, the transformation of capitalism into socialism. Again, the question of how successful is the

CPSU's propaganda exercise is frequently answered in terms of how much those who attend classes and lectures absorb of the subject matter of their lessons. But the important point may not be what they learn; it may be simply that they are there. To feel that it is right (if tedious) to turn up now and then to talks organised by the party's ideological apparatus (or indeed to vote in elections, the results of which are known in advance) is evidence of an ideology at work. If a bit of knowledge about surplus value goes in, so much the better; if not, a little social cementing will have been achieved by the class having met and the duty of teacher and pupil fulfilled. For ideology is every bit as much about what social and political comportment seems right and what wrong, as it is about the ultimate cosmological justification for these sentiments.

In what follows, this chapter concentrates on two topics of current relevance to the study of ideology in the Soviet context: first, the relationship between ideology and culture; and secondly the political use of ideology in the Soviet Union. The aim is not to enthrone any one particular approach to the place of ideology in Soviet politics, but to suggest which of the many possible approaches are helpful, in the sense of promoting a clear economic and helpful account of the Soviet political system. Since both of these topics have a relevance extending well beyond the confines of that system, it is important to begin by emphasising those features of Soviet history and of Soviet society that give the study of ideology in the context of Soviet politics its particular salience.

2.2 THE IMPACT OF HISTORY

Over the years, the Soviet Union has developed a rigidity in economic and political life that was evident enough in the inertia of the Brezhnev years, but which has had a more recent illustration in Gorbachev's acknowledgement of the difficulties of instituting change in Soviet society. The Soviet Union is also a highly authoritarian state in which there are strict controls, both formal and informal, over the generation and diffusion of ideas. In such circumstances, to say that the Soviet Union's revolutionary origins have a continuing relevance may surprise. It must, nonetheless, be said. The Great October lies not far in the past and its shock waves are still being felt. The rigidity of the Soviet system has been due, at least in part, to the nervousness engendered by revolutionary turbulence and to the difficulties of transition from an even more recent Stalinist phase that was itself a period of acute revolutionary change.

Revolutions have a logic of their own, and ideology is an important part of that logic. First, in revolution the antagonists will, in Mannheim's words, 'seek to annihilate not merely the specific beliefs and attitudes of one another, but also the intellectual foundations upon which the beliefs and attitudes rest'.[4] In this struggle, however, the ideas of the revolutionaries have a different status from those of the defenders of the old order. The old beliefs and attitudes, though under attack, are familiar and are hallowed by memory. The revolutionaries, on the other hand, whilst they are aware of the strength of the values that they are assulting, have no social memory to put in their place. For it they have to substitute a future. Certain implications follow from this. As Michel Verret has pointed out in another context, the problem is that in presenting a picture of the future they will unconsciously reintroduce elements of the rejected social past. Moreover, these elements will be distorted through the effort to avoid contaminating the new with the old.[5]

Secondly, what the latent beliefs of the past are exchanged for is a self-conscious and aggressively asserted doctrine based on the texts that constitute the revolutionary frame of reference. There emerges an ideology that, in Bernard Williams' words, is 'creed-like' as opposed to 'tacit'.[6] This familiar (though gradually declining) feature of Soviet life is a clear corollary of the revolutionary process in Russia. What is involved is a complex interaction between ideology and culture that is inherent in the revolutionary situation.

At the same time, efforts are made to provide a new memory, a new set of valued symbols and new attitudes. Alfred Evans, in his study of Soviet school histories, has shown how this happened in the Soviet case and also how time brought changes, ever newer 'new' memories being imposed upon the older 'new' memories: 'The heroic efforts of struggle and sacrifice have receded further into the past' and the present (the 1970s) 'has been separated from the romantic–heroic period by increasingly thicker layers of history interpreted in terms of material progress, stability and consensus'.[7]

Further, revolution must be seen as a threefold process. A revolutionary force that has acceded to power must then consolidate that power; and once it has secured itself against counter-revolutionary forces and revolutionary rivals, it must then map out and address a strategy for the future. The ideas of the revolution undergo a significant change during this process of development. Before and during the accession to power, the revolutionaries can present whatever picture of the future they like. Afterwards they can go on saying what they wish, but they cannot go on *doing* what they wish – in Baechler's words 'lying becomes an inevitable ingredient of the exercise of power. This is why people's relationship with the ideology is not the same before the taking of power, during the early stages of exercising power and in the routine exercise of power'.[8]

The revolutionary vision of the future serves different purposes – and more importantly different people – at the different stages of this revolutionary process. Until it is put to the test in a post-revolutionary situation, the rhetoric of the revolutionaries can be read in various ways by various social groups. In the end, however, it will be put to political use in securing loyalty to a new regime in a situation in which a pre-existing basis of legitimacy has been swept away, and in which the revolutionary leadership can no longer count on the spontaneous support of the forces that brought it to power. It is for these reasons, among others, that the Soviet Union's revolutionary origins provide, even today, an essential clue to understanding ideology in the Soviet context, and the political uses to which it is put.

A second factor is the Soviet Union's relationship with the developing world. Since 1917, the Soviet Union has been the centre of an expanding communist universe, but it was not until more than halfway through the century that the close link between communism and the movement of the developing world against the West became manifest. By that time the Soviet Union was no longer a poor nation, but the link had none the less been forged. The implications of this fact for any discussion of the ideology of the Soviet Union or of the CPSU are of the first importance.

These implications are best illustrated by considering three possible interpretations of the Russian revolution. From one point of view, it represented the first occasion on which a Marxist party had achieved state power. That revolutionary struggle, and the policies that the Bolsheviks subsequently adopted, can be placed in the context of a European debate about the revolutionary transformation of capitalism into socialism, a debate that had its origins in a European Marx and in which Lenin was a prominent participant. From this point of view, the Russian revolution was above all about socialism.

From a second point of view, the Russian revolution and its aftermath can be seen as an early but highly influential example of the fight-back by the poorer nations of the world against the economic penetration and superior firepower of the West. Half European, half Asian, with a growing industry heavily funded by the foreigner and an army of which it was said it took ten Russians to fight one Western solider, Russia shared the predicament of the less developed world, even though its statesmen, many of its writers, and certainly its Bolsheviks, situated themselves and their country in a European framework. From this point of view, the Russian revolution and its upshot were above all about national freedom, and cultural and economic development. It was the first in a series that was continued in China, Cuba, Vietnam and beyond.

Thirdly, the Russian revolution can be seen simply as an internal adjustment arising from the failure of the tsarist structure to accommodate social change and increasing social pressures. Soviet society, in this view, is a continuation of Russian history into a new phase.

These three views of the Russian revolution are a matter of emphasis; they are not, of course, mutually exclusive. Each of them represents one facet of the Soviet Union's history. But it is imperative to separate them analytically if a proper perspective is to be gained on the ideology of the CPSU. The reason is quite simply that if the *sources* of Soviet ideology are sought, they will be found to be not one, but many. There are elements that derive from the Marxist canon, there are elements that derive from the developmental situation ('catching up and overtaking the West' and 'socialism equals Soviet power plus the electrification of the whole country' compared with the dictatorship of the proletariat) and from the Soviet Union's links, either perceived or real, with its less developed clients and allies; and there are elements that are drawn quite simply from the national past. To say that the Soviet Union has a Marxist ideology is to say something about Soviet ideology – something that in certain contexts might be the essential consideration – but it is by no means all that there is to say. To use the extended term 'Marxism–Leninism' itself is to acknowledge this.

A corollary of this multiple derivation is that elements of the CPSU's ideology drawn from one source coexist and at times conflict with elements drawn from other sources, and it does not help understanding if ideology is attached to a single one of these sources, to the express exclusion of the others. Consider the following statement about literary policy in the Zhdanov period: 'Although national motifs continued to make their appearance in these essays, it is clear that Zhdanov consciously subordinated them to the claims of ideology'.[9] Here expressions of nationalism are seen as conflicting with ideas hostile to nationalism which Zhdanov chose to draw from the Marxist armoury, but (quite wrongly) only the latter are attributed to ideology.

Sometimes the different sources of the CPSU's ideology are presented sequentially – with good cause, since the relative emphasis has shifted between them at important turning-points of Soviet history, of which the period around 1924 is of particular significance. Thus Daniels, asking the most helpful question of all: 'What is the actual content of Soviet ideology?', notes that the question is not often asked, since the answer seems so clearly to be given by the corpus of Marxism–Leninism, but that an answer must acknowledge that 'the ideology has not survived the successive phases of the revolutionary process as a factor of constant value.'[10] Evans' study of Soviet textbooks suggests, on the other hand, a view of the CPSU's ideology as simultaneously containing differing strands in the Stalinist period – 'a mixture of social transformation with economic growth and nationalism'.[11] But we do not need to choose between these two views. Ideological shifts can be a matter of a changing balance of elements drawn from different sources. What is important is that any account of the content of the CPSU's ideology at any time must take into account the following points:

1. It is far from abnormal for conflicting elements to coexist within the ideology of a political party or a society. It is a question of which element is uppermost or can prevail at any given time.
2. That question is not an abstract matter but concerns political choices made by actual people, by actors on the political scene. It is *people* that need ideology, that make it, and that use it.
3. If themes of nationalism and national development came to the fore in the Stalinist period in the Soviet Union (under whatever impulses or as the result of whatever rivalries between groups) that does not mean that they were absent during Lenin's lifetime.
4. The rhetoric of Marxism–Leninism, in acting as an umbrella under which shifts in relative emphasis of the various elements of the CPSU's ideology have taken place, has served to conceal the extent of these shifts. Each item of that rhetoric is a carapace – to employ Rignano's term – the occupant of which is liable to change from time to time. It is the rhetoric that conceals the process whereby the CPSU came to use the same ideas that were associated with change in the revolutionary period (and continue to accompany change in the case of other parties in other places) to justify lack of radical change in the Soviet Union during and since the Stalinist years.

These three aspects of the Soviet Union's history, then, are of importance for an understanding of ideology in the Soviet context. First, the effects of the revolution and its aftermath; secondly, the strategy of economic and cultural development that the party adopted; and thirdly the Soviet Union's relationship with a communist movement that has been dominated by the confluence of communism with the 'national liberation movement'. In turning now to the relationship between ideology and culture, it is the first of these aspects – the impact of revolution – that most commands attention.

2.3 IDEOLOGY AND CULTURE

It was noted above how a vigorous discussion on Soviet ideology in the 1960s was followed by an equally vigorous discussion about Soviet political culture in the 1970s, with very little attempt being made to link the two. The failure to do so is all the more surprising in that it is hard to define political culture in a way that does not impinge on the conceptual territory of ideology. This does not mean, however, that the relationship between the two constructs is simply stated. In this section, the factors that should inform any statement of that relationship will be examined, beginning with a point made above about the nature of revolution, in relation to the specific case of the Russian revolution and its aftermath.

Revolution involves an assault on a culture. It also involves a conflict between rival ideologies. For the first of these, whilst the Bolsheviks saw as one of their major aims the elimination of certain influences of the past, and whilst some of them were thoroughly familiar with the societies of Western Europe, they were nevertheless children of the culture of tsarist society. This was bound to affect the manner in which the assault on the culture of the past was conducted, with both over-reaction and an unsuspecting carry-over of traditional values playing their part. In the mixture of change and continuity that revolution presents, the element of continuity is provided by the insidious intractability of the pre-revolutionary culture, which is to be seen not only in the attitudes of the defenders of the old order, active or passive, but also in the content of the revolutionaries' discourse and policy alternatives.

As for the conflict between rival ideologies, it was suggested above that the values of tsarist society and the ideas with which the Bolsheviks aimed to supplant them differed not only in their content, but in other ways besides: the old ideas and beliefs were familiar and were invested with a lingering value stemming from folk memory, despite the contradiction between those values and the material demands that the revolutionary masses were making at the point of revolution. The new ideas had little basis in the social memory; they were to an extent foreign and by definition novel; they were aggressively asserted; in rejecting the past they laid emphasis on the future. They existed, in fact, at the point of revolution as a *project*. And whilst it is not difficult to discuss the ideology of tsarist Russia in terms of the culture of that society, the appearance on the scene of an ideology having the character of a project introduced a different situation that called for different treatment.

Before the revolution, the culture of tsarist Russia was congruent with the ideology promoted by the political and social authorities through the

Church, the educational system, the army and the manipulation of political symbols. The revolutionary ideology, being without roots, had to be provided with them, and in the next section the way in which this has been done will be examined. That, however, took time; and whilst this lengthy process was taking place, other means had to be found of anchoring the new ideas and patterns of behaviour. The emphasis on textual sources, the generation of slogans and of a vigorous poster art, the cult of the personality of the founding fathers of the ideology, the publication of a new dictionary to enshrine new definitions, all played a part in this process of anchoring new values.[12] The effects of this early assertiveness are still present in more than vestigial form, although the self-consciousness might be expected to diminish with the passing of time. This has indeed been the case, and Gorbachev's words on ideological work to the 27th Congress of the CPSU, with their emphasis upon improving the quality and reducing the quantity of the party's ideological endeavours, and on avoiding 'scholasticism, pedantry and dogmatism' – if they are more than a routine headmasterly chiding – may mark a step in the direction of just such a diminution of self consciousness.

The Western literature on the CPSU's multifaceted drive to change political attitudes and behaviour has tended to avoid the term 'ideology'. Whatever the term is used to connote this drive matters much less, of course, than acknowledging the full historical value of the confrontation between the bearers of an existing culture and a new élite which, though formed in that culture, has set out to implant a new one and to create the 'new socialist man'.[13] Archie Brown, for example, in his edited symposium on *Political Culture and Communist Studies*, distinguishes between a dominant, an élite, and an official political culture. The last of these 'represents official norms, desiderata, and political goals rather than societal values and beliefs', and Brown calls for study of the interrelationships between the three, rightly pointing out that 'no detailed study has been undertaken yet'.[14] Here the all-important distinction between a project and the results of its propagation is made; and yet the term 'ideology' is dispensed with. The question is whether or not it matters to dispense with it.

There are a number of reasons for maintaining that it does matter a great deal. The first is that to conduct the discussion in terms either of culture or of ideology alone fudges the question of the relationship between the two. Treatments of ideology have admittedly been riddled with conflicting definitions and charged with *parti pris*. Furthermore the senses in which Soviet sources use the term, and the very particular way in which ideology is institutionalised in the Soviet Union, might suggest that other terms be used in analysing the Soviet Union's political system. None of this, however, justifies leaving a very interesting debate about ideology hanging in the air without relating it to a more recent one about political culture. Secondly, there is the simple lexical point that words serve to mark distinctions. If the term 'culture' is made to work too hard, it loses some of its analytical value for making useful distinctions.

To confuse a project for a culture has, in the Soviet case, unfortunate results. In particular, it blurs the perspective on a very specific aspect of the Russian revolution and Soviet development, namely the way in which the party has put itself above society and above class, originally so as to institute social change, and then to maintain the new order, including its own place in that new order. It has done this in a very particular way that is historically novel, though the pattern has since been reproduced in many parts of the world. The party's authoritarian control over the means of communication and the use it makes of that control are of great historical interest and importance; all the more reason for sifting out the party's programmes from the results of those programmes. The results are susceptible to a discussion in terms of culture. For the programmes we dispose of another term that allows us to preserve the distinction, and that term is ideology.

There is a further reason for detaching ideology from a notion of an official political culture. The Soviet Union is linked to a world-wide Marxist movement in which it wields immense authority, but which, nevertheless, extends beyonds its sphere of control. It is ideology that binds the units of a movement together, in a manner that bridges cultures. We are clearly here in a realm far removed from the political culture of a single society, however influential. But the elements of that linking ideology form the basis of the suggested Soviet 'official political culture'. These elements enable a Soviet citizen to relate what is happening at home in the Soviet Union to what is happening in the wider world in the twentieth century. To term them ideology when they are seen in this broader role, but an official political culture when they turn up in programmes run by the CPSU at home is not entirely satisfactory.

There can be no doubt that the preoccupation with cultural factors in general, which developed in the 1960s and 1970s, enriched the discussion on communist politics. The discussion would have been further enriched if it had been related to the earlier discussion on ideology and had not displaced it. It should be possible to retain the scheme of a pre-revolutionary political culture giving place, after a period of revolutionary turbulence, to a modified or new culture, and to add to it a parallel or overlapping analysis of the impact of an aggressively-asserted revolutionary ideology on the pre-revolutionary political culture and on the pre-revolutionary ideology which that culture secreted. In Mary McAuley's words, we could 'spell out the message coming through the ideology, trace the changes in it and relate them to the practice of the rulers'.[15] There could then follow the discussions, which we have not had to an adequate extent, on the relationship between ideology and culture in communist politics, and on the question of whom it is appropriate to regard as the bearers of ideology and of culture in communist countries.

It is an interesting fact that, while political scientists have been busy extracting from the sociological concept of culture a notion of political culture that they have often, if not always, assumed could be detached from culture in the broad and analysed separately, there have been sociological developments that do the reverse: the psychological, attitudinal factor that are of relevance to political processes and structures have been sought more widely in the broader cultural matrix. Space does not allow a full treatment of what might be termed the sociological contribution to a discussion of ideology in the Soviet Union, which has hitherto been mostly either philosophical or political. Two aspects of it, however, must be mentioned.

First, in so far as treatments of Soviet ideology in the 1960s were concerned with language, the focus was, with some exceptions, on the highly formalised vocabulary of official texts and pronouncements. The discussion was not, on the whole, particularly profound. Foucault's seminal treatment of discourse has offered a much more secure basis for relating language to ideology, an offer that has been taken up so far chiefly by his own compatriots.[16] Language is the fundamental conveyer of ideology, and a revolutionary epoch provides an exceptional laboratory for the study of language in that role. In less turbulent times, language secretes an ideology; the latter can be revealed by studying the matrix of meanings that a language comprises. But in revolution words not only acquire new meanings; language can be used as a political instrument to inculcate new values and to reinforce a still insecure revolutionary ideology.

Secondly, our ideas of what is to count as ideology in Soviet politics have not included, to the extent that they should, the entire realm of ritual and the mythos. The recent emphasis on language has had as one of its effects to bring this, too, within the discussion. In the words of François Saint-Ouen: 'a particular logic flows (from the discourse), in which memory, events and symbols are all involved. A discourse is what gives events their sense, and presents the future in relation to the past.'[17]

There has been in the past a widely accepted notion that a reverence for symbols, for heroic personages and heroic events, for rituals concerned with the calendar or with marriages and other civic events great and small somehow conflicts with values contained in the Marxist canon and is therefore not acceptable as ideology. But if in the CPSU's ideology an exaggerated concern for ritual and symbols clearly coexists with an equally exaggerated veneration of Marxist texts which might seem to question such a concern, this must be accepted as a fact of life, and a part of the evidence that the analyst must deal with. As for the exaggerations involved in both cases, we have seen that a revolutionary party, being unable to use the social memory as a support for its ideas, compensates by creating its own mythos and by asserting it with particular vigour. This aggressive and self-conscious assertion of symbols, and this constant reference to hallowed texts, had already been severely modified in the Soviet Union, and may be expected to decline further as the revolution continues to recede and as a Soviet culture more congruent with the values that the party has been promoting emerges. Research that reveals the extent to which this is taking place, of the kind carried out by Evans and referred to above, is now particularly valuable.[18]

Finally, we have encountered in this section at least three reasonably distinct senses of the term 'ideology': first, ideology as an overall view of the world and of man's place in it, the 'key to history or the solution to all the "riddles of the universe"'; secondly, ideology as the revolutionary project, involving doctrines, slogans and programmes of political education; and finally the mythos – symbols and rituals that are mostly local in nature (the Great October, the figure of Lenin, and approved patterns of behaviour when visiting his mausoleum), but which are related through the rhetoric to the wider scheme. If it be doubted that the last category really counts as ideology it is instructive to consider the case of the 'Leninist principle of democratic centralism'.

This originally purely local pattern of party and then social organisation is linked in authoritative Soviet texts to Marx's view of the path to communist society.[19] The phrase itself has a high symbolic value as a rallying cry both conjoining and evoking unity and solidarity; it reveals a very particular collectivist psychology in which the well-being of the organism is preferred to the well-being of its parts; and it provides a guide to what kinds of political actions are acceptable and what not. As a mode of organisation it also happens to have proved productive in less developed countries whose élites are, or see themselves as being, in a situation analogous to that of the Bolsheviks at the point of the Russian revolution. It clearly must be accounted a part of the CPSU's ideology. The refrain must once again by rehearsed that one understanding of what constitutes ideology does not exclude another. There is room for several discussions around that chameleon term. We must now turn to consider in greater detail the second of the senses of term listed above: the Bolshevik project, and the historically novel manner in which the CPSU has developed the 'creative use of ideology'.

2.4 THE POLITICAL USES OF IDEOLOGY

One of the problems of dealing with ideology in Soviet politics is the double use that Soviet sources make of the term – first as 'false consciousness', in the sense that Marx and Engels gave to that expression, and secondly as a political instrument appropriate to the tasks of the party in constructing communist society. Moreover, the programmes of political education run by the CPSU under the rubric of the 'creative use of ideology' have a markedly local and national colouring that seems hard to reconcile with the universal concepts of Marxism.

It was noted above, however, that it is not surprising to encounter, in the Soviet context as in any other, differing notions of what constitutes ideology. It has to be accepted that Soviet sources attach great significance to both of the above definitions. It is for us to discover why they are deemed so important, and what light they throw on the role of ideology in the Soviet political system. In this section, it is the second of these Soviet presentations of ideology that will concern us: ideology as a political instrument.

Soviet experience since the revolution presents a number of very compelling reasons for taking seriously the Soviet view of the instrumental use of ideology. First and foremost, Soviet history offers a valuable example of an ideology being promoted deliberately and with dynamism by a political leadership. It illustrates, in fact, the close relationship between ideology and power. Four tasks in particular that the Bolsheviks had to address at different stages of Soviet development favoured the creation of a structure of political education reaching down to the roots of society. The first of these tasks was to secure in people's minds the identity of the new social order. The second was to legitimise the party's rule. The third was to integrate society, or rather to reintegrate it, after the dissolution that the revolution and the Civil War had wrought. The fourth was to mobilise the masses for the tasks of national construction in circumstances of acute austerity. A relationship between ideology and power, which is present in less pressing times, gained a further dimension in insurrectionary revolution in the circumstances of the Russia of 1917, and in the development drive that followed. Morover, the phases through which Soviet development has passed serve to illustrate with great clarity the fact that ideology is not generated in the abstract, but is always the ideology of a group, organisation or class. The programmes and the doctrine that the CPSU transmits have been the product of the party's theorists, and the shifts in these programmes and doctrines have to be related to the shifts in power relations within the CPSU.[20]

This feature of ideology in Soviet politics was the corollary of a revolutionary process, in which the introduction of new ideas in a period of social flux gave place, in a later period, to the authoritarian assertion of the ideology. In these circumstances, far from being latent in society, ideology has been, and remains, a political tool in the hands of a political leadership. Soviet spokesmen make no bones about this aspect of what they see as an important part of the party's leading role: 'The fulfilment of our economic and social plans depends to a tremendous extent on the ideological back-up, on how ideology helps to fulfil the key tasks of social development', wrote Chernenko in 1983, approving 'Lenin's requirement that communists' ideological and organizational work should be an organic whole'.[21] Even Gorbachev, in his 'new look' speech to the CPSU's 27th Congress, acknowledged the work of the 'tens and hundreds of thousands of propagandists, agitators, political instructors, circles and seminars, newspaper and magazine runs in the millions, and audiences of similar proportions at lectures', although, given the emphasis in his speech on improving the quality and reducing the quantity of the party's ideological output, there may well have been a touch of sarcasm in his comment that 'these figures are truly impressive'.[22]

Secondly, the programmes of political education that the party organises illustrate the fact that if the CPSU's ideology is Marxist, this is Marxism in a localised form, and doubly so. On the one hand, it is fruitless to think of Marxism as having some objective or ideal existence detached from the perceptions that Marxist parties and individuals have of it. The ideas of the Russian Marxists necessarily refracted Marx's ideas, accommodating them to a Russian context and to the Russian language. In the case of Bolshevik thinking, mention has already been made of the rather obvious example of the party's leading role; outlined in Lenin's work before the revolution, it was to live on as a central element of the CPSU's ideology.

This fundamental refraction of Marx's ideas through the Russian theorists was given a further dimension in the need to secure the link between party and masses by means of programmes of political education. To be comprehensible to the masses the ideology had first to be simplified. But not only that; it had also to be given an emphatic local colouring. If the idea of the vanguard party emerged as one Marxist's local response to the universal problem of adapting a Marxist analysis to the revolutionary struggle, the party's teaching took the process one stage further. It provided illustrations from the lives of individual and local leaders, making those leaders, the party itself, and the idea of the party's leading role familiar to a population whose introduction to Marxism followed the reverse track – starting with Stalin's virtues, passing through the importance of the party in Soviet life and of the party's role in communist construction, and so to the Marxist texts themselves – which, of course, would in the case of most people not be reached, except in the most schematic form.

Moreover, if the ideas of Marx were abstract, external to Russia in their origin, and (so far as the simple populace was concerned) remote, other elements of the ideology that formed the content of the CPSU's propaganda were from the start purely local, and thus familiar. This was true, above all, of the mythos that was being created – the soviets, the Great October, Lenin, democratic centralism, and the values associated with these and other symbolic institutions, events and 'principles' – and was being projected vigorously and self-consciously by the new revolutionary élite.

Thirdly, the political uses to which ideology has been put in the Soviet Union, in reflecting the shifts in power relations in the CPSU, illustrate also the way in which an ideology can not only feature as a project for change, but also justify inertia and become a support for the power of an existing leadership. This, of course, is the distinction that Mannheim made between Utopia and ideology; and it is one of the chief reasons why it is important, in analysing ideology in Soviet politics, to start not with the label of Marxism but with the questions of what the components of the CPSU's ideology are at any given time, who is formulating it, and for what purposes.

This leads to a fourth, and in many ways the most remarkable, aspect of the political use of ideology in the Soviet Union, namely, the immense size and political weight of the establishment that is charged with packaging and propagating the CPSU's ideology, and in filtering or suppressing rival ideas. So influential and pervasive is this establishment that it merits the closest attention in any discussion of ideology in the Soviet context. Certain features of its structure and ways of operating are worth spelling out.

The most striking features are its sheer size and the extent of its ramifications. Attention has naturally focused on the Central Committee's Department of Propaganda, but other departments of the Central Committee clearly play a crucial role in ideological matters, including the Department of Culture, Science and Education, the International Information Department and the Main Political Administration of the armed forces. This mighty central apparatus is but the hub of a wheel with many radiating spokes, including the party's local *agitprop* organs, the entire education system, the mass organisations, the Znanie society and similar bodies, certain of the institutes of the Academy of Sciences, and the party's own schools and research establishments. The nature of the linkages at the centre of this network, and the roles of particular individuals, are gradually becoming better known to outside observers. The attention that the party's apparatus is currently attracting will no doubt enhance our knowledge of these links, the importance of which is proportional to the importance of doctrine in Soviet life. In fact, within the party's apparatus, which lies at the heart of the system of politics with which the Soviet Union has endowed the world, there are, in turn, two central functions. The first is control of nominations to responsible posts. The second is control over communications, that is, ideological control, both in the sense of control through the institutions that purvey the ideology, and control of the ideology by protecting it from discrepant voices and by keeping its message clear.

Further, so vast an establishment has been subject to specialisation. For the sake of clarity, three broad functional specialisations should be noted. Firstly, there are the teachers and instructors. This most numerous category of ideological workers must itself be broken down into those who are on the staff of the party committees at the various levels, and of the armed forces' political administration; those who are paid from other sources, including a large part of the entire educational establishment; and the great army of volunteers.[23] The number of people involved, and the kind of audiences that they have faced over the years, go a long way to explaining the dogmatising of the leadership's pronouncements and doctrines.

Secondly, there is the function of shaping the doctrines and 'packaging' them for popular consumption. At the highest levels these are roles of the greatest political importance, about which we are beginning to establish some of the details. It is now possible to identify not only the theorists and officials, but also the institutions and bureaux that count in the shaping of the doctrine, even if our knowledge of how the final choice of a key phrase is made still has to depend upon more or less respectable rumours[24] and if a good deal still remains obscure about the precise way in which influence passes between the theorists based, for example, in institutes of the Academy of Sciences, and the higher officials of the Central Committee's ideological departments. And thirdly there are what might be termed the ideological policemen and controllers. These include most prominently the censors (in both party and state instances), officials in charge of appointments, and the KGB itself.[25]

Mention should be made also of the importance, for achieving a position of supreme power, of having held an ideological brief within the Secretariat of the Central Committee. Mikhail Suslov was for a long time credited with the role of ideological 'overlord', though in his case this did not lead to the general secretaryship. In the cases of both Chernenko and Gorbachev, however, that rather ill-defined role of ideological overlord was a clear stage in their progression to power, and it is this same role that has more recently conferred so great an authority on Egor Ligachev.

A final consideration concerns the major shift in power and property relations that resulted from the Russian revolution. That revolution was extreme in the extent to which power and property were removed from corporate and individual hands and held as a single pool by the force that had emerged triumphant from the revolutionary process. Ever since the revolution, the CPSU has held an effective monopoly of power in political, economic and ideological terms. The trend of recent comment has been to modify this view; the monopoly in none of these fields is complete and has been subject to change. But the extent of the party's power of control remains remarkable. This fundamental historical fact affects the discussion on ideology in a number of ways.

The question arises, first, how this scooping of the pool of political and economic power came to be so extreme. No doubt the Marxist ideas of the Bolsheviks had something to do with it. But there were other factors, such as the historical centralisation of the Russian state, and the stunted growth in Russia of those social forces in the middle ranges of society, which in the French case had dominated the revolution. To attribute the party's present dominance of Soviet society to Marx, even by way of a Leninist refraction, is elliptical in the extreme.

Moreover, whilst analysis has tended to focus on the political and economic aspects of this dominance, the ideological aspect is no less important. The party's theorists have had to rationalise the party's monopoly over the vast pool of centralised power, and to make that rationalisation stick. Thus works appear, for example, expressly linking democratic centralism with central command planning and with the party's leading role, and in turn linking all these Soviet inventions with the Marxist thesis by defining socialism and democracy in terms of them.[26]

The central consideration from the point of view of the instrumental use of ideology, is that the political, economic and ideological monopolies reinforce each other. Just as the plan has the force of law, so the party's doctrines are effectively constitutional acts, and share in the authority that the party's position in society provides.[27] What makes life difficult for the outside observer is that the party insists that things are otherwise, that it does not govern, and that its pronouncements do not have constitutional authority. In other words, it is party doctrine to conceal the status of party doctrine.

This interdependence between the political, economic and ideological spheres is central to the role in the Soviet political system not only of ideology itself, but of the whole ideological establishment. What is involved is far more than an abstract link between the party's ideology and its policies. It is a matter of institutional relationships of the principles on which the legal and penal systems function, of the foundation on which the power of the central leadership rests. From that interdependence stems a particular way of thinking – one that converts the dissenter into either a traitor or a madman.

The way in which this works is of the greatest importance. The general link between the ideological and political spheres in the Soviet system can be expressed as a link between the content of doctrines on the one hand, and on the other of their political status and of that of their framers. In a situation of effective monopoly not only do the framers of the doctrines enjoy a privileged status, but so too do the doctrines. This situation is internally self-supporting: the doctrines not only guarantee the power positions of the leadership, but also promote their own doctrinal status. That is, they will not only establish what is to be considered orthodox, but will also promote a strong belief in the value of orthodoxy itself. In this way revisionism, from being an ideological category, becomes a political one; and in the taboo on fractional activity the political and ideological factors merge completely.

It is this fusion of the political and ideological spheres that gives party congresses their particular salience in the life of communist parties. Congresses proclaim the authority and the oneness of the leadership (a minority becomes an 'anti-party group' or a 'gang of four') and at the same time the oneness of the doctrine. Society's leadership is confirmed and at the same time the line is proclaimed for the immense ideological network. This, of course, has been said many times before, but it bears repeating for three reasons. First, the changes that commentators have discerned in the Soviet political processes since Stalin died have not significantly modifed this situation, which continues to be a major characteristic of Soviet political life, and indeed of that of most communist parties; secondly, because the discussion about political culture, whilst it has not questioned this basic fact, has caused a distraction from it by abandoning an existing terminology for a less appropriate one; and finally because occasions such as the Solidarity crisis in Poland, in revealing how essential to the system is this link between the political and ideological apparatuses, suggest that the formation of doctrine in the Soviet Union merits the closest attention.

2.5 CONCLUSION

It should by now be clear what are the helpful approaches to ideology that this chapter has sought to identify. The first is to give due weight to historical factors in a society whose institutions and political processes still heavily reflect a period of revolutionary turbulence and change. The second is to ask the right questions, such as those suggested in the introduction to this chapter – questions which test the assumptions that are made about ideology and which start from the people who collectively generate and transmit the ideology of the CPSU. Thirdly, our analysis and research should focus on the CPSU's vast ideological establishment, which provides so many of the clues to understanding the link between ideology and politics, the ways in which ideology becomes localised, and the ways in which it is not only generated, but also packaged and transmitted. Fourthly and finally, we should give much more attention to the actual content of the doctrine that is transmitted in this way.

NOTES

1. Quoted in Bernard Crick, *In Defence of Politics* (Harmondsworth: Penguin, 1964), p. 98.
2. Among the works that deserve particular mention are Franz Schurmann, *Ideology and Organization in Communist China* (Berkeley and London: University of California Press, 1966); Jerome M. Gilison, *The Soviet Image of Utopia* (Baltimore, Md: Johns Hopkins University Press, 1975); A. Ross Johnson, *The Transformation of Communist Ideology: the Yugoslav Case 1945–1953* (Cambridge, Mass.: MIT Press, 1972); and Ray Taras, *Ideology in a Socialist State: Poland 1956–83* (Cambridge University Press, 1984).
3. See Hough in H. Gordon Skilling and Franklyn Griffiths, eds. *Interest*

Groups in Soviet Politics (Princeton University Press, 1971), p. 69.
4. Karl Mannheim, *Ideology and Utopia* (London: Routledge, 1960), p. 57.
5. M. Verret, 'Mémoire ouvrière, mémoire communiste', in *Revue française de science politique* (*RFSP*), vol. 34, no. 3 (June 1984), pp. 413–27.
6. Bernard Williams, 'Democracy and ideology', *Political Quarterly*, vol. 32 (1961) no. 4, pp. 374–84.
7. Alfred Evans Jr., 'Trends in Soviet secondary school histories in the USSR', *Soviet Studies*, vol. 28, no. 2 (April 1976), pp. 224–43, at p. 238.
8. Jean Baechler, *Qu'est-ce que l'idéologie?* (Paris: Gallimard, 1976), p.58.
9. John B. Dunlop, *The Faces of Contemporary Russian Nationalism* (Princeton University Press, 1983), p. 24.
10. Robert V. Daniels, 'The ideological vector', *Soviet Studies*, vol. 18, no. 1 (July 1966), p. 71.
11. Evans, 'Trends in Soviet secondary school histories', p. 233.
12. On the first major post-revolutionary dictionary published under the editorship of D. N. Ushakov see Michael Waller, 'The -isms of Stalinism', *Soviet Studies*, vol. 20, no. 2 (October 1968), pp. 229–34.
13. This process has been particularly well treated by Stephen White in his *Political Culture and Soviet Politics* (London: Macmillan, 1979).
14. Archie Brown (ed.), *Political Culture and Communist Studies* (London: Macmillan, 1984), p. 177. For further reference to an 'official political culture' see Archie Brown and Jack Gray (eds), *Political Culture and Political Change in Communist States* (London: Macmillan, 1977), pp. 8ff., and Stephen White in the same work, p. 35. For a studious determination not to allow the term 'ideology' to intrude into a discussion of a revolutionary assult on established values, see Gabriel Almond, 'Communism and political culture theory', *Comparative Politics*, vol. 16, no. 1 (January 1983), p. 137.
15. McAuley in Brown (ed.), *Political Culture and Communist Studies*, pp. 25–30.
16. Michel Foucault, *L'archéologie du savoir* (Paris: Gallimard, 1969). See also Verret, 'Mémoire ouvrière', and D. Labbé, 'Le discours communiste', *RFSP*, vol. 30, no. 1 (February 1980), pp. 46–77.
17. 'De la matérialité du discours aux espaces discursifs', *RFSP*, vol. 34, no. 3 (June 1984), pp. 428–48.
18. On these aspects of the CPSU's ideology see Christel Lane, *The Rites of Rulers* (Cambridge University Press, 1981) and Christopher A. P. Binns, 'Revolution and accommodation in the development of the Soviet ceremonial system', *Man*, vol. 14 (1980), no. 4 and vol. 15 (1981), no. 1.
19. For one example among many, see V. M. Lavrichev, *Demokraticheskii tsentralizm – dialekticheskii printsip organizatsionnogo stroeniya KPSS* (Moscow: Mysl', 1971).
20. See Nigel Harris, 'The owl of Minerva', *Soviet Studies*, vol. 18, no. 3 (January 1967), pp. 328–39, at pp. 329–31.
21. *World Marxist Review*, 1983, no. 11, p. 6.
22. *Pravda*, 26 February 1986, p. 10.
23. See White, *Political Culture*, ch. 4; Gayle D. Hollander, *Soviet Political Indoctrination* (New York: Praeger, 1972); Jerry F. Hough and Merle Fainsod, *How the Soviet Union is Governed* (Cambridge, Mass.: Harvard University Press, 1979), ch. 11.

24. The part played by Fedor Burlatsky, for example, in the formulation and adoption of the doctrines both of the 'state of the whole people' and of 'developed socialism' seems to be generally accepted.
25. See John H. Miller, 'The top Soviet censorship team?', *Soviet Studies*, vol. 29 (1977), no. 4, pp. 590–8, and Sidney Monas and Ronald Levaco on cinema censorship in *Studies in Comparative Communism*, vol. 17 (1984–5), nos. 3 and 4, pp. 163–84.
26. N. A. Moiseenko and M. V. Popov, *Demokraticheskii tsentralizm–osnovnoi printsip upravleniya sotsialisticheskoi ekonomikoi* (Leningrad: Lenizdat, 1975) and Lavrichev, *Demokraticheskii tsentralizm*.
27. The 1977 Soviet Constitution, for example, included a formal reference to democratic centralism, which until then had been a constitutional matter only in the party. Constitutional lawyers had for some time accepted the *de facto* constitutional status of the 'Leninist principle': see V. I. Vasilev, *Demokraticheskii tsentralizm v sisteme sovetov* (Moscow: Yuridicheskaya literatura, 1973).

3 Political Ideologies in the Soviet Union: Reflections on Past Attempts to Understand The Relationship between Ideas and Politics

ALFRED G. MEYER

For the last forty years, I have been a student of Engels and Marx, their ideas and theories, and how others have interpreted and sought to apply them. What originally attracted me to this study was, among other things, the fact that, in the United States in the period immediately following the Second World War, Marxism and its various transformations were not considered worthy of systematic exploration. My professors sought to convince me that Marx had made no significant or lasting contributions to any branch of theory and that, at best, one might study his writings as examples of the aberration of the human spirit. None the less I set out, very much without guidance and therefore in a rather haphazard fashion, to explore this body of theory, both in its original form and as transformed by Lenin. I discovered a system of thought expressed in language rather different from that used by my teachers, but very much worth studying. My writings in this field have always been a conscious attempt at translating this language, trying to communicate its meaning to the uninitiated, taking these ideas seriously, and making sense out of them. I have done this not only because Marx, Engels, Lenin and other contributors convey important insights and thus can teach us much about ourselves, but also because these ideas, in turn, have become historic forces, impulses, guides, or constraints to action. The term ideology seems to me to carry the implication that ideas should be studied in their relatedness to action.

Precisely which body of ideas is being referred to when we talk about Soviet ideology is not at all clear, as will be discussed in this chapter similarly, the nature of the relationship between the ideology (however defined) and political action has always been controversial. In the article I published in 1966, I wrestled with both problems; and in retrospect it seems to me that what that article did primarily was to express my confusion.[1] I defined Soviet ideology as the body of doctrine taught in courses on dialectical and historical materialism, political economy, scientific communism and the history of the party, in short, the sum-total of what the new Programme of the CPSU describes as 'the scientific world view . . . the basis of which is constituted by Marxism–Leninism as a well integrated system of philosophic, economic and socio-political positions'. In the article, I discussed a number of features of that doctrine which seemed to me worth noting: that it was both rigid and flexible; that both the political leadership and the masses of the population seemed to be deeply committed to and yet quite cynical about it; and that it was equally plausible to understand it as a guide to action or as a mere public relations device. I further stressed discontinuities in Soviet ideology. Just as the party of Stalin and his successors was a very different organisation from that of Lenin, so Soviet ideology since the 1930s, I suggested, was markedly different from that of the early revolutionary period, even though the transformation was obscured by the use of vocabulary first placed into circulation by Marx and Engels. Anyone looking beyond the formal continuities is likely to agree that they have become empty shells drained of the old, and ready to be filled with new, contents.

Once this is recognised, we must dismiss as disproven the persistent belief that Soviet politics can be understood primarily as the effort on the part of the communist party leadership to put Marxist or Marxist–Leninist ideas into practice – a belief which I label 'ideological determinism'. To be sure, the Russian revolution like many other revolutions was a process in which spontaneous as well as organised action by broad masses of radicalised people was channelled with the help of the revolutionary ideology of the party that came to power. But in all such revolutions harsh reality soon prompts drastic changes in the dreams, hopes and expectations that the ideology expressed. Those who cling to the original hopes and dreams, if indeed they are allowed to survive, then talk about the revolution betrayed.

In my 1966 article, I speculated about the residual effect of the revolutionary ideas on present-day leaders in the Soviet Union and suggested that adherence to this Holy Writ imposed limits on the range of policies they might adopt; Marxist–Leninist ideology, I suggested, functioned as a brake on arbitrariness. Since then I have tried to find examples of policies that the official ideology would forbid them from implementing, and I have come up with only two: lifting censorship and permitting citizens to form associations freely. In other words, the Communist Party is firmly committed to fairly tight control over the organised activities of their citizens and over the ideas they might express. So broad a principle of rulership, however, is compatible with many ideologies and cannot or need not, therefore, be derived from Marxism.

Beyond such an all-encompassing principle, one can, of course, identify certain policies that the Soviet leadership has fairly consistently preferred over others that might have been available. But I would argue that such preferences, which constitute the pattern or style of Soviet rule, can be explained by determining factors extraneous to the Marxist heritage, such as Russian political culture, accumulated experiences of the Soviet state and the nature of large complex bureaucracies. Hence my rejection of the theory that Soviet behaviour today can be explained by reference to that ideological heritage.

The theory of ideological determinism has appeared to be a plausible explanation of Soviet behaviour to so many scholars and politicians because the vocabulary of Marxism–Leninism continues to function as the official language of politics. The terminology introduced into philosophical and social-science discourse by Engels, modified by Kautsky, Plekhanov and Lenin (among others), and virtually codified in the Stalin era, continues to be the vocabulary that must be used in discussions of public issues. Like all language systems, of course, the one used in the USSR functions to some extent as a screen through which the users perceive the world. All linguistic conventions are conducive to the imposition of some artificial order on reality by highlighting some aspects of it and obscuring others. In this fashion, by alerting Soviet policy-makers to certain phenomena and blinding them to others, routine thinking in terms of the official doctrine may, indeed, have an effect on actions taken or not taken; and if orthodox phrasing is strictly enforced, the effect may be significant. Twenty years ago I suggested that, in a world that was rapidly changing, new perceptions would come into conflict with orthodox language conventions, impelling some groups of people to stretch the limits of orthodoxy or even to break out of its confines altogether. I referred to this as an incipient conflict between science and ideology. Today I am no longer sure whether such terms ought to be used. Instead, I would simply point out that Soviet thinking is becoming more and more differentiated, both in its effort to understand or interpret the world and in its endeavour to define values and establish priorities, and I would refrain from calling some interpretations scientific and others ideological. I will come back to this point below.

The growing differentiation of thought in the Soviet Union came up in a slightly different context as well: I discussed the functions of the official doctrine as a device both to legitimise the regime and to socialise its citizens for participation in societal life. On the basis of both observation and deductive reasoning, I suggested that this effort could be expected to be more intensive the closer one came to the top of the stratification pyramid. I also argued that, as the Soviet Union became more prosperous, powerful and securely established, the system would need doctrinal rigidity less than during the process of construction and trying to acquire legitimacy under circumstances of severe austerity. Hence I expressed the belief that we could expect the indoctrination effort to become more and more a routine and a ritual, akin to Sunday sermons or Independence Day oratory. This too implies that within the boundaries of the officially sanctioned vocabulary a widening spectrum of views can develop.

In previous decades I would probably have called this the 'erosion' or 'emasculation' of Soviet ideology. In a recent survey of Soviet philosophy, James P. Scanlan has suggested that this kind of differentiation, although perhaps more obvious today than a few decades ago, is indeed a process that has gone on for a long time. Scanlan demonstrates that the officially approved philosophical tenets and formulations lend themselves to widely divergent interpretations and also that Soviet philosophers are quite skilled in making the officially sanctioned phrases express the opposite of general party doctrine.[2] In an article I published not long ago, I suggested that the boundaries to stretching or amending the official language have at times been drawn tightly and at other times loosened, and that virtually all professional discourse in the Soviet Union involves the continual testing of these boundaries.[3] If that kind of testing goes on within a scholarly discipline, the issues in dispute may be quite technical and seemingly unpolitical. But even seemingly technical disagreements may have political implications; and even if they do not, it has become apparent that within Soviet society a process of differentiation has begun which allows us to distinguish an ever widening spectrum of *political* opinions. They crop up in various places, most noticeably, perhaps, in historical journals and in works of fiction.

Soviet literature in recent years, for instance, has dealt with such touchy issues as squalor on the *kolkhoz* and discontent among the working class. Science fiction writers have allowed themselves to cultivate the grotesque and to indulge in daring political fantasy. Orthodoxies about art and literature, about the 'positive hero' and the obligatory happy ending have come under fire. Historians have openly debated Stalin and Stalinism, as well as other important phases in Soviet history, such as the New Economic Policy in the 1920s and the history of the Red Army. These and other themes have become symbols around which divergent ideological positions and programmes have begun to crystallise. However tentatively and hesitatingly, therefore, observers of the Soviet political scene have begun to identify 'left', 'right' and 'centre' views within the party and professional élites: reformers and conservatives, modernisers and traditionalists, Westernisers and those who wish to keep all things western out.[4] Furthermore it has become apparent that, in addition to such a left–right spectrum, the Soviet Union harbours a liberational underground that constitutes a far left; it contains people subscribing to liberal, democratic, socialist and anarchist views. There is also a far right, allegedly with sympathisers in high places, that preaches a romantic Russian nationalism, harsh disdain of the West and other views reminiscent of Slavophile populism, the nativist ideology of the pre-revolutionary Black Hundreds and the reactionary journalism of Fedor Dostoevsky. In a provocative recent book, Carl Linden has suggested that the range of ideologies to be observed in the current Soviet Union stretches from anarchism to neo-fascism and is, therefore, no less wide than the ideological spectrum in Western Europe and North America.[5] Such a startling assertion would have to be tempered, however, by observing that, for the time being, it would be quite impossible to assess the relative strength of any of such ideological orientations.

So far, I have discussed the official ideology of the Soviet Union, Marxism–Leninism, as a fairly inflexible code of communication with which, however, widely ranging ideas can be expressed. Hence, much of the orthodox adherence to the doctrine that the regime demands turns out to be an insistence on form rather than content. If that is correct, we might be tempted to ask whether the party leadership is sincere in its commitment to this official doctrine. In my 1966 article I referred to this only in a footnote in which I referred to D. D. Comey's distinction between 'naïve,' 'honest' and 'cynical' commitment: 'naïve' party leaders would believe that ideology really determines policy; 'honest' ones would be aware that the fit between ideology and practice is imperfect; and 'cynical' ones would manipulate the doctrine for the purpose of *post hoc* rationalisation. In my 1985 article I presented this question as a paradox: both among the top leaders and within the citizenry as a whole, some observers have noted that deep commitment to the official ideology can coexist with blatant violations of its tenets. Members of the élite can endorse principles of socialist democracy, even while showing their contempt for the masses. Average citizens may profess their adherence to Marxism–Leninism, even when it becomes apparent that their knowledge of its contents is woefully deficient. They remind us of those Americans who loudly proclaim their allegiance to the US Constitution but don't know anything about it. Cynicism and deep commitment may very well be quite compatible, and perhaps they even reinforce each other. We will return to this phenomenon further below.

Up to this point I have used the term 'ideology' to mean the official doctrine, Marxism–Leninism, as taught to Soviet citizens in different degrees of intensity. In passing, I have also used it to denote the specific views subscribed to by people occupying various positions within the variegated political spectrum today being observed in the Soviet Union. In pointing this out, am I continuing to express my own confusion? Or is the relationship between ideas and action, or between the printed and preached word and actual states of mind, so difficult to understand that we must use a terribly slippery term and thus reproduce our confusion?

Let me intensify the confusion by pointing out that the term 'ideology' has at times been used in a very general sense to refer to a specific mindset attributed to a society's ruling class or élite. Most students of society take it for granted that any group's perception of reality and definition of values are related to its role within the society, and many further assume that ruling élites are by their own position rendered unable to recognise basic flaws within the system over which they rule, including their own approaching obsolescence. Karl Mannheim referred to this allegedly inevitable blindness of ruling élites as 'ideology'. This proverbial inability of people wielding power to see beyond their narrow and short-range interests may well be aggravated in our century by the complexity of contemporary society and by the bureaucratic structure of modern administration systems. In short, the Mannheimian concept of ideology imples the attribution of irrationality to rulers, top bureaucrats, and other members of élites.

Mannheim treats this as a recurrent phenomenon afflicting all societies. If we agree with him, and if we thus attribute 'ideological' thinking to the ruling establishment in the Soviet Union, we can once again observe that this kind of ideology need not be explained by the influence of the Marxist–Leninist heritage. Whether they call themselves Marxists or not, the assumption here is that power corrupts the minds of all those who wield it.

All this is worth mentioning, first, because I sense that even though my 1966 article omitted all references to this understanding of the concept of ideology, it may well have been there as an undercurrent. Consequently, I have now used the term 'ideology' in three distinct meanings. Note, however, that the last interpretation – ideology as ruling class blindness or irrationality – is not subject to verification. In order to demonstrate that any social group lacks rational understanding, we would have to possess some universally accepted standard of rationality. That, however, does not exist.

To be sure, critics of the Soviet system, both inside and outside the USSR, may be able to point to contradictions, unresolved problems, inefficiencies and injustices plaguing the Soviet system. Yet when such a claim is made by people outside the Soviet system, their critical views are often themselves 'ideological', meaning, in this case, that they express the ideology of the Cold War. And that, in turn, deserves some additional comments.

There are strong undercurrents in both of the articles I have been reviewing here, reflecting one more reason by I have been drawn to the study of Soviet thought. One of these is my long-standing endeavour to study Soviet history and politics in a comparative context. I have always placed myself in opposition to those who regarded the Soviet state as a phenomenon quite unlike all other states and the Russian revolution unique among the great revolutions of the last several centuries. Hence, when I attribute 'ideological' thinking to the Soviet élite (in the Mannheimian sense), I take it for granted that ruling élites *everywhere* are prone to indulge in self-deception; if I consider the concept of the 'revolution betrayed' to be meaningful, I would stress that all revolutions will be betrayed even while they are being 'fulfilled'. Hence, all utopias give way to ideologies, and all ideals are amended by 'realism'. Similarly, all revolutions are likely to have resulted from mixtures of mass unrest and 'ideologies'. Furthermore, modern industrial societies, whether they recognise private and corporate property and citizens' rights, or whether they entail command economies and citizens' duties, do share many features and many problems and, to the hypothetical visitor from another planet, must look more similar than dissimilar.

The more I have toyed with this idea, the more intensely I have felt the Cold War to be an aberration, a delusion, a disastrous mistake likely to ruin all of human civilisation. While the causes for the forty-year conflict between the Soviet Union and the United States have been very complex, ideology has to a significant degree intensified the tension. In the United States, this has been the ideology of anti-communism, a set of assumptions about contemporary world politics which is naïve and crude, yet preached by demagogues and scholars, taken for granted by the overwhelming majority of citizens, and having a deplorable impact on foreign and domestic politics.[6] In short, when I place the study of Soviet politics into a comparative framework, with particular attention to parallels between the USSR and the leading western nations, one comparison that emerges is that between ideology in the USSR and ideology in the West.

Ideological conflict is a recurrent phenomenon in history. Often it has taken the form of religious conflict, that is, enmities and wars which were fought on the basis of some religious urge, for the sake of ideas and ideals rather than in the pursuit of power, influence, territory or riches. Consider the religious struggles of the seventeenth century, the Crusades, or the wars of extermination between Athanasians and Arians, where the ostensible cause of the dispute was the struggle over the proverbial iota in the formulation of the Nicean Creed. In each of these cases, the world was plagued by long and bloody conflicts in which several protagonists professed to be fighting for ideas, for the purpose of spreading a good message of salvation. Historians may, of course, justifiably point out that these professions should not be taken at face value, that they may have been public relations devices designed to whip up enthusiasm and gain support, or that, even if the political leaders actually *believed* they were fighting for noble causes, they were in fact contending for power, wealth and territory, with the religious or ideological doctrines serving as self-legitimation devices. Historians might give plausibility to such debunking of religion as the motive, by pointing out that even in the allegedly religious wars of the seventeenth century, Catholic and Protestant rulers were allied, or that throughout European history Christian rulers quite readily allied themselves with Moslem princes against other Christian sovereigns. If, despite this, many leaders in the seventeenth century honestly believed they were fighting for their religion, rather than for naked power or some other material benefit, then we would be able to characterise them as 'ideologists' in the Mannheimian sense of the word, which suggests that these political actors had delusionary self-images. In this view, ideological wars and religious conflicts are not essentially different from any other political conflict, except that they are accompanied and justified, and indeed often intensified and prolonged if not instigated, by the hold that religious or political ideologies have on the actors involved.

The conflict-ridden relationship between the two major super-powers and their respective allies since the end of the Second World War has often been regarded as an ideological conflict. Conventional Western analysis has portrayed it as a conflict between an open-minded and a mind-controlling world, hence one between a set of systems that is free of ideology and one that possesses an ideology to which it socialises its citizens and which it seeks to spread. I am sure I need not refer to the wealth of literature published in North America and Europe during the last forty years that take such an interpretation for granted.

Yet I have increasingly convinced myself that this is a false distinction. To be sure, political discourse in the Soviet Union, to be permitted, must observe fairly well-defined boundaries of form and content, while in the United States virtually anything can be said or printed with impunity. But within the political and academic 'establishment', that is, among those Americans in politics and in the universities who mattered, the spirit in which the Soviet Union and all things related to Marxism and communism were discussed has been that of religious or ideological fanaticism. Most of the principal assumptions made about the Soviet Union by presidents and presidential advisers, by senators, journalists and other opinion makers, have been coloured by this fanaticism. The one-dimensional image of the entire world that has resulted from this ideology of compulsive anti-communism has led the United States into a whole series of self-defeating policies. Indeed, when I survey the foreign policies of the two super-powers in the last two or three decades, it seems to me that, by and large, the Soviet Union has pursued a cautious, unadventurous policy based on a carefully weighted set of priorities. To express this in the jargon of contemporary political science: the USSR has shown itself to behave like a 'rational actor'.[7] In contrast, the United States and its allies have behaved much more like ideologists, that is, like people obsessed by delusions, including the delusion that the chief threat presented by the USSR was ideological.

Lest I myself sound like a foaming-at-the-mouth ideological fanatic, let me qualify this by pointing out the perils of accusing anyone, communist or anti-communist, American or Soviet, of harbouring delusions. Such an accusation cannot be supported by evidence that would be acceptable to all. One person's delusion is another person's perception of reality. My statement about the 'ideological' nature of US policies, even though it might be supported by vast quantities of supporting evidence, ultimately remains a subjective judgement.

And so do all statements attributing 'ideological' thinking to political actors anywhere, so that once again the slipperiness of the term 'ideology' is brought out. To the extent that it implies 'false consciousness' or 'self-deception', it is based on the arrogant assumption that the user of the term is thinking correctly, has the right consciousness, and therefore knows the truth. I happen to be in sharp disagreement with many people who are active in politics, both those in Moscow and those in Washington. I claim the right to voice this disagreement and to posit my own judgement against theirs. But only history will decide ultimately which of us harboured delusions, or whether Soviet orthodoxies were more or less ideological than current 'mainstream' thinking in the United States.[8]

The dangers inherent in such a highly-charged, subjective use of the term 'ideology' can be averted by using it in a somewhat more objective sense, in anthropological fashion, as it were. It then becomes synonymous with political culture. That is, ideology then is simply defined as the values any individual or group or nation professes, their ideas concerning the ideal or desirable political institutions, their notions of citizenship, rights, duties, participation, their attitudes towards authority or the nature of the constituency to which those in authority should be response, and similar attitudes. For every nation and for every nation's ruling élite, it may be possible to define a set of such beliefs, assumptions and attitudes that seem generally shared and thus constitute its ideology. It seems to me that there is such a body of beliefs and assumptions that can be attributed to the Soviet élite and to those many Soviet citizens who more or less accept the system or take it for granted.

Thus understood, Soviet ideology is an ideology of modernisation. Its adherents assume that becoming modern is desirable, and they would measure modernity by technological development, urbanisation, the educational level of the population and a variety of similar indicators, including perhaps a rising gross national product and adequate defence capability. In the case of the Soviet élite, the commitment to modernisation seems to include also the cult of bigness, a preference for centralisation and command, and the belief that science can solve all human problems. I like to call this an 'engineer's mentality'; and this 'engineer's mentality' applied to societal problems results in the commitment to bureaucratic forms of organisation and management. People who have made this 'engineering' approach to the solution of problems part of their own thinking like to refer to themselves as 'realists'.

In describing this as the core of contemporary Soviet ideology, I am once more stressing its affinity to the ideology reigning in the American political, administrative and academic élites. Lenin, one of the pioneers of this approach to problem-solving, often stressed his indebtedness to western efficiency specialists, from Walter Rathenau to Henry Ford and Frederick W. Taylor. One should, however, stress the distinctions between Soviet and American ideologies. Indeed one may well argue that Soviet ideology is *substitute* Americanism, that is, a self-conscious, organised effort to copy achievements which in capitalist societies were made in unplanned fashion on the basis of private or corporate initiative. The Soviet leadership hopes to copy these achievements through a concerted effort organised by the state, and under conditions of severe austerity. In this substitute capitalism, the state functions as the principal entrepreneur, and the guiding ideology thus turns into an ideology of organised entrepreneurship, with the political superstructure trying to build itself a material base.

Further, while the American conception of citizenship stresses rights against the state and entitlements against society, the Soviet idea of citizenship focuses on duties and obligations. It includes a stern work ethic, as well as the expressed desire that citizens will participate as much as possible in public life away from their place of work. Moreover, even though Soviet rhetoric continues to suggest that all citizens are equal and that every person's labour is of equal worth to society, the prevailing political ethos takes it for granted that the society is stratified with regard to material rewards, prestige and degrees of authority over others. Soviet ideology assumes that good citizens will respect the resulting hierarchies, that they will subordinate themselves willingly, even though they should also be vigilant towards malfeasance in high places. Finally, it encourages all citizens to compete with one another for advancement and for the rewards that come with it: authority, prestige and higher living standards. As Vera Dunham has so convincingly shown in her *In Stalin's Time* (1976), two attitudes often considered as American as apple pie – careerism and consumerism – are accepted parts of current Soviet ideology.

Of these two attitudes, the new Programme of the Party, adopted at its 27th Congress in March 1986, appeals only to the people's hunger for consumer goods, but in many other ways codifies the ethos I have summarised above quite clearly. In specifying how the further development of Soviet society is to be promoted, it repeatedly gives pride of place to the application of the newest technologies and in addition stresses the most efficient mobilisation of human productive potentials. Even in its definition of the ultimate goal it makes the same points: communism is defined, as Lenin described it, as the maximum development of all productive forces, including technology and human creativity. Affirming the work ethic, the Programme implies that under communism free, unrewarded work for the benefit of the community will have become the motive force for all citizens. 'Work, discipline and order will save the Soviet regime,' was the title of a pamphlet Trotsky wrote in 1918. Work, discipline and the observance of rules are, still today, stressed by the Programme.[9]

Despite the copious obeisances that the Programme makes to Marx, Engels and Lenin and to the glorious revolutionary mission pursued by the Soviet state, little is left of revolutionary expectations. Beyond stressing the hope for greater affluence through the application of modern technologies and hard work, plus the promise of increased participation in public life by all citizens, the new Programme refuses to dwell on the nature of the coming communist society in any detail. It merely states that the gradual transformation (*pererastanie*) from socialism to communism is determined by objective laws of societal development that one must not fail to acknowledge, and goes on to warn that this process must not be unduly speeded up.[10] Indeed, while the Programme adopted twenty five years ago during the Khrushchev administration had visualised that communism would have arrived by 1980, and while it had confidently predicted that by that time the state would have begun to wither away, the new Programme identifies the key political problem of the present time as being 'the development and strengthening of the Soviet socialist state.'[11]

The entire Programme, with few alterations, could, in fact, fairly easily be imagined as an excessively lengthy speech by an American corporate chairman of the board explaining at his stockholders' meeting the measures that must be taken to ensure the corporation's survival in the face of Japanese or Taiwanese competition. Even the language of the Programme, the language of Soviet ideology, has been infused with terms that are similar to American corporate or bureaucratic jargon, such as *mobilizatsiya* (mobilisation) or *infrastruktura* (infrastructure).

In the article I published in 1985 I attempted, in cursory fashion, to trace various elements of current Soviet ideology to their historic roots, and I suggested that those ideas which Soviet ideology most obviously shares with current American values had come into Soviet thinking from Marxism: the worship of science, technology, rationality and bigness, the work ethic, the stress on the need to accumulate productive capital, and the urge to modernise by destroying traditional cultures.[12] But the political–administrative *style* of carrying out such a programme of modernisation has been inherited from a political culture that is specifically Russian, having its roots in age-old Russian experiences, attitudes and modes of government. I might be tempted to call the resultant ideology of the Soviet Union national in form and entrepreneurial in content were it not for the fact that political–administrative forms are not mere formalities or differences in style, but are painfully substantial: the manner or style in which leaders and followers, bureaucrats and citizens, the powerful and the powerless deal with each other is a very concrete fact of daily intercourse. A country's political style is far more than mere form. Moreover, the work and production ethic prevalent in the Soviet Union goes beyond politics. By emphasising such traditional bourgeois virtues as sobriety, respect for (socialist) property, frugality and marital fidelity, it embraces the totality of people's lives. How deeply is this ethic of work, abstinence, and obedience to authority ingrained in these people?

There is a good deal of evidence that would lead one to question the sincerity of their commitment to this ideology. For instance, while the ideology proclaims the working class to be the leading and most enlightened class in society and attributes all the virtues of the collective work ethic to its members, there is good reason to assume that in fact the leadership has contempt for the workers and sees them as drunkards, lazy, stupid and rebellious. Moreover, similar contempt for the working class seems widely spread throughout the population, including the industrial working class itself. Similarly, the official rhetoric about friendship between the nationalities that make up the Soviet population is in conflict with ethnic prejudices harboured by many members of the leadership and, again, by millions of ordinary citizens. The official proclamations of gender equality conceal old-fashioned patriarchal attitudes shared by many, and the sympathy expressed for the peoples of the Third World masks a good deal of racial antagonism.

As for the general population, there is evidence that the Soviet people are increasingly oriented towards private values: their own and their children's careers, work that is easy and carries prestige, consumer goods, hedonism, sex and alcohol. The general population shows many other attitudes that worry the leadership: admiration for the West, low respect for public property, poor work discipline, unwillingness to serve in the armed forces, reluctance to accept officially assigned positions, and many similar attempts to evade their duties.

Vladimir Shlapentokh, in an unpublished paper, has called attention to this phenomenon, which he considers a growing trend that will ultimately produce a crisis of legitimacy.[13] At the same time, he acknowledges that such a crisis need not destroy the fabric of society. He suggests that a distinction be made between two sets of values, in effect, two ideologies, to which the people of the Soviet Union subscribe: 'values for me' and 'values for others'. The 'values for others' are the ethics of the official ideology, while the 'values for me' are the pragmatic values by which people in the USSR live in reality.

For example, the bureaucratic managers firmly believe that rules must be enforced, but they also know that they themselves must break rules if they are to perform their functions successfully. People are genuinely indignant about the corruption practiced by others, but engage in corrupt dealings themselves; they extol the family and practice adultery; they denounce drunkenness but themselves drink to excess. Similarly, the leadership tolerates many kinds of behaviour which violate official norms, as long as such deviancy produces results.

While one result of this double morality may be the general spread of cynical contempt for the official ideology, Shlapentokh seems to believe that in the long run it works very well for the regime because it creates mass pressure for conformity to official ideological standards, or a public atmosphere that enforces compliance with official values. Where everyone chimes in with the publicly proclaimed norms, and does so in all sincerity, it would be rash indeed to challenge them openly. Thus the universal profession of the official ideology acts as a general enforcer of party norms and does this quite effectively. If, none the less, it makes sense to distinguish between two ideologies in the Soviet Union, an official one and real one, with both the leadership and the masses of the citizenry professing the former and living by the other, then it might also be plausible to assume that the people fully conscious of the discrepancy, exploring it and laying the conflict open, are, perhaps by definition, the intelligentsia. The intelligentsia in Russia have always been the ones who uncovered hypocrisy and sham; they have always functioned as the conscience of society, conscience being that feeling of discomfort which is generated by dissonance between professed ideas and actual life.

At a conference I attended recently, the term 'national culture' was mentioned so many times, and with so much imprecision, that some participants suggested that it should be banned from scholarly discourse altogether, whereupon my friend Hans Rogger remarked that to make the meaning of the term precise was as impossible as to accurately describe the odour of some strong cheese: we do not know how to describe it, but we certainly do know it is there. That remark might fittingly be made about the concept of ideology as well.

Ideology 'is there' in many forms, as an official doctrine laid out in textbooks and as a range of ideas concerning society, politics and citizenship that may or may not coincide with this textbook doctrine. In what forms it is active in the minds of Soviet people in various walks of life can be studied only through a multiple screen of obstacles, including our own ideological assumptions, and at best we are left with inferences or impressions. Of one thing I am sure: no simple statements about the nature of Soviet ideology or its relationship to people's actions will ever be plausible, for we must take it for granted that people in the Soviet Union have minds that are just as complex, contradictory, compartmentalised, biased and confused as those of people in other parts of the world.

NOTES

1. The functions of ideology in the Soviet political system', *Soviet Studies*, vol. 17, no. 3 (January 1966), pp. 273–85.
2. James P. Scanlan, *Marxism in the USSR. A Critical Survey of Current Soviet Thought* (Ithaca, NY: Cornell University Press, 1985).
3. 'Assessing the ideological commitment of a regime', in Joseph L. Nogee (ed.), *Soviet Politics: Russia after Brezhnev* (New York: Praeger, 1985).
4. See Alexander Yanov, *The Russian New Right: Right-Wing Ideologies in the Contemporary USSR* (Berkeley, Cal.: Institute of International Studies, 1978). See also the same author's *The Drama of the Soviet 1960s: A Lost Reform* (Berkeley, Cal.: Institute of International Studies, 1984).
5. Carl A. Linden, *The Soviet Party-State: The Politics of Ideocratic Despotism* (New York: Praeger, 1983).
6. My most forceful statement of these views has been made in 'An anti-anti-communist looks at defense', in Bernard Eissenstat (ed.), *The Soviet Union: The Seventies and Beyond* (Lexington Books, 1975).
7. For a very persuasive study making this point, see Marita Kaw, 'Taking sides and taking risks: Soviet conflict involvement 1950–1983', doctoral dissertation, University of Michigan, 1985. See also William Zimmerman, *Soviet Perspectives on International Relations, 1956–1967* (Princeton University Press, 1969), which traces the professionalism of the Soviet foreign service establishment.
8. Some years ago I talked with a Polish economist, a specialist on Western economies. I asked him whether he had foreseen the recession that was then plaguing the world economy, and he said that he had not. I expressed mock astonishment that someone trained as a Marxist had not been alert to the certainty of setbacks in capitalist economies, but found out that, after studying political economy, Marxist-style, he had been retrained in western econometrics, which, one might argue, serve to close as well as open the user's eyes to different aspects of economic life. One could assert that this Polish colleague had exchanged one methodology or one paradigm for another; one could argue instead that he had exchanged one ideology for another. What one would not have a right to say, however, would be that he had exchanged ideology for science.
9. *Programma Kommunisticheskoi partii Sovetskogo Soyuza. Novaya redaktsiya* (Moscow: Politizdat, 1986), Part I, Chapter I, para. 6.
10. Ibid., Part I, Chapter I, para. 9.
11. Ibid., Part II, Chapter IV, para. 6.

12. 'Assessing the ideological commitment of a regime', in Nogee, ed., *Soviet Politics: Russia after Brezhnev*.
13. Vladimir Shlapentokh, 'Social values in the Soviet Union: major trends in the post-Stalin period', Report presented to the National Council for Soviet and East European Research, June 1984.

4 Ideology and System-Building: the Experience under Lenin and Stalin

GRAEME GILL

Most scholars of ideology have distinguished between two different types of belief systems. These have been accorded various labels, including 'pure' and 'practical' ideology (theory and thought), 'doctrine' and 'ideology', and 'fundamental' and 'operative' ideology.[1] The distinction which these labels reflect is between a body of philosophical principles and assumptions about the nature of reality and of historical change on the one hand, and on the other a set of tenets which are designed to link these principles and assumptions with existing reality by constituting an 'action program'[2] through which the adherents seek to realise those principles and assumptions in action. The more fundamental principles and assumptions combine together to constitute a social theory which has as its principal characteristic an explanatory orientation. The ideological tenets will be drawn from the body of social theory, but they will tend to be much less complex than the principles from which they spring. Indeed, one of their chief characteristics will be to rationalise or simplify the complex propositions of the social theory so as to enable them both to be understood and acted upon by those who may not have the philosophical training or insight to get to grips with the social theory as a whole.

The line between social theory and ideology is, in practice, unclear and fluctuating. Both interact in ways which can bring changes to them both. If an ideology is to remain vibrant and relevant over time, it must undergo change, react to new situations, experience 'creative development'. However, if the ideology is to sustain the integrity of its link with the social theory, it can develop only in ways which are consistent with the propositions of that social theory. But a social theory will usually consist of a wide range of propositions, not all of which are at any one time instrumental in the generation of an ideology. Some may lie dormant, perhaps for a very long period of time, before being called to play a part in the process of ideological change and development. In this way, depending upon the richness and diversity of the social theory itself, an ideology may develop in ways quite different from its immediate past without doing violence to its relationship with the social theory, simply by drawing upon elements of that theory previously unutilised. Furthermore, the social theory may itself grow and change over a period of time through the processes of accretion and ideological development. As the ideology develops and changes, elements may move from the sphere of ideological action programme to that of the grand theory from which the ideology initially sprang. This has clearly been the case in the Soviet Union with many of the writings of Lenin. Thus it may be very difficult in any particular case to distinguish clearly between the fundamental, explanatory-oriented principles of the social theory and the more action-oriented tenets of the ideology.

While the social theory may provide a basic underpinning for the political system as a whole, the ideology will play a more prominent and activist role in the operation of the system. The ideology will be expressed in the speeches and writings of political figures at many levels of the system, in many of the decisions taken by the ruling bodies, through party programmes like that recently adopted by the CPSU, and through much of the literature of both a political and non-political nature. However in a highly centralised and authoritarian system like that of the Soviet Union, it is principally through the leaders' speeches and writings that the main developments in the ideology are expressed. Ideological change may be initiated here at the apex of the system or, if it emerges elsewhere (such as in works emanating from academic or ideological institutes), it must be ratified here. It is, therefore, principally through this medium that the development of the ideology will be charted. The role of ideology in the course of system-building in the Soviet Union is best seen in terms of two broad areas of concern, legitimation and policy-making. These will be looked at in turn.

4.1 IDEOLOGY AND LEGITIMATION

The men who led the party to power in October 1917 were committed Marxists. They believed totally in the enterprise upon which they were engaged and they accepted the claims for scientific rigour which were attached to the Marxian system of analysis. For them, the Marxist focus upon class analysis was the means of laying bare the laws of historical development and thereby making it possible, through a study of those laws, to understand the path of social development. Part of the Marxian analysis, as it was widely accepted in Marxist circles throughout Europe in the first decade and a half of this century, was the view that socialism would come about only after society had achieved a high level of industrial development and after capitalism had developed to its maximum extent. This involved acceptance of the Marxian notion of stages of historical development: from feudal to bourgeois to socialist. With the single major exception of Trotsky, who as early as 1906[3] argued that an industrially backward country like Russia could telescope the bourgeois and proletarian revolutions together and thereby move from the feudal into the socialist phase, all leading Russian Marxists accepted that Russia could attain socialism only after an extended period of capitalist development.

Within this intellectual context the October revolution, proclaimed in the name of the proletariat and of socialism, was confronted with a major problem: how could a socialist revolution occur in such an economically-backward country, and how did this fit in to the accepted notion of stages of historical development? Furthermore, did the development of socialist revolution in Russia show the claims for the scientific nature of Marxism to be false? This clear lack of consonance between the theory and the claims made for October thus called into question both the nature of the enterprise upon which the Bosheviks believed themselves to be engaged and the validity of the theory upon which their whole world view rested. This problem was addressed in the development of the ideology after October 1917.

A beginning had been made on the theoretical reconciliation of these positions even before the Bolsheviks had gained power. In his famous April theses, Lenin had startled friends and foes alike by rejecting the notion of distinct stages of development and enthusiastically adopting (without openly acknowledging it) a position similar to Trotsky's on the telescoping of the stages of the revolution.[4] Such views aroused significant opposition in the party, opposition which remained largely submerged throughout the April–October period, but which surfaced at the time of the Bolshevik seizure of power. Expressing fears that were probably more widespread in the party than Lenin cared to acknowledge, Zinoviev and Kamenev opposed the proposed seizure of power some two weeks before it was carried out[5] and, in the immediate aftermath of the October Revolution, various leading Bolsheviks opposed Lenin's determination to rule alone rather than in coalition with other socialist forces in the country.[6] The principal objection of these groups was that Russia was not yet ripe for a socialist revolution. In the event of such a revolution bringing the Bolsheviks alone to power, the party would find itself isolated and would have to resort to terroristic means to survive. This simply reflected the absence of the necessary preconditions for socialism.

Lenin's most complete answer to this line of criticism is to be found in the debates with the Left Communists over the Brest–Litovsk peace treaty.[7] Lenin argued that the international development of capitalism had made it possible for revolution to break out in the 'weakest link' of the capitalist chain, the capitalist state with the lowest levels of capitalist development, and that such a revolution would act as the catalyst for the revolution in the more advanced states. It was to be through this unrolling of the international proletarian revolution that the preponderance of petty bourgeois elements in the 'weak link' country would be counteracted by the weight of the world proletariat, thereby overcoming the difficulty posed by national backwardness and subsuming it within the worldwide socialist advance.[8] The fate of the Russian revolution was therefore directly dependent upon revolution in the advanced capitalist world; it was this which would transform the minority position of the proletariat in Russia into a majority position across the globe. In an immediate sense, therefore, the task of the rulers of Russia was to ensure that the revolution gained a 'breathing space', that it did not succumb before international revolution came to its rescue. Practically, this meant signature of a peace treaty with the Germans, regardless of its predatory nature.

The Left Communists, with Bukharin as their leading standard-bearer, agreed with much of Lenin's position.[9] They rejected any notion of Russia being able to develop independently toward socialism, because the petty bourgeois threat posed by the predominantly peasant population could be overcome only by the support given to the Russian proletariat by the world proletariat following world revolution. But where the Left Communists differed from Lenin was in arguing that there could be no peaceful coexistence between Russia and the West: either the new heartland of proletarian revolution would assist in the overthrow of western capitalism or it would be devoured. Furthermore, they argued, current conditions were conducive to revolution in Western Europe and the Bolsheviks should actively seek to foster such revolution. In the meantime, radical measures had to be introduced domestically to check the power of the petty bourgeois forces and advance the proletarian cause.

The nub of the Left Communist argument with Lenin was the issue of how long the socialist revolution could remain without degenerating under domestic pressure in the absence of international revolution. Lenin's answer to this question was non-committal, although his comments suggest that he thought that such revolution would come sooner rather than later. For the Left Communists, the answer was more unequivocal: the Russian revolution could not long survive the absence of international revolution and all efforts should be made to facilitate its appearance. Although Lenin's position carried the day, the enthusiasm with which sections of the party greeted War Communism suggests that there was significant sympathy for the Left Communist warnings on the danger of degeneration.

The ideological legitimation of the revolution as a holding operation until international revolution enabled the advance to socialism to be resumed with vigour was facilitated by War Communism and the conviction that this was a move in the direction of the transformation of social and economic relations in a socialist direction. However, a major crisis in this type of formulation emerged with the introduction of NEP in March 1921. This involved a substantial reversal of the trend under War Communism, including the reintroduction of the market mechanism as the principal motor force of a large part of the economy and the return of significant parts of the economy to private hands. This was a clear strengthening of those petty bourgeois forces about which there had been such concern in the party and is reflected in the way in which NEP was sold to the party as a temporary retreat, a withdrawing from the field so that the socialist forces could regroup, grow stronger and then launch another attack against the citadel of capitalism.[10] This setback was accompanied by the recession of prospects for world revolution. The failure of the Hungarian and German revolutions and of the Red Army's advance on Warsaw, plus the absence of even a glimmer of revolutionary activity in the other advanced capitalist states, seemed to condemn the Russian revolution to a long period of isolation. The question of the fate of the revolution was once again cast in stark terms: how long could the revolution last in such circumstances?

The response to this question, towards which Lenin was edging in the last months of his political life, foreshadowed a major shift in the ideological position of the party. The basis of this shift was a re-evaluation of the nature of both NEP and international revolution. The earlier view of NEP as a temporary retreat was now replaced in Lenin's view by the belief that this could constitute a viable road to socialism.[11] Lenin placed his faith in the cooperative movement, through which he believed the peasants would grow into socialism. He envisaged NEP as the guiding principle of a long transition period, but it was a transition which could not be completed in Russia alone. Lenin did not lose his view of socialist society as an international society. However the direction in which Lenin now looked for international succour changed. With the industrial proletariat of the West showing no signs of revolutionary ardour, Lenin turned to the East, to the colonial peoples of Africa and Asia, to provide the salvation of the revolution. The contradictions of international capitalism were such that the national liberation movements of the colonial world were the most likely allies of the Russian proletariat in the quest for socialism. Russia had to hold out against the pressures of international capital until the suppressed peoples came to their aid. In the meantime, the Russian proletariat should go about building towards socialism through NEP.[12]

This change in orientation was taken up widely within the party, but was particularly promoted by the right of the party led by Bukharin.[13] Under the guidance of this 'most outstanding theoretician of the party',[14] the vision sketched by Lenin was moulded into the basic ideological framework for political and economic development for much of the decade. For some years, the mainstream of debate took place within an acceptance of the NEP framework. But beneath the general acceptance, there remained a strong residue of distrust of NEP and the implications it had for Russian development. This rested upon the same sorts of concerns about the effects of seizing power in a peasant country that had been voiced earlier by the Left Communists, fear about the corrupting effects of the petty bourgeois peasant environment and the strengthening of capitalist tendencies through the operation of market forces. Although such concerns were evident from the outset of NEP,[15] it was not until the debate over socialism in one country, in the middle of the decade, that the newly-emerging orthodoxy was confronted by a fundamental challenge.

The notion of socialism in one country was developed by Stalin during the autumn of 1924. In the published version of a series of lectures he presented at Sverdlov University following Lenin's death, Stalin presented what was at that time the orthodox position: although the proletariat could seize power in one country, they could not achieve the final victory of socialism without the assistance of the proletariat in several advanced countries.[16] However Stalin soon amended this in a way which, theoretically, was quite significant.[17] He now argued that Russia could fully build socialism itself without having to rely on the international proletariat. Socialism was no longer contingent upon events outside Russia's borders. The context of this change on Stalin's part reflects much more a move for factional advantage than a carefully considered handling of the theoretical issues. Stalin's new line was in direct conflict with the internationalist position advocated by Trotsky, and although the latter could claim ideological consistency on his side in this issue, the decision ultimately on which line to adopt was determined by considerations of power politics, and here the advantage lay decisively with Stalin. The new formulation was taken up enthusiastically in many parts of the party and soon became official writ.[18]

The change wrought by Stalin had no necessary consequences for economic policy. Bukharin, who supported the notion advanced by Stalin, could continue to maintain that socialism could only be built at the speed dictated by the peasant, thereby supporting a continuation of NEP policies. Increased levels of industrialisation, like those demanded by Trotsky and Preobrazhensky, would also have been consistent with this notion, as was shown at the end of the decade. In foreign policy, too, there were no necessary consequences from this change in direction. No one argued that world revolution was not a desirable thing, nor that efforts should not be made to foster it. Indeed, Stalin vigorously argued[19] that the achievement of socialism in Russia would not be secure while the possibility of armed intervention by the capitalist world existed. Thus, while the change was significant in factional terms, symbolically drawing to Stalin's banner those who sought a direct rather than a contingent path to socialism and isolating Trotsky as someone who seemingly lacked confidence in the creative energies of the Russian proletariat, it had no immediate and necessary consequences for considerations of economic or foreign policy. But its main significance was at the ideological level because it decisively overturned the established orthodoxy by declaring that socialism could be built finally in Soviet Russia in the absence of world revolution.

This shift in the ideological position was consummated some eleven years after it was introduced, with the adoption of a new state constitution in 1936. This proclaimed the Soviet Union to be a socialist state and enshrined as one of its guiding principles the aphorism enunciated by Marx 'from each according to his ability, to each according to his work'.[20] The formal announcement of the achievement of socialism effectively ended the argument at the heart of much of the ideological discourse during the early years of the life of the Soviet regime, the fate of the revolution. With socialism achieved, that question was no longer relevant.

The passing from the scene of this question should have left the way clear for the emergence of another issue of crucial importance for the development of the system. Important as it was, the achievement of socialism was only one step on the path to the gaining of full communism. However, the means whereby this transition was to be achieved did not emerge as an ideological issue of major importance under Stalin, nor had it been dealt with in an exhaustive fashion by his forebears. Although Stalin touched upon this question in his final published work,[21] his vague formulations added nothing to the established wisdom that once socialism had been achieved, communism would be reached simply by proceeding along the lines laid down in the achievement of the earlier stage. Communism was merely a further extension of socialism, and although the transformation would be long and difficult, no major structural changes were necessary for its achievement. Although under Khrushchev much more attention was devoted to the question of the transition to communism, especially in the party Programme of 1961, little was said that brought this position into question.

The legitimation of October through the claim that socialism could be achieved in one country created further ideological problems, relating principally to the continued presence and role of the party-state structure. The first problem was methodological. It concerned the relationship between the political structure of a society and the productive forces at work in the society. Among students of Marx interpretations of the relationship between these have differed widely, ranging from a crude economic determinism, whereby the former is totally determined by the latter, to a more sophisticated view which emphasises the interaction between the two parts. But even those who have adopted the latter position, thereby providing for a degree of autonomy for the state from its economic foundations, have acknowledged that ultimately the conditioning effect of the productive forces is crucial for the development of political forms. While Russia was awaiting imminent world revolution, the relationship between political structure and economic forces was not a theoretical problem. The Bolsheviks were brought to power by the contradictions in world capitalism and therefore the shaping of the political form in Russia was not solely subject to the essentially petty bourgeois nature of economic relations in that country. Indeed, when the international revolution subsumed the backward state of Russia, the problem posed for the political form by the capitalist nature of the society would be transcended. However, when the likelihood of international revolution receded and the Bolsheviks shifted towards an acceptance of the view that they could build socialism in Russia alone, a methodological problem emerged. If ultimately the political form was determined by the productive forces dominant in the society, and if those forces were primarily capitalist in nature, how could a political form emerge which was both dedicated and able to develop the country along socialist lines? The methodology of Marxism, the social theory from which the Bolsheviks' ideology grew, therefore seemed to deny the very possibility of a group like the Bolsheviks being able to guide Russia in its move toward socialism.

Lenin solved this dilemma by amending the original premise. In essence, he argued that where the productive forces were insufficiently developed, and therefore the cultural conditions did not exist for the building of socialism, the proletariat could seize power and then go about creating those prerequisites.[22] This was a major change because it denied the primacy of the productive forces, but it was the sort of change which was essential if the ideology was not to be too far out of step with reality in Russia. Without it the enterprise upon which the Bolsheviks were engaged would have been impossible in their own terms.

Recognition of the role the political form was to play in the creation of the socialist society raised the further question of the fate of the state. Little had been written about the state in the post-socialist revolution period; Marx's references were scanty[23] and although Lenin had devoted one whole publication to this question on the eve of October, it was not meant as a blueprint for the future.[24] Nevertheless there was a general understanding within socialist circles about the withering away of the state. Indeed, this was seen as one of the key characteristics of the transition towards socialism. However, in post-1917 Soviet Russia few were prepared to argue for a weakened state structure. In theoretical terms, the justification for the state remaining powerful after the socialist revolution was related to the notion of continuing class struggle. The outline of this argument was sketched out by Lenin in *The State and Revolution* where he argued that the state needed to remain strong because the establishment of the dictatorship of the proletariat did not lead to the disappearance of class struggle, but merely to its transformation into new forms.[25] It followed from this that the state, the dictatorship of the proletariat, had to remain powerful to be an effective weapon in this struggle. The argument was extended further by Stalin. Towards the end of the decade, Stalin argued that the dictatorship of the proletariat was 'the sharpest form of class struggle' and that under that dictatorship the class struggle became 'even more fierce' than it was before.[26] This was because the greater the advances made, and therefore the closer the approach to socialism, the greater and more intense became the opposition and resistance of the capitalist elements and the sharper the class struggle.[27] It followed, therefore, that class struggle was at a higher level of intensity on the eve of socialism than it had been at any time before under the dictatorship of the proletariat. Classes would be eliminated and the state would wither away only after the class struggle had been intensified and state power had been strengthened to the utmost. A strong state was essential to overcome the increased opposition of hostile class elements.[28]

This position rested on the premise of the antagonistic interests of classes in Soviet society. That premise disappeared with the formal achievement of socialism in 1936. Henceforth the social structure of the USSR was held to consist of two classes, the working class and *kolkhoz* peasantry, and one stratum, the intelligentsia. What made these social groupings different from the classes which preceded them was that the contradictions between them were non-antagonistic and involved no fundamental conflicts of interest like those which had generated the class conflict of earlier epochs. This changed the nature of the state. Henceforth, in a step foreshadowing Khrushchev's notion of the 'all-people's state', the state was deemed to be of a special type, being the servant not of one section of society but of society as a whole. Its task was thus not the protection of the interests of one class, but the promotion of the interests of all. Furthermore, although the internal danger from hostile class forces had now evaporated, the Soviet Union was still confronted by the dangers posed by capitalist encirclement. This had been a major point of emphasis during the 1920s as well,[29] but in the absence of class conflict within it took on greater significance. While the dangers posed by capitalist encirclement remained, and therefore while the revolution remained restricted within national borders, it was the state's task to protect socialist society from its outside enemies.[30] The state was thus not to disappear under socialism, but was to remain to guide the transition into communism and to protect that transition against a hostile, capitalist world.

While the continued presence of a powerful state could be justified in this way, different sorts of ideological developments were required to legitimate the position and role of the party. From the outset, the state was formally known as a 'dictatorship of the proletariat', a phrase lacking in precision, but one which seemed to involve the rule of the working class. But in practice, the nucleus of the new system was the party. The ideological basis for this was the notion, rooted in the early Lenin, of the party as the vanguard of the proletariat. Although there is some tension within Lenin's pre-1917 writings about whether the party should be highly centralised and controlled from above or much more open to the control of the working class,[31] an élitist view of the party remained a prominent strand in his thought. Lenin fully accepted the orthodox position of European Marxism at the turn of the century, that class consciousness had to be brought to the proletariat by socialist intellectuals. The party was to be the bearer of that consciousness, which was essential if the proletariat was to take a leading role in the revolution. This type of argument clearly retained some validity in Russia after the October Revolution because of the low level of development and the consequent absence of class consciousness among wide ranks of the Russian working class.[32] Possession of theoretical sophistication brought with it understanding of the laws of historical development and thereby the capacity better to perceive the interests of the class and to pursue them successfully.[33] This perception of the party as the most advanced section of the class, as the vehicle of class interests, provided a ready theoretical basis for single party dominance. Rule by the party was equated with rule by the class, without the exact relationship between the two ever being clearly specified.

The capacity of the party to guide the class in its move towards socialism remained the foundation of its claim to rule.[34] But like the justification for the state, this principle was undercut by the proclaimed achievement of socialism. Once it was assumed that communism would flow automatically from the structures established during the socialist epoch, the guiding role of the party seemed less secure. If the transition was automatic, why was a guide needed, and therefore why should the party retain its political monopoly? This question was never squarely faced under Stalin, although two tentative lines of justification do appear in Soviet writings. The first was simply to reiterate the point that the party was leading the society towards communism,[35] that it enabled the overcoming of the difficulties encountered along the way, and was therefore essential at least until communism was achieved. The other line of argument accorded to the party an important role in reconciling those non-antagonistic differences which did exist between the three social groupings of which Soviet society formally consisted. The party thus appeared as a sort of broker between social interests in the society. It was this sort of argument which laid the basis for the attempt made under Khrushchev to deal with this problem: the party was defined as a social organisation rather than a governmental one, and therefore as a body which would not wither away under communism, but would remain to carry out the social functions it was currently performing.

The ideology thus provided a means of legitimation for the major components of the Soviet system, the party and the state, and for the foundation and continued existence of the system itself. This central place in the system's legitimation programme virtually ensured that the ideology would become a key factor in any élite conflicts which emerged. If the party's right to rule rested upon ideological claims to a special form of knowledge and understanding, it followed that positions of leadership within the party likewise involved that knowledge. As a result, conflicts over political power became intricately intertwined with questions of policy and ideology. Such conflicts may have been motivated by a genuine disagreement on ideological grounds, but even if they were not, the intentions of the combatants needed to be clothed in ideological garb. From the revolution until the end of the 1920s, all of the successive disputes at the pinnacle of Soviet power were conducted principally in ideological terms or through arguments which had ideological assumptions as their bases. The Left Communists' fear of the degeneration of the revolution in the absence of international revolution, the Democratic Centralists' concern with bureacratisation, the Workers' Opposition's claims about the effects of the erosion of the position of the working class, the arguments of the Left and United Oppositions about bureaucratisation, the need for international revolution and the role of the peasant domestically, and the arguments of the Right Opposition regarding the continued relevance of a NEP programme of development all stemmed from the ideological fund with which the system was invested. The ideology became the principal mode of discourse of Soviet politics. However, this mode of discourse, and the part ideology played in political conflict, changed substantially over the first decade and a half of the system's life.

Initially conflict took place in the party within an environment in which the ideology was a fluid body of assumptions, precepts and tenets. There was no standard against which individuals' interpretations of particular points could be measured, no orthodoxy which was clearly specified and to which all had to bow. Even Lenin, although the most prominent leader and the one whose views regularly prevailed on the most important issues of the day, was not considered an ideological authority in the sense that his views were treated as unchallengeable writ. There remained scope within the party for ideological differences of major dimension, including conflicts over major ideological precepts. While the participants in such conflicts were convinced of the correctness of the views they were espousing, they also recognised that there was no clearly established orthodoxy that all could see immediately and that ideological differences were therefore bound to develop. The *de facto* legitimacy of holding and expressing ideologically divergent views was reflected in the fact that generally those who disagreed with the leadership on ideological grounds did not forfeit their right to continued party membership, as the cases of the Left Communists and the Democratic Centralists illustrated.[36] The ideology remained a vibrant, developing body of theory. However the fluidity and flexibility disappeared during the 1920s and 1930s as a dogmatic orthodoxy emerged, principally under the impact of élite conflict.

The factional conflicts that emerged among the leaders following the removal of Lenin from active political life in 1922 differed from the earlier bouts of conflict by being much more directly related to the question of personal access to political power. While all of the earlier opposition groups were, through the import of the claims they made, challenging the current policy line and thereby calling into question the right of those who made policy to continue to do so, the post-1922 conflicts took place in the context of the need to replace Lenin. This problem was evident in the minds of all of the protagonists. The quest to replace the founder of the system was a major stimulus to the rigidification of the ideology and its transformation into an orthodoxy.

Two principal processes were at work in the ideological sphere during the 1920s: a personalisation of ideology and a transformation of its form into a catechismic state. The personalisation of ideology involved the projection of Lenin as a fount of ideological orthodoxy. This was part of the general cult of Lenin which developed and expanded throughout the 1920s,[37] linking Lenin with an increasingly mythologised view of the foundation of the regime and his words and actions with the ineluctable march toward communism. Lenin's doctrinal statements now became formally sacrosanct and subject to no question or, at least officially, revision. Whoever sought to wield high political power was thus obliged to do so only in Lenin's name; the epithet 'leninist' soon emerged as the highest praise, while that of 'anti-leninist' was the greatest condemnation.[38] By the end of the 1920s, the holding and propagation of views deemed to be anti-leninist became grounds for expulsion from the party.[39] As a symbol, Lenin and his thought were supreme.

The transformation of ideology into a catechism involved a process of codification, the reduction of a complex mass of ideas to a more standardised set of principles which was much more readily available to wider circles of the party than was the existing bulk of Lenin's writings. In the mid-1920s both Stalin, through his *Foundations of Leninism*, and Zinoviev, through his *Leninism: An Introduction to the Study of Leninism*, sought to present and expound Lenin's ideas and thereby to lay claim to Lenin's mantle. The difference in approach of these two works is stark: in contrast to Zinoviev's more sophisticated handling of the material, Stalin's presentation of 'leninism' is much simpler and more basic, well suited to one of the tasks for which it was employed, the political education of new party members. But what is important for current purposes is that the choice of which of these different types of interpretation was to be accepted as the legitimate account of Lenin's views, and therefore as the orthodox line of the party, was decided not through a consideration of the intellectual integrity of each as an expression of Lenin's views but through considerations of a more political nature. It was the victory of Stalin in the élite struggles of the 1920s, a victory due at least partly to the attractiveness of the ideological positions he espoused, that elevated his interpretation of leninism into a position of orthodoxy. The clearest reflection of this was the emergence of the cult of Stalin during the 1930s. This was a multi-faceted phenomenon, but one of its principal elements was the projection of Stalin as the direct descendant of Lenin.[40] The symbol of Stalin was transformed from 'the best pupil of comrade Lenin' into 'the Lenin of today', with the result that Stalin became the fount of ideological orthodoxy himself and a direct source of the official ideology, Marxism–Leninism. The two processes, personalisation and catechisation, thus came together. The ideology became in large part what Stalin chose to define as ideology, thereby creating an orthodoxy which was defined ultimately by the utterances of one person.

The transformation of the ideology in this way is related to changes in the nature of the membership of the party during the 1920s and 1930s. The nature of the party was completely transformed by the entry of very large numbers of recruits during this period. The party increased from 390 000 in 1918 to 1 677 910 in 1930 and to 3 399 975 in 1940.[41] This rapid expansion brought into the party large numbers of people who were ideologically untutored and whose knowledge about, and understanding of, the ideology was rudimentary at best. Many lacked the basic essential of literacy.[42] They entered a party in which ideological rectitude was an established virtue and a high level of what was called 'political literacy' a requirement for all party members. Indeed, throughout these two decades, the party press was full of complaints from the top about the deficient levels of political literacy of the rank-and-file and exhortations to the membership to rectify this. Major programmes of political education were set in motion to achieve this end. Furthermore, the environment for these new members was one characterised by constant warnings from above about the need to beware of the effect of alien class influences, to reject and root out the hostile petty bourgeois influences which endangered the party and which stemmed from the socio-economic situation in which it found itself. These sorts of considerations created clear political reasons encouraging ostentatious commitment to the ideology on the part of the newcomers, over and above any deep personal commitment on purely ideological grounds. Open and obvious commitment to the ideology was one means of seeking security within this situation of uncertainty. Such considerations would have facilitated the transformation of the ideology discussed above. The simplified version offered by Stalin would have been far more attractive to those with bare literacy than the more sophisticated offerings of Zinoviev or, later, Bukharin, while the personalisation of ideology made the commitment to it much easier by linking it with a personalised authority figure. The low cultural level of much of the party membership was thus an influential factor in shaping the course of ideological development over this period.

But attention must also be turned to the leadership to explain this trend of development in the ideological sphere. The ideology was particularly important to the first generation of post-revolution leaders, those who played leading parts in the wide-ranging debates of the 1920s. There is little reason to doubt that, at least for most of them, commitment to the Marxist method of analysis and to the future type of society envisaged in that analysis was genuine. They had surmounted many difficulties in pursuit of its ideals and it had sustained them through the darkest days. Their thoughts and perceptions, indeed their whole approach to life, was filtered through their ideological commitment. The strength of this commitment, and the belief that through this body of ideas the future could be built, constituted a powerful bond linking them and their actions to Marxian theory. It was therefore very important for them to be able to justify their actions in Marxian terms and thereby to show how the positions they adopted had been reached through application of scientific Marxist analysis to the question at hand. Association with the theoretical basis proved the correctness of their current conduct. Furthermore, the ability to defend their positions in ideological terms involved a judgement about the theoretical veracity of their whole political career, of the past in which they had helped to shape the development of Marxism and of their own personal positions in the succession of ideological struggles which preceded the revolution. The question of Marxism was thus an acute personal issue for most of these leaders.

Among this first generation of Bolshevik leaders there were a number with high levels of skill as theoreticians, a capacity finely honed in the intricacies of ideological debate in the period of the underground. Lenin, Trotsky, Bukharin and perhaps Zinoviev were the leading figures of this group, standing clearly above their leadership colleagues in this regard. However if one looks at the leading group in the 1930s there are no equivalents of these people. People like Kaganovich, Molotov, Kalinin, Voroshilov, Mikoyan and Andreev were clearly not significant thinkers, while the pretensions of Stalin in this regard were also highly exaggerated. The low profile that most of this group adopted in the theoretical discussions of the 1920s, and the ponderous nature of their interventions when they did become involved, reflects a group for whom the skills of ideological discourse and debate were less important than for those who preceded them. This does not mean that they may not have been true believers, deeply committed to the Marxist mode of analysis and the ideal associated with it. Doubtless some were; but it is true that their lack of ideological sophistication facilitated the transformation of the ideology in the ways sketched above. Lacking the ideological grasp and confidence of their forebears and supporting Stalin politically, this group encouraged the rigidification of the ideology and its transformation into orthodoxy.

4.2 IDEOLOGY AND POLICY

The discussion of the rigidification of ideology and of its importance for the ruling group leads directly to the question of its role in policy-making. Much has been written on this question, often in extreme and simplistic terms. Some have maintained that the Bolsheviks were purely pragmatic, manipulating ideology merely to legitimise actions and decisions taken on other grounds. Ideology is, in this view, merely a rationalisation for action.[43] At the other extreme is the view, much less current than it was, that the Bolsheviks were driven purely by ideological fanaticism, that their actions took little or no account of reality, and that the course of Soviet development was ideologically determined.[44] Both of these positions, in a much more moderate form, have some validity. Ideology has been used to justify policy, but it has also played a part in the moulding and formation of policy, and it is important to distinguish between these two roles. Similarly, in the policy formation role, it is important to distinguish between the effect ideology could have in providing a general orientation towards a method of analysis of problems, and any direct policy prescriptions which could follow from the content of the ideology.

The ideology's provision of a general orientation towards policy questions was not a mechanistic process. The leaders did not perceive a problem and then go to some 'holy book' to seek the solution. The ideology was built in from the outset, an intrinsic part of the initial perception and understanding of the problem at hand. Rather than being an external factor, the ideology constituted the framework or set of categories through which the Bolsheviks sought to understand the world about them. The most important aspect of this was class analysis. Use of this as a method of analysis of social reality focused attention upon basic social and economic processes at work in the society, directly linking economic and political developments with those processes which were believed to be at the heart of the society's development. This meant that policies were evaluated and alternatives discussed primarily in terms of their class implications and, given the pre-1936 interpretation of class relations within the Soviet Union as basically antagonistic, it is little wonder that policy alternatives were seen in terms of their impact upon the ongoing class struggle. As a mode of analysis, this process was largely unconscious, a means of reasoning and arguing which was part of their world view. It would be inadvisable, therefore, to believe that the conscious manipulation of simplistic ideological symbols which took place particularly in the 1930s and 1940s reflected a similar simplicity in the intellectual framework used by those who made the decisions of most import for the society. If ideology had a simplistic public face, that does not mean that its cognitive role in regard to the political leaders was similarly simplistic.

Provision of a general orientation to questions does not involve the determination of precise policies. Nevertheless, an interpretation of a situation which stems from any ideological position will have built into it a bias against certain sorts of policies and in favour of others. This it was with the Bolsheviks. To take one example, that of the attitude to the peasantry: for Marx, this was a backward class, which inevitably put a brake upon the progressive aspirations of the working class. Despite the more favourable view which Lenin adopted at times,[45] for the Bolsheviks the alliance with the poor peasantry was at best an unfortunate necessity. It was an alliance which demanded certain policies and concessions, and it was one which, notwithstanding Lenin's change of heart in 1922 and the position symbolised by the Right Opposition throughout the 1920s, did not sit easily with many Bolsheviks' understanding of what they were about. This uneasiness is reflected clearly in the alacrity and enthusiasm with which wide ranks of the party took up the policies of War Communism and agricultural collectivisation and in the way in which NEP initially had to be sold to the party in terms of a temporary retreat. Without the ideologically-based distrust of the peasant, mixed up as it was with that of private ownership, these sorts of reactions would have been much less likely. Without this ideological background, the solution of the crisis of NEP through an extension of the market mechanism would have been much more acceptable to a wider range in the party than it was.

The ideology thus clearly militated against certain types of policies, in particular those which would have strengthened capitalist elements in Russia, and in favour of certain other types. But this does not mean that the ideology provided clear and compelling guidelines in areas of major concern nor that its influence was necessarily decisive, as the introduction of NEP illustrates. The ideology did not offer any clear blueprint for reaching communism. Marx's comments about the institution of socialism are neither specific nor detailed, and in any case he did not foresee the type of situation in which the Bolsheviks found themselves. Nor did Lenin devote much time to this question prior to 1917, and even his major venture into this field, *The State and Revolution*, was motivated less by a concern with laying out the path of future development than with correcting what he saw to be the mistaken theoretical conceptions of some of his colleagues. What these offered were generalised views of the future, but they lacked any clear prescriptions about the concrete means through which this future could be attained. Some attempts were made ideologically to come to grips with this problem, the most notable being *The ABC of Communism* by Bukharin and Preobrazhensky, the theses of the Left on industrialisation and economic development during the 1920s, and Bukharin's exposition of NEP as the road to socialism. All of these involved policy prescriptions, and the continued recognition of them as all lying within the broad compass of Bolshevism simply reflects the diversity and flexibility of the ideology at this time. It shows the way in which different sorts of policy directions could flow from the ideology. The choice of any one particular policy line would thus result not from any mystical inner dynamic of the ideology, but from hard political and economic choices in situations in which the perception-structuring role of ideology was evident. The decisions at the end of the 1920s on pressing ahead with collectivisation and industrialisation provide a good case in point. Here the ideology, as represented by the pro-NEP line espoused by the Right, offered reasonably clear directions about how the crisis of NEP might be overcome, through a strengthening and expansion of its basic principles. But the ideology also provided a set of assumptions about the nature of private property and the present and about the capacity of the proletarian dictatorship to create the conditions for the move to socialism which were consistent with a move against the private principle towards a more collectivist type of arrangement, without, however, predetermining the sorts of policies which should bring this about.[46] Thus while the ideology retained some diversity, it did not impose policy prescriptions upon the decision-makers.

Once the ideology became transformed into an orthodoxy and thereby lost its pluralist elements, it may seem that it would have been more important in laying out guidelines for future policy. However what was important about the ideology during this period was its direct and immediate association with the most powerful political figure in the land. With the content of the ideology effectively being subject to definition by Stalin, the capacity of the ideological heritage to impose serious constraints upon decision-making at the apex or the system was very limited. But for those at lower levels, this development would have made the ideology even more directly and immediately relevant to decision-making than it had been before. If Stalin's words automatically entered the canon of Marxism–Leninism, all of the directions he gave became by definition ideological in nature, with the result that the ideology involved precise policy guidelines. But of course this merely reflects the way in which the ideology had changed fundamentally from what it had been in the early years of Bolshevik rule; it had been captured by an individual and used by him as an instrument of rule over those who were formally his colleagues.

There is one aspect of the relationship between ideology and policy which has not yet been mentioned and in which the relationship is much more direct and immediate than that sketched above. This is the shaping of the development of various areas of intellectual life through the imposition upon them of ideological controls. Perhaps the most important of these from the party's viewpoint were history, philosophy and the social sciences. The imposition of a Marxian methodology produced results which, in some respects, were of positive benefit in stimulating the development of the discipline. But what had a profoundly negative impact was the prohibition of the use of other forms of analysis and the imposition of a party line upon these disciplines. In history and philosophy, both of which were particularly badly affected in this way, this began from the earliest period of Bolshevik rule, to be followed by art, literature and the humanities in general. Neither political science nor sociology developed as a separate discipline during this period. Controls were also placed upon the natural sciences, but these tended to come somewhat later than in the social sciences and humanities, which had a more direct bearing upon both systemic legitimacy and ideological integrity. However the baleful effects of such controls were no less for their later introduction, as the experience of the Lysenko affair clearly demonstrates. In all areas of intellectual endeavour, the imposition of 'scientific' ideological principles, and the crude interpretation of them, hamstrung Soviet development.

If the diversity and fluidity of the ideology was the main reason why it did not play a policy prescriptive role in the first decade and a half of the system's life, this also facilitated its task of policy justification. The claim that the party, and through it the dictatorship of the proletariat, could build socialism in Russia laid an obligation upon the party to demonstrate advance in that direction. If success was not forthcoming from the party's efforts, doubts were thrown upon the legitimacy of the revolution and of the system, and also upon the intellectual integrity of the ideology. As a result, policy and decisions had to be justified by reference to their contribution to the building of socialism, to the pursuit of communism. All of the twists and turns of policy, regardless of what had gone before, had to be justified by this claim. In one sense, the justification was self-fulfilling. If one accepted that the party, through its ideology, could understand the laws of history and thereby lead the country into the communist dawn, it was sufficient for the party to adopt a policy for it, by definition, to be justifiable in these terms. When the ideology became an orthodoxy and stemmed from Stalin's mouth, this became even more the case. This type of argument was clearly facilitated by the lack of precise directives provided by the ideology. Indeed, had policy prescriptions been evident in the ideology, this task would have been more difficult. The absence of such prescriptions has meant that the ideology has been immensely flexible in its role as a vehicle to legitimise policy.

The final question that deserves from consideration is the relationship between ideology and populace. From the time the Bolsheviks came to power, a conscious effort was made to propagate their ideological precepts among the populace at large. Early attempts to spread ideological education were limited by the weak development of the mass media network and the generally low literacy levels. As these matters were improved, and as the party invested more effort in its ideological work, much larger segments of the populace were drawn into direct contact with the ideology. But for those who did not contemplate public careers or who were not destined to rise into managerial positions, open commitment to the ideology was probably unnecessary. All that may have been required for much of this time was silent acquiescence, although the sort of enthusiasm evident at the time of the First Five Year Plan shows that such a course of action was by no means universal. The absence of satisfactory studies of popular perception and belief at this time makes adequate conclusions about the level of popular commitment to the ideology impossible to draw. However, one factor which should counsel against acceptance of the bland conclusion that the ideology had become embedded in the society by the middle of the Stalin period is the way in which that ideology was handled during the war. When the political leaders appealed to the population to rise up and throw out the German invaders in 1941, that appeal was couched not in terms of Marxism–Leninism, but of nationalism. The symbolism of the war harked back to Russian national heroes like Nevsky, Suvorov and Kutuzov, and the overriding emphasis was on saving the motherland. A loosening of control over resurgent nationalism, both in Russia and the other regions of the USSR, reflects a clear decline in the profile of the ideology in the society and suggests that the ideology was still far from becoming completely dominant as the belief system of the USSR.

Ideology was thus a major feature of the Soviet system's development during the first decades of its existence. It constituted a mode of discourse by providing the method of analysis and the categories of discussion for coming to grips with all of those questions which confronted the Soviet leaders. As such, it was fundamental to political debate. Furthermore it fulfilled a basic legitimation function for the system as a whole, for its major component parts, for those who exercised political power in the system, and for the policies which emanated from leading circles. But it could only continue to perform these functions if it continued to develop, and when it ceased to do so its ritualistic aspects became dominant. It was Khrushchev's task to restore ideological dynamism, and it was because he was successful in doing this that the ideology was able to develop in the ways discussed in the other papers in this collection.

NOTES

1. These terms come from, respectively, Franz Schurmann, *Ideology and Organisation in Communist China* (Berkeley: University of California Press, 1968), V. Zaslavsky, 'Socioeconomic inequality and changes in Soviet ideology', *Theory and Society*, vol. 9, no. 2 (March 1980), and Martin Seliger, *The Marxist Conception of Ideology* (Cambridge University Press, 1977). They are discussed further in Ray Taras, *Ideology in a Socialist State: Poland 1956–1983* (Cambridge University Press, 1984), ch. 2.

2. The term comes from Zbigniew K. Brzezinski, *Ideology and Power in Soviet Politics* (New York: Praeger, 1962), p. 4.
3. These views were spelled out initially in his work 'Results and Prospects' of 1906 and more fully in 'Permanent Revolution', published in 1928. See *The Permanent Revolution and Results Prospects* (London: New Park Publications, 1962).
4. For discussions of Trotsky and Lenin, see Baruch Knei-Paz, *The Social and Political Thought of Leon Trotsky* (Oxford: Clarendon Press, 1978) and Neil Harding, *Lenin's Political Thought, Vol. 2: Theory and Practice in the Socialist Revolution* (London: Macmillan, 1981).
5. Their letter is reprinted in Ann Bone (ed.), *The Bolsheviks and the October Revolution. Minutes of the Central Committee of the Russian Social Democratic Labour Party (Bolsheviks) August 1917–February 1918* (London: Pluto Press, 1974), pp. 89–95.
6. For example, see Nogin's declaration to VTsIK on 4 November 1917. This is reprinted in John L. H. Keep (ed.), *The Debate on Soviet Power* (Oxford: Clarendon Press, 1979), pp. 77–8.
7. There were actually three parties to the dispute, but the difference between Lenin and Trotsky was essentially tactical, concerning how the negotiations with the Germans should be conducted.
8. See Lenin's comments in *Sed'moi ekstrennyi s"ezd RKP(b). Mart 1918 goda. Stenograficheskii otchet* (Moscow, 1962) pp. 11–16.
9. *Sed'moi s"ezd*, pp. 24–40. The Left Communist theses are outlined in *Kommunist*, 20 April 1919, pp. 4–9.
10. *Desyatyi s"ezd RKP(b). Mart 1921 goda. Stenograficheskii otchet* (Moscow, 1963), pp. 403–15.
11. 'O kooperatsii', *Polnoe sobranie sochinenii*, 5th ed., 55 vols. (Moscow, 1958–65), vol. 45, pp. 369–77.
12. For an official statement of this turning towards the East, see Bukharin's speech to the XII Congress: *Dvenadtsatyi s"ezd RKP(b) 17–25 aprelya 1923 goda. Stenograficheskii otchet* (Moscow, 1968), pp. 264–71. For Lenin's view, see his 'Luchshe men'she, da luchshe', *Pol. sob. soch.*, vol. 45, pp. 401–6.
13. The best study of this is Stephen F. Cohen, *Bukharin and the Bolshevik Revolution. A Political Biography 1883–1938* (London: Wildwood House, 1974).
14. In Lenin's words. 'Pis'mo k s"ezdu', *Pol. sob. soch.*, vol. 45, p. 345.
15. For example, *Odinnadtsatyi s"ezd RKP(b) Mart–aprel' 1922 goda. Stenograficheskii otchet* (Moscow, 1961), pp. 16–17, 103–4 and 116–17.
16. I. V. Stalin, 'Ob osnovakh leninizma', *Sochineniya*, 13 vols. (Moscow, 1947–53), vol. 6, pp. 106–7.
17. See his 'K itogam rabot XIV konferentsii RKP(b)', *Sochineniya*, vol. 7, pp. 113–16. It is spelled out at greater length in 'K voprosam leninizma', *Sochineniya*, vol. 8, pp. 60–75. The original statement of autumn 1924, which was amended in the way discussed here, was significantly watered down in reprintings of the text of Stalin's original address. See Robert H. McNeal, *Stalin's Works. An Annotated Bibliography* (Stanford University Press, 1967), pp. 110–11.
18. It was formally adopted at the XIV Conference of the party in March–April 1925. See *Kommunisticheskaya partiya Sovetskogo Soyuza v rezolyutsiyakh i*

resheniyakh s"ezdov, konferentsii i plenumov TsK (Moscow, 1953), vol. 2, pp. 47–50.
19. 'K voprosam leninizma', *Sochineniya*, vol. 8, pp. 65–6.
20. Articles 1 and 12. Also see Stalin's 'O proekte konstitutsii Soyuza SSR', in his *Sochineniya*, Tom 1 (XIV), ed. R. H. McNeal (Stanford: Hoover Institution, 1967), pp. 149–50.
21. 'Ekonomicheskie problemy sotsializma v SSSR', ibid., Tom 3 (XVI), pp. 188–245.
22. 'O nashei revoliutsii', *Pol. sob. soch.*, vol. 45, pp. 379–82.
23. For one discussion of this, see Neil Harding, 'Socialism, society and the organic labour state', in Neil Harding (ed.), *The State in Socialist Society* (London: Macmillan, 1984), esp. pp. 3–4.
24. Finally written in July–August 1917, this was designed as a response to what Lenin saw to be the erroneous veiws on the state of Kautsky and Bukharin. See Marion Sawer, 'The genesis of State and Revolution: Lenin and left Marxism', *The Socialist Register 1977* (London: Merlin Press, 1977), pp. 209–27. Compare with Harding, *Lenin's Political Thought*, vol. 2, ch. 6.
25. 'Gosudarstvo i revolyutsiya', *Pol. sob. soch.*, vol. 33, pp. 1–120.
26. 'O pravom uklone v VKP(b)', *Sochineniya*, vol. 12, pp. 30 and 32.
27. 'O pravom uklone v VKP(b)', pp. 34–9 and 'Ob industrializatsii i khlebnoi probleme', *Sochineniya*, vol. 11, p. 171.
28. 'Itogi pervoi pyatiletki', *Sochineniya*, vol. 13, pp. 210–11.
29. See, for example, Stalin's reports to the 14th and 15th Congresses: *XIV s"ezd Vsesoyuznoi kommunisticheskoi partii (b) 18–31 dekabrya 1925g. Stenograficheskii otchet* (Moscow–Leningrad, 1926), pp. 27–8, and *Pyatnadtsatyi s"ezd VKP(b). Dekabr' 1927 goda. Stenograficheskii otchet* (Moscow, 1961), vol. 1, pp. 43–53.
30. Stalin even argued that the state might continue once communism has been achieved if capitalist encirclement remained. See his report to the XVIII Congress: *XVIII s"ezd Vsesoyuznoi kommunisticheskoi partii (b). 10–21 marta 1939g. Stenograficheskii otchet* (Moscow, 1939), pp. 35–6.
31. For example, compare 'Chto delat" and 'Takticheskaya platforma k ob"edinitel'nomu s"ezdu', *Pol sob. soch.*, vol. 6, pp. 1–192, and vol. 12, pp. 221–38.
32. For example, see Lenin's comments at the VIII Congress where he acknowledged that the low cultural level meant that the soviets were not organs of administration *through* the workers but *for* the workers by the advanced section of the proletariat. *Vos'moi s"ezd RKP(b). Mart 1919 goda. Protokoly* (Moscow, 1959), p. 62.
33. Initially this did not involve claims for infallibility, but with the growth of the leader cult and the tactical exigencies of the struggle against the opposition, such claims become firmly embedded.
34. For an explicit statement of the party's task to lead the move into socialism, see Stalin's report to the XVI Congress. *XVI s"ezd Vsesoyuznoi kommunisticheskoi partii (b). Stenograficheskii otchet* (Moscow, 1931), pp. 47–8.
35. In the Preamble to the party Rules of 1934, the party is described as ensuring 'the successful construction of socialist society', in those of 1939, 'the successful construction of communist society'. *KPSS v rez.*, vol. 2, pp. 775 and 923.
36. What was forbidden initially was organisation to further such views. As the

ideology was transformed into an orthodoxy, the holding of heterodox views was also forbidden.

37. For a general discussion, see Nina Tumarkin, *Lenin Lives! The Lenin Cult in Soviet Russia* (Cambridge, Mass.: Harvard University Press, 1983).
38. On the political aspects of this in the 1920s, see Graeme Gill, 'Political myth and Stalin's quest for authority in the party', in T. H. Rigby, Archie Brown and Peter Reddaway (eds), *Authority, Power and Policy in the USSR* (London: Macmillan, 1980), pp. 98–117.
39. For example, see the call in *Pyatnadtsatyi s"ezd*, p. 155.
40. For an ideological justification of Stalin's position, see K. Popov, 'Partiya i rol' vozdya', *Partiinoe stroitel'stvo*, January 1930, pp. 3–9.
41. T. H. Rigby, *Communist Party Membership in the USSR 1917–1967* (Princeton University Press, 1968), pp. 52–3. The number of people who entered the party was actually greater than these figures indicate because of the high levels of membership loss during the period.
42. On educational levels, see Rigby, *Communist Party Membership*, ch. 13.
43. One problem with this interpretation is why there were such battles over questions of ideology and ideological change in the early years after the revolution if there was no belief in the ideology.
44. Adherents of this view tend to be very selective in what they emphasise to support their case. For example, the seizure of power and the introduction of NEP are difficult to fit into the fundamentalist interpretation of Marxism which such commentators adopt.
45. Lenin did see the poor and middle peasantry as playing a positive role under proletarian leadership in the move towards socialism.
46. Despite the claims of some. See for example, Leszek Kolakowski, *Main Currents of Marxism* (Oxford University Press, 1978), vol. 3, p. 41.

5 Developed Socialism and the New Programme of the CPSU

ALFRED B. EVANS

Throughout the history of the Soviet state, Marxist–Leninist ideology has attempted to define the current stage of development of Soviet society and show the relationship between trends of change in the current stage and the attainment of the higher phase of communism. Lenin came to view the prolonged institutionalisation and stabilisation of socialist relations as a necessary prerequisite for progress toward communism. In the early years of Stalin's rule it was assumed that the Soviet Union was at such a rudimentary state of economic development as to make the goal of communism highly remote. However, in 1952 Stalin asserted that the USSR had begun a new, higher stage of development, and authored the notion that socialism would pass to communism through a series of distinct stages. Khrushchev departed from Soviet tradition by announcing at the end of the 1950s that the Soviet Union had entered the stage of direct transition to communism, and left the Communist Party of the Soviet Union with a Programme elaborating on this conception of the full-scale construction of communism. By introducing the concept of developed socialism, Brezhnev repudiated the argument that Soviet society was in a transitional stage and initiated a reassessment of the nature of the entire phase of socialism. Brezhnev also launched plans for the preparation of a new Party Programme describing developed socialist society. Since Brezhnev's death, Soviet leaders have honoured his pledge to adopt a new Programme for the CPSU, but have advocated a more realistic interpretation of the process of improvement and perfection of developed socialism.

5.1 BACKGROUND

While Marx and Engels fairly often discussed the means of transition from capitalism to communism, they usually made no effort to distinguish between the separate stages of development of society which would follow the proletarian revolution. In 'The Critique of the Gotha Programme', Marx did make a clear distinction between a 'first phase of communist society', in which the claim on the means of consumption would reflect each individual producer's labour, and a 'higher phase of communist society', in which goods would be distributed to members of society according to their needs.[1] Marx apparently envisioned the first phase of the new society as a period of fluid, revolutionary transformation of capitalism into communism. He explicitly derived the necessity for such a period of transition from the remaining influence of capitalism: 'What we have to deal with here is a communist society, not as it has *developed* on its own foundations, but on the contrary, as it *emerges* from capitalist society; which is thus in every respect, economically, morally and intellectually, still stamped with the birthmarks of the old society from whose womb it emerges'.[2] As a result of the heritage of capitalism, society in the transitional phase would combine some principles of communism, such as social ownership of the means of production, with some concessions to capitalist psychology, such as material incentives for labour; 'these defects are inevitable in the first phase of communist society as it is when it has just emerged after prolonged birthpangs from capitalist society'.[3] Thus Marx conceived that the essence of the first phase of communism would be determined by the interaction of the features of communism and capitalism, and that the dynamic of transition in that period would be the progressive, continuous replacement of capitalist forms by communist patterns.

Lenin's speeches and writings were the principal source in Russian Marxist thought of the notion of the necessity for the stabilisation and institutionalisation of features distinctive to the first phase of communism. Even before the Bolshevik Revolution, Lenin, who referred to the lower phase of communism as 'socialism' and usually called the higher phase simply 'communism', acknowledged in *State and Revolution* that 'politically, the distinction between the first, or lower, and the higher phase of communism will in time, probably, be tremendous'.[4] He also emphasised that the transition from the higher to the lower phase would be a protracted process, whose duration could not be predicted in advance.[5] After October 1917, Lenin steadily postponed even further into the indefinite future the time when Soviet Russia was expected to arrive at full communism. In fact, he argued that Soviet society had not even entered the first phase of communism but that the October Revolution had inaugurated a period of transition from capitalism to socialism, when the birth marks left by the pre-revolutionary setting were being effaced and the socialist sector of society was being strengthened and expanded.

5.2 STALIN

It was left to Stalin to have the honour of announcing in 1936 that the Soviet Union had reached the first phase of communism. In his speech of November 1936 proposing a new constitution for the USSR Stalin declared that socialist ownership had become dominant throughout the country's economy, so that a society which was basically socialist had been constructed in the Soviet Union.[6] Though it followed, according to the logic of Marxist theory, that the next step was the realisation of communism, Stalin displayed an aversion to discussion of the means and timing of movement to the higher phase. Stalin in his November 1936 speech rejected the suggestion that the draft of a new constitution should include a description of the goal of building communism; he insisted that a constitution should only register and solidify that which has already been attained, while the marking out of goals for the future should be left for a 'programme'.[7] Though Stalin's remarks might have served as a reminder that the claim that the Soviet Union had reached socialism rendered the existing Party Programme (adopted in 1919) obsolete, he mentioned no plans for writing a new programme. During the remainder of the Stalin period, Soviet society was ostensibly considered to be engaged in the 'gradual transition' (*postepennyi perekhod*) to communism, but in actuality the works of Soviet ideologists during the years of mature Stalinism implied that Soviet society had entered a long period of preparation of the preconditions for the transition to communism. The avoidance of discussion of the features of the transition to the higher phase suggested a tacit awareness of a fundamental conflict between the requirements of the consolidation of the institutions of socialism and the demands of a transformation of socialist into communist relations.

Stalin regarded the development of the Soviet system from the middle of the 1930s on as *neuklonnyi*: consistent, in the sense of being steady, unswerving, and undeviating. Stalin sought to maintain the continuity of policies established by his decisions of the late 1920s in favour of the collectivisation of agriculture, forced-pace industrialisation, and intensification of the state's control of society. Each Five Year Plan was to be followed by another in an endless series extending the pattern of development embarked on at the time of Stalin's triumph. *Neuklonnyi* progress meant the linear accumulation of existing assets, the continual movement in the same direction. The problem was to reconcile the continuity of the development of socialism in the Stalinist perspective with the belief in the transition to communism promised by the classics of Marxism. At the 18th Congress of the Soviet Communist Party in 1939, Stalin boasted of the 'further consolidation of the Soviet system' and called for further sacrifices on behalf of investment in 'the utmost expansion of our socialist industry'.[8] The Congress elected a comission which was supposed to prepare a new programme for the party. However, the commission neither produced the text of a new programme nor reported publicly on its work, presumably because the Second World War was soon to remove from consideration any optimistic plans for the future.

The attempt to bring the official statement of the goals of the CPSU up to date was resumed at the 19th Party Congress in 1952, which, like the 18th Congress, chose a commission which was assigned the task of rewriting the party's programme. The new committee also failed to report on its work, perhaps because of Stalin's death a few months later. However, some hints as to his intentions for a new programme were offered by Stalin in his essays published shortly before the 19th Congress, under the title *Economic Problems of Socialism in the USSR*. In fact, the resolution adopted by the 19th Congress establishing a commission to revise the party's programme declared that the new programme should follow the suggestions in Stalin's newest work.[9]

In *Economic Problems of Socialism in the USSR*, Stalin revealed his vision of a new stage of development of Soviet society. His most explicit statement on the conditions for the transition to communism in the USSR was presented in his criticism of the alleged theoretical errors committed by an economist, L. D. Yaroshenko. According to Stalin, Yaroshenko's chief error was his supposition that arranging a rational organisation of productive forces would make possible an abundance of products and the achievement of communism. Stalin rejected the assertion that an abundance of goods and distribution according to need could be brought about readily, without establishing the necessary preconditions through the development of productive forces and relations of production. 'Comrade Yaroshenko does not understand that before we can pass to the formula, "to each according to his needs", we shall have to pass through a number of stages of economic and cultural re-education of society'.[10] Stalin specified that three 'main preliminary conditions' would have to be satisfied in order to 'pave the way' for a transition to communism. First, it was necessary to ensure 'a continuous expansion of the production of all social production, with a relatively higher rate of expansion of the production of means of production'.[11] With this point Stalin emphasised that a high rate of investment in the growth of industry, and the priority for investment in the production of capital goods, would be maintained. Secondly, it would be necessary to eliminate the difference between collective farm property and state property, and to replace the production of commodities by a system of exchange of products under the control of the central government or some other central agency.[12] Stalin stressed the transitory status of collective farm property and commodity circulation, observing that such factors were already beginning to hamper the development of productive forces, and would become more of an encumbrance with the passage of time. The third condition mentioned by Stalin was such a 'cultural advancement of society as will secure for all members of society the all-round development of their physical and mental abilities'.[13] By 'cultural advancement' Stalin meant an increase in popular education, to be associated with the shortening of the working day, the freeing of the citizen from a life-long tie to a single occupation, a radical improvement in housing conditions, and at least a doubling of the real wages of workers and employees.

A careful reading indicates that Stalin was describing not the process of transformation of socialism into communism, but the process of establishing the conditions to be satisfied prior to undertaking such a transformation. Stalin warned that the Soviet Union would have to pass through 'a number of stages' before realising communism.[14] His discussion of the programmatic tasks ahead of Soviet society pertained to the 'main preliminary conditions' necessary in order to *prepare* for the transition to communism.[15] Stalin's thesis was that the Soviet Union was beginning a stage of preparation for the transition to communism, to be followed by a later stage (or series of stages) in which the transition would be carried out. It was Stalin who introduced into Soviet ideology the idea that the development of socialism might be divided into several different, consecutive stages, and who suggested in 1952 that the USSR was on the threshold of a stage that was distinct and separate from the earlier period of socialist industrialisation and the future stage of realisation of the potential of communism.

Economic Problems of Socialism in the USSR sketched out Stalin's guidelines for progress within the new stage of growth, in order to chart the trends of change in Soviet society in the foreseeable future. An easing of the burdens which the drive to increase industrial capacity had imposed on the people of the USSR was not a prospect for the immediate future. In an earlier section of *Economic Problems of Socialism in the USSR*, Stalin had warned that giving priority to the production of consumer goods over the manufacture of capital goods would destroy 'the possibility of the continuous expansion of our national economy, because the national economy cannot be continuously expanded without giving primacy to the production of means of production'.[16] The first condition to be satisfied in preparation for the transition to communism, according to Stalin, was the consistent growth of gross production, with a higher rate of growth for the production of capital goods than for total economic output. A main theme of the new stage of development was to be the preservation of a high rate of saving and investment, making possible the expansion of Soviet industrial capacity at a rate sufficient to overtake the Western capitalist economies.[17]

The further intensification of the state's control over society was the second trend Stalin foresaw for Soviet society in the imminent future. Stalin expected that at some time the state-owned sector and the collective farm section of the economy would merge into 'one all-embracing production sector', while the circulation of goods as commodities bought and sold on the market would disappear, probably to be succeeded by a system of exchange of products under the supervision of 'a single *national* economic body'.[18] He declared that the elimination of the distinction between state ownership of productive property and collective farm ownership was 'a matter of paramount importance'.[19] In enumerating the second condition for preparing the way for communism, he made it clear that he considered beginning the elimination of collective farm property and commodity circulation to be an immediate necessity: 'these factors are already beginning to hamper the powerful development of our productive forces, since they create obstacles to the full extension of government planning to the whole of the national economy, especially agriculture'.[20] Stalin conceived of social transformation primarily in terms of changes in formal relations of property ownership and patterns of economic administration, consisting of the extension of state ownership of production and centralised control of distribution throughout the whole economy.

Stalin's vision of the future did not emphasise the promise of material abundance that often had been featured very prominently in discussions of the higher phase of communism. As we have noted, he argued strongly against granting a higher priority to the production of articles of consumption in Soviet economic policy. In addition, his warning that before distribution according to need could be instituted, Soviet society would have to pass through 'a number of stages' of change, implicitly cautioned against anticipating a high level of abundance in the near future. Finally, Stalin chose to mention as the third preliminary condition for the higher phase, not reaching an affluent level of consumption, but ensuring sufficient 'cultural advancement', or education, to make possible for Soviet citizens 'the all-round development of their physical and mental abilities', providing the qualities needed to make them more productive workers.[21] Stalin did say that housing conditions should be 'radically improved' and that the real wages of workers and employees should be 'at least doubled'.[22] While abundance did not occupy a place of importance among Stalin's goals for Soviet society, neither did asceticism. There is no reason to think that austerity was ever an end in itself for him. Also, it would have been virtually impossible to achieve the enormous expansion of output desired by Stalin and to stimulate substantial increases in the productivity of labour without granting a significant rise in the real wages of Soviet workers. Nevertheless, Stalin clearly regarded the expansion of production as a more important objective than the enhancement of the standard of consumption in Soviety society in the years for which he was making plans.

Another criterion of advancement to communism de-emphasised by Stalin was the reduction of social and economic inequality. He described the distinction between town and country in the USSR as consisting 'mainly and chiefly' of a difference in forms of property ownership (state property versus collective farm property)[23] rather than differences in conditions of labour or standards of living, which suggested that changes in property relations rather than the removal of social–economic inequality were necessary for progression toward the higher phase. Stalin took pains to insist that even in the future not all the distinctions between industrial and agricultural labour, or between mental and physical labour, would disappear; only the 'essential' distinctions would die off, because 'the conditions of labour of the managerial staffs and those of the workers are not identical'.[24] For the first time it was argued that some distinctions between major groups and strata, including the distinction between management and labour, would persist even in a fully communist society. In the stage of development in which Soviet society found itself in the early 1950s, the real wages of workers and service personnel would be raised, Stalin said, by increasing cash wages and reducing the prices of consumer goods.[25] Those measures would lead to the growth in incomes of the Soviet population in a manner calculated to heighten the emphasis on material incentives to labour and preserve differentials between higher and lower wages. (Stalin did not seem to notice the difficulty of combining such a policy with the elimination of the use of money). The trends ahead within the new stage of development would rule out the possibility of decreasing inequality in consumption by introducing distribution according to need.

Stalin's projection of goals for the new stage reflected his conception of development within socialism as *neuklonnyi* – consistent, linear, and unswerving. The stage initiated by Soviet society was one not of transition to communism, but of the further consolidation of socialism. The trends of that higher stage of socialism were to be the logical extension of the pattern of change established in the Soviet Union by the early 1930s, during the period of the first Five Year Plan and collectivisation of agriculture. As Robert C. Tucker observes, Stalin sought after the Second World War to reimpose the general line of the policy of the 1930s.[26] *Economic Problems of Socialism in the USSR* communicated Stalin's determination that the Stalinist general line would remain dominant in the future, within the stage of development defined by his analysis.

Implicit in Stalin's analysis was an awareness of the underlying tension between the further consolidation of the features of Soviet socialism and the transformation of social relations involved in the realisation of communism. Stalin tried to relieve that tension to a considerable degree through the use of two devices. First, he postponed the final and culminative period of transition by lengthening the duration of the phase of socialism, which he divided into several stages of change. Second, he assimilated the higher stages of development to the characteristics of the lower stage.[27] Increasingly, his vision of the future of socialism, and even of the ultimate goal of communism, became more consistent with the implications of the direction of the policy pursued by the Soviet regime during the early period of socialism. Nevertheless, success in fulfilling Stalin's demands for Soviet society in its new and higher stage of growth would raise more sharply the question of resolving the inherent contradictions between the strengthening of the state's control over society and the Marxist classics' prediction of the withering away of the state, and between the preservation of differences in economic reward and the vision of the distribution of goods on the basis of need. While Stalin left his successors with the conception of a new and distinct stage of advancement within the limits of socialism, a theoretical contribution which was to be put to use by both Khrushchev and Brezhnev, in postponing the advent of the transition to communism Stalin left the reconciliation of the requirements of continuity and transformation to be dealt with by future generations of leaders.

5.3 KHRUSHCHEV

Within a few years after becoming the head of the Soviet Communist Party, Khrushchev hinted that the transition to communism in the USSR was much closer than Stalin had suggested. At the 20th Congress of the CPSU in 1956, he declared that the USSR was in a position to surpass the most advanced capitalist countries in per capita production in 'an historically very short period'.[28] Stalin had mentioned overtaking the capitalist countries in production as a long-term goal to be associated with the fulfilment of the prerequisites for communism. At the same Party Congress, Khrushchev further encouraged the expectation of dramatic advancement by saying that 'we have climbed to such summits, such heights, that we can see the wide vistas leading to the ultimate goal, a communist society'.[29] The 20th Party Congress, like each of the two preceding congresses of the CPSU, selected a commission which was instructed to prepare a new party programme.

At the 21st Party Congress in 1959, Khrushchev announced that the Soviet Union had entered a new period of development, the stage of the 'full-scale construction of communist society'.[30] Like Stalin in 1952, Khrushchev argued in 1959 that the development of Soviet society had reached a new stage. Khrushchev observed that the level of development of the Soviet economy in his time was qualitatively superior to that of the early 1930s. He was impressed with the distance travelled by the Soviet Union in economic development since the time of the early Five Year Plans. He noted that by the 1950s the Soviet Union had become a mighty industrial power, and concluded that 'today our level, our potential, and our possibilities are different'.[31] Discarding the caution expressed in Stalin's view of the prospects for Soviet society, Khrushchev characterised the stage of 'full-scale construction' as a period of direct transition to the higher phase: 'the Soviet people have entered a new period of historical development in which socialism grows into communism'.[32]

Khrushchev's conception of the stage of transition from socialism to communism was expounded in the new Programme of the Communist Party of the Soviet Union, which was adopted by the 22nd Party

Congress in 1961.[33] This new Programme, the third in the history of the party, promised that between 1961 and 1970 the Soviet Union would surpass the United States of America in per capita production, that between 1971 and 1980 the material and technical base for communism would be created, and that by 1980 a communist society would be built 'in the main' (*v osnovnom*) in the USSR. The 1961 Party Programme contained more specific details of the transition to communism than had been offered by Soviet sources before, and departed from Soviet ideological tradition in announcing a timetable for the achievement of the higher phase. The new Programme ended with the words, *'The party solemnly proclaims: the present generation of Soviet people will live under communism'*.[34]

In the analysis of the relationship between socialism and communism in Soviet ideology during the early 1960s, the key term was *posledovatel'-nost'*, or consistency. Development from socialism to communism was regarded not simply as the continuous extension of previous trends, but as *posledovatel'nyi* – consistent, proceeding in successive stages, with achievements resulting logically from established conditions. The characteristics of communist society would not be identical to those of socialist society, but they would be the logical consequence of the accomplishments of socialism. According to Khrushchev, the classics of Marxism–Leninism 'emphasised that communism is not separated from socialism by a wall, but that they are rather two phases of the same socio-economic formation.'[35] The socialist and communist phases belonged to the same formation, characterised by social ownership of the means of production and the absence of exploiting classes. There were important elements of similarity between the lower and higher phases, such as collective ownership and the growth of production. However, there were also 'essential distinctions' between socialism and communism with respect to the degree of material abundance, the distribution of material benefits, relations between social classes and the role of the state in society. Khrushchev's notion of consistency took into consideration both that the transition to communism involved major changes and that 'communism grows out of socialism and is its direct continuation'.[36] On balance, his formulation tended to minimise the difficulties of transition.

A crucial point in Khrushchev's interpretation was his insistence on the transitional nature of socialism. He argued that socialism did not develop on its own foundations. The building of socialism began amid the social and economic conditions created by capitalism, so that socialism bore the impression of the old order from which it had sprung. Socialism's imperfections were the result of the remaining influences of presocialist historical phases. Communism, however, did develop on its own foundations. The construction of the basis of full communism took place in socialist society, after the foundations of the communist socio-economic formation had been laid. Fully developed communism would not reflect the influence of capitalism. The phases of socialism and communism within the same socio-economic formation were distinguished from each other by their level of economic development and maturity of social relations. In Khrushchev's theory, socialism had no logic of its own other than that which would find its conclusion in the achievement of communism, while the perfection of socialism had no meaning apart from its transformation into communism.

The period of the full-scale construction of communism was thought to include trends of three varieties. First, those features common to both the socialist and communist phases of the communist formation would continue to develop. Secondly, the potential of those features distinctive to the socialist phase would be exhausted, leading to the 'atrophying of old forms of life'.[37] And thirdly, new features distinctive to the phase of communism, already visible as sprouts or shoots (*rostki*) in socialist society, would grow stronger, beginning to replace distinctively socialist features. The stage of full-scale construction of communism would be one of the interweaving and interaction of old and new forms.

Khrushchev spoke of three main tasks to be accomplished during the full-scale construction of communism. The main economic task would be to build the material and technical base of communism. The principal social task would be the elimination of distinctions between social classes, resulting in the creation of a classless, communist society. In politics, society would prepare itself for the 'complete implementation of the principle of communist self-government'.[38] Khrushchev introduced a change in the Soviet understanding of the relationships between the tasks of communist construction. Stalin had tended to speak of a sequence of tasks, with construction of the material–technical base of communism preceding qualitative changes in social relations and political institutions. Khrushchev indicated that economic, social and political changes would proceed more or less simultaneously, with change in each area contributing to the success of change in other areas. Socialist society would tackle the tasks of economic, social, and political transformation at the same time. However, Khrushchev still maintained that the most crucial task was that of building the material–technical base of communism; and he did not promise that each of the main tasks of full-scale construction of communism would be completely resolved within the same span of time. While the material–technical base of communism would be built within twenty years, the full merging of social classes would take longer, and the withering away of the state might take even longer.

By 1980, the USSR would have become a basically communist society, that is, communist society whose foundations had been constructed. This basically communist society would take up the work of finishing the construction of communism. The features of communist society would be realised fully only after the finishing (*zavershenie*) of communist construction. In short, in Khrushchev's view, socialism was an historical phase consisting of two stages – basic socialism and the full-scale construction of communism – and communism would be a phase that also would include two stages, basic communism and finished communism. The distinction between the first and second stages to come within the communist phase relieved Soviet ideologists of the necessity of promising the completion of all processes of transformation from socialism to communism by the early 1980s. Nevertheless, Khrushchev had infused the transition to communism with operational significance. The boldness and optimism of his predictions seem startling today.[39]

5.4 THE CONCEPT OF DEVELOPED SOCIALISM

In the first few years after Khrushchev's fall from power in 1964, Soviet sources placed less emphasis on the claim that the USSR was in the stage of full-scale construction of communism and on the specific timetable for economic achievement set forth in the Party Programme. However, there was evidence of some reluctance in the Soviet leadership to abandon the promises of the 1961 Programme. Even in November 1967, in his speech on the fiftieth anniversary of the October Revolution, Leonid Brezhnev used the phrase 'full-scale construction of communism' and implied that the Programme represented a solemn pledge undertaken by the party. Brezhnev insisted that 'the entire path travelled by our country over half a century has shown convincingly that the word of our party does not diverge from its deed. The Third Programme of the party – a programme of construction of the foundations of communist society – will also be fulfilled'.[40] Yet in the same speech, Brezhnev for the first time made conspicuous use of the term, 'developed socialist society' (*razvitoe sotsialisticheskoe obshchestvo*), and hinted that developed socialism was a new and distinct stage of development.[41] During subsequent years, it became apparent that developed socialism was a replacement for Khrushchev's concept of the full-scale construction of communism.

The occasion of the full-blown introduction of the idea of developed socialism was Brezhnev's report to the 24th Congress of the CPSU in 1971. In that address, Brezhnev proudly announced that 'the developed socialist society, of which in 1918 V. I. Lenin spoke as the future of our country, has been built by the self-sacrificing labour of the Soviet people'.[42] During the next few years, a large number of works by Soviet authors established developed socialism as the orthodox characterisation of the stage that had been reached by Soviet society in the 1960s. The new Constitution of the USSR adopted in 1977 reaffirmed that a developed socialist society had been built in the USSR, and that developed socialist society was a 'logically necessary stage on the path to communism'.[43] At the 26th Congress of the CPSU in 1981, Brezhnev revealed plans to write a new Party Programme expounding the features of developed socialism. While conceding that the Programme ratified in 1961 'on the whole correctly' expressed 'the regularities of social development', he noted that twenty years had passed since its acceptance, and suggested that the document had become somewhat outdated. Brezhnev reported that experience since 1961 had indicated that the Soviet Union was advancing to communism through developed socialism, and urged that that conclusion should be 'duly reflected' in the party's Programme.[44] The delegates to the 26th Congress instructed the party's Central Committee to prepare the draft of a new version of the Party Programme to be considered at the next Congress.

A general trend of Soviet Marxism–Leninism from 1917 to the present has been the gradual extension of the time required to reach the ultimate objective of communism. The major deviation from that trend occurred during the Khrushchev years, with the assertion that Soviet society had begun a direct transition to communism. The concept of developed socialism replaced Khrushchev's thesis of the full-scale construction of communism and signified a substantial postponement of the period of transition to communism. Theorists of developed socialism emphasised that socialism was not a brief stage, but a long historical phase consisting of an orderly succession of stages. They added that developed socialism was itself a prolonged stage.[45] With the introduction of the concept of developed socialism, Khrushchev's schedule for attaining communism was quietly but decisively rejected.

The addition of a further stage on the way to communism implied a re-evaluation of the nature of the entire phase of socialism. Previously it had been assumed that socialism was a transitional state of society's development, combining features inherited from capitalism with the characteristics of immature communism. In that perspective, the development of socialism consisted of the fading of the birth marks left by capitalism and the strengthening of communist relations. The maturation of socialism had no logic other than that of the progressive realisation of communism. Socialism could not develop on its own basis, since, as a stage in the growth of the communist socio-economic formation, it must develop on the basis of the principles peculiar to that formation and fully expressed in the functioning of the higher phase, communism. The belief that socialism would be a period of fluid transition was derived from Marx's works. However, theorists of developed socialism described socialism as a distinct, relatively independent phase of historical progress, and emphasised that there were important, qualitative differences between socialism and communism.

Anatolii Butenko, for instance, argued that socialism was 'not at all a temporary combination of features of immature communism and "birthmarks of capitalism", but a social order, characterised by socialist features, signs and principles, united in their social nature'.[46] Socialism, after being established and firmly consolidated, developed on its own basis; it was based on socialist relations of production, and functioned according to its own laws. The essence of the process of development and maturing of socialism was that the features and properties inherent in socialism were 'disclosed more fully, they become more mature, and the regularities and principles of socialism receive ever greater scope for their manifestation and utilisation'.[47] The features distinctive to socialism were not to be regarded as the result of the influence of capitalism, as therefore somehow evil, and to be purged from society as rapidly as possible; what was most distinctive to socialism was contributed by its own development, and should be consolidated and expanded as much as possible.

Butenko argued that there were sharp differences between tendencies which pertained to the development of the socialist phase on its own basis and those which would be revealed during the direct growth of socialism into communism. He criticised other Soviet theorists for having devoted attention mainly to the regularities of the growth of socialism into communism, while having neglected the principles of development proper to the socialist phase. In other words, he contended that during the contemporary period the consideration of the transition to communism was less important than the study of the maturing of socialism. Butenko's position was unusually forthright. However, approval of his argument was suggested by the statement in the 1977 Constitution that in the stage of developed socialism, socialism developed on its own basis.[48]

The thorniest problem faced by Soviet theorists of developed socialism was that of the relationship between the trends of the current stage and the transition to communism. The further consolidation of socialism and the perfection of the socialist relations would have seemed to preclude entry into the transition to the higher phase, since the further institutionalisation of socialist relations could hardly be compatible with their replacement by communist patterns. Yet Soviet leaders continued to insist that change within the stage of mature socialism prepared the way for the transition to communism. When introducing the concept of developed socialism at the 24th Party Congress, Brezhnev said that the construction of a developed socialist society permitted the Soviet Union to 'begin the practical resolution of the great task, posed by the Programme of the party and by its latest congresses – the creation of the material–technical base of communism'.[49] Suslov in 1971 directed Soviet social scientists to study not only the problems of developed socialist society but also 'the scientific substantiation of the ways and means of its gradual growth into communism'.[50] To abandon the claim that Soviet society was moving towards communism would shatter the party's self-conception and raise severe theoretical doubts about the justification of its role. The assertion, repeated by Soviet leaders in every period from the October Revolution to the present, that the party is guiding Soviet society towards communism, provides the ultimate goal for social development, justifies the party's leading role, and furnishes an essential link between the heritage of Marx and Engels and contemporary Soviet ideology. The hesitation and uncertainty of party leaders during the late 1960s in approaching the definition of the current stage is evidence that the decision to postpone the onset of full communism, however unavoidable, was not taken lightly.

Paradoxically, since proclaiming the advent of developed socialism, Soviet leaders have continued to urge Soviet scholars and ideologists to show in detail the ways in which developed socialism will grow into communism. Suslov was particularly emphatic on that point. In 1975 he identified the question of the further development of socialism and its transformation into communism as having 'first level significance'. He contended that reaching developed socialism made the study of the transition to communism more timely. 'When the Soviet people under the leadership of the Communist Party constructed a developed socialist society, the concrete problems of its further progress and transition to communism became the order of the day both theoretically and practically'. He added that 'the party does not limit itself to the characterisation only of that which already is, which has become actually existing. In its documents is also given a scientific elaboration of the ways of the growth of socialism into communism, of the maturing of future forms of communist society'.[51] Yet, after having led up to the subject, Suslov said nothing about the way in which developed socialism might generate the growth of communist social relations. His message was only exhortatory.

Brezhnev attempted to provide a decisive answer to the question of the relationship between developed socialism and communism in his speech on the final text of the new Constitution in October 1977. He described mature socialism as a 'relatively long state of development on the path from socialism to communism', but went on to say that 'the knowledge and utilisation of all the possibilities of developed socialism is at the same time the transition to the construction of communism. The future does not lie beyond the limits of the present. The future is rooted in the present, and, resolving the tasks of today – of the socialist present – we are gradually entering tomorrow – the communist future'.[52] The assertion that the future did not lie beyond the limits of the present was in agreement with the view that Soviet society still faced the long and difficult task of solving the problems encountered in the socialist phase of development. At first glance, it might seem that Brezhnev had said that resolving those problems was identical with moving into the phase of communism. However, closer examination of his remarks reveals a more complex thesis. He did not say that 'the knowledge and utilisation of all the possibilities of developed socialism' constituted in themselves the transition to communism, but that the knowledge and use of the possibilities of the present stage were at the same time the transition to the *construction* of communism. In other words, the present stage was to make its contribution to the achievement of communism largely through the preparation of the preconditions for a future transition.

This was the traditional interpretation of the meaning of the statement that Soviet society was already engaged in a gradual transition to communism, the position taken by Stalin from 1936 to 1953. Khrushchev broke with this tradition with his announcement that Soviet society had entered a stage of direct transition to communism, in which the continued accumulation of the prerequisites for the higher phase would be accompanied by the dialectical replacement of socialist relations by communist relations. Brezhnev declared that the achievement of developed socialism would permit the Soviet Union to turn to the resolution of 'the great task, posed by the Programme of the party – the creation of the material–technical base of communism'.[53] But in actuality the task set by the Party Programme of 1961 was not only the building of the material–technical base, but the creation of communism itself. With the introduction of the idea of developed socialism, Soviet leaders implicitly abandoned the conception of the present stage as one of direct transition and adopted a view of the relationship between the perfection of socialism and the emergence of communism as indirect.

A few Soviet writers in the 1970s predicted that developed socialism would be succeeded by another stage of socialism, postponing to that still later stage of highly developed socialism the process of transition to communism. The most authoritative sources have attempted to discourage such a conclusion, perhaps fearing that the introduction of still more stages on the way to communism might appear ludicrous. However, making a clear distinction between the present stage and a still later stage would help to resolve the apparent contradiction between the further institutionalisation of socialism in the present and its replacement by communism at some time in the future. In line with his argument for separating the consideration of the further development of socialist relations from the description of their transformation into communist relations, Anatolii Butenko suggested that the direct transition to communism would come about at a later, separate, historical stage, when the potential of socialism had been exhausted and a much higher level of advancement of productive technology had been reached. 'Only in the concluding stages of socialism . . . inevitably will unfold the intensive process of elimination of those features which are inherent only in socialism and the creation of those elements which, coming to replace the former, are characteristic only of communism', he argued. But that would 'inevitably be a whole historical stage of qualitative and complex changes in social life'.[54]

Though mainstream sources disavowed the thesis that another stage of socialism would follow developed socialism, those sources in fact largely adopted the substance of Butenko's position. Richard Kosolapov, for instance, ventured the notion in the early 1970s that developed socialism itself might contain two sub-stages, in the first of which the drawing closer together of forms of socialist property and of social classes would take place; and in the second of which forms of property would merged into one and society would become classless.[55] Kosolapov's scheme of subdivision of developed socialism was cited with approval in the authoritative work, *Developed Socialist Society*, in the late 1970s.[56] Kosolapov went on to become editor of the party's theoretical journal, *Kommunist*. In 1981 an article in *Kommunist* by a leading Soviet historian, M. P. Kim, endorsed the idea of delineating two stages in the growth of socialism into communism.

> In the first stage, in all the substantial changes in socialist reality will dominate, evidently, the regularities, principles, and norms of socialism. (Attempts ahead of time to limit their action would mean an unjustified forcing of events and harmful haste.) Only in the following stage, when socialism will attain higher perfection and all the necessary prerequisites for the transition to communism will be created, will socialist regularities, principles and norms give way to communist ones. In those two stages the transformation of the first phase into the second will be carried out on two different historical levels with significant peculiarities.
>
> In the first stage, when the centre of emphasis will fall on the general perfection of the socialist organisation of society, on strengthening its principles and norms, that transformation will have an *indirect (oposredovannyi)* character, that is, the transition to communism will not be thought of as other than through the strengthening and full realisation of the demands precisely of socialism. In the second stage the transformation of socialism into communism should have a *direct (neposredstvennyi)* character, that is, the transition to the second phase will be completed by means of the replacement of the principles and norms of socialism by the principles and norms of communism. That, obviously, will begin when socialism fully exhausts its creative possibilities and decisively creates all the prerequisites of its transformation into communist society.[57]

Soviet society was still considered to be in the period within developed socialism in which the possibilities of socialism had not been exhausted. The tasks of direct transformation had in this way been postponed to some point in the indefinite future.

5.5 DEVELOPED SOCIALISM AFTER BREZHNEV

The commitment to present a new Programme to the next party congress was reaffirmed by each new leader of the Communist Party of the Soviet Union in the early 1980s. Though Andropov did not mention plans for a new Programme in his major article in *Kommunist* in February 1983, he did report in his address to a Plenum of the Central Committee of the CPSU in June 1983 that a new version of the Party Programme was being prepared 'on the basis of a decision of the 26th Congress'.[58] Chernenko wasted no time in revealing his interest in the writing of a new programmatic document; immediately upon assuming the post of

General Secretary he spoke of the new Programme, and added that 'the Central Committee attaches enormous importance to its drafting'.[59] The promise that the 27th Party Congress would adopt a new version of the Party Programme was repeated frequently in Chernenko's speeches during his brief tenure in office.[60] The same promise was made in Gorbachev's speech at the conference on Soviet ideology in December 1984 and his remarks to the Central Committee meeting which elected him as head of the party organisation in March 1985.[61] The new version of the Third Programme of the Communist Party of the Soviet Union was published in draft form in October 1985 and, after public discussion on a grand scale, was approved in its final form by the 27th Party Congress, which met in late February and early March 1986.[62]

Andropov's and Chernenko's statements on the preparation of a new Party Programme were coupled with criticism of the ideas embodied in the 1961 Programme. In June 1983 Andropov accorded the Programme adopted in 1961 much the same faint praise it had been given by Brezhnev at the 26th Party Congress, saying that 'the present Party Programme . . . on the whole correctly characterises the laws governing world social development and the goals and fundamental tasks of the struggle of the party and Soviet people for communism'. However, Andropov engaged in a repudiation of the offical Programme that was unprecedented for the head of the party by adding, 'some of its provisions – this must be stated bluntly – have not fully withstood the test of time, since they contained elements of isolation from reality, running ahead, and unwarranted detail'.[63] While Brezhnev had merely implied that the current Party Programme was outdated, Andropov argued that it had been wrong in some respects from its very inception.

Chernenko picked up the same theme in his speech to the June 1983 Central Committee Plenum, charging that 'during a certain period . . . an oversimplified view was held of the paths and timing of the transition to the higher phase of communism. Hurrying our dream, so to speak, certain theorists and propagandists tried to smooth out the uneven spots in the path we are following and lost touch with the real conditions of life'.[64] The period of oversimplification and excessive optimism alluded to by Chernenko was obviously that of the early 1960s, when the Programme of full-scale construction of communism was framed. Chernenko repeated his criticism of the over-optimistic expectations of the Khrushchev period in this remarks in April 1984 on the preparation of the new Programme.[65] He also warned against burdening the new Party Programme with excessive detail: 'none of us, naturally, is prepared to ask Gosplan or any other organisations to name the concrete date of finishing the period of developed socialism. In general in such a document, as we all agree, one should not abuse figures, or any sort of details'.[66] In fact, the new Party Programme generally avoids specific predictions and timetables of the sort that featured in the 1961 document.

The speeches and writings of Soviet leaders in the years since Brezhnev's death have constantly insisted on the necessity of realism in the assessment of the problems and prospects of contemporary Soviet society. In fact, the stress on realism was evident in a speech delivered while Brezhnev was still alive and which foreshadowed the themes of later statements: Andropov's address on the anniversary of Lenin's birthday in April 1982. On that occasion Andropov cautioned that 'it is important to combine boldness and flexibility in solving objectively urgent problems with a precise, strictly scientific evaluation of what has been achieved, without underestimating or exaggerating our forces and possibilities'.[67] In the tradition of Leninism, the two main errors that are possible in the domestic policies of a Communist party–state are running ahead of existing conditions and resting on what has been achieved. Andropov made it clear which of those deviations he considered to be the more important to guard against in February 1983, when he warned that any attempts 'to run ahead to communist forms of distribution . . . can and do create undesirable phenomena' and urged, 'we must soberly consider where we stand . . . to see our society in real dynamic, with all of its possibilities and needs is what is now demanded'.[68] In June 1983 Andropov called for a 'realistic analysis of the existing situation' in the new Party Programme.[69]

Chernenko underlined the same point in the Central Committee meeting in June 1983, insisting that social science research should 'take existing reality, with all of its pluses and minuses, as its point of departure and must reveal the objective laws of social development more fully'.[70] In April 1984, Chernenko added that the Party Programme should provide a realistic description of developed socialism and cautioned that 'if attention, as Lenin said, is shifted to "the relatively remote, beautiful and rosy future", then often we lose sight of the more imminent tasks of the difficult, concrete transition and approach to that future'.[71] Gorbachev joined in the advocacy of realism in December 1984, affirming that 'the assessments and conclusions that have been made caution against running ahead and against confusing what exists with what should be achieved'.[72] The emphasis on realism in the words of recent Soviet leaders has been designed to prepare the Soviet people for a new Party Programme that does not promise an imminent transition to communism in the USSR, and has opened the way for increasingly frank criticism of the problems that had built up under Brezhnev.[73]

Andropov and Chernenko took pains to emphasise that developed socialism was a prolonged stage of development, and endorsed the thesis that developed socialism would contain distinct, successive sub-stages of advancement. Those conclusions were prefigured by Andropov's declaration in April 1982 that 'our country is at the beginning of this long historical era, which in turn will have its own periods and its own stages (*stupeni*) of growth'.[74] Virtually the same statement was repeated in Andropov's article in *Kommunist* in February 1983.[75] Andropov stressed the distance still separating Soviet society from full communism, noting in June 1983 that 'we still have a long way to go to reach that goal'.[76] In the Central Committee meeting of June 1983, Chernenko expressed his agreement with the assertion that Soviet society was only at the beginning of the stage of mature socialism.[77] If the USSR has still not advanced past the beginning of the period of developed socialism, which the Soviet system is said to have entered about twenty years ago, then that stage must be a very long one indeed. That conclusion was affirmed by Chernenko, who declared in December 1984, 'it is clear that the improvement of developed socialism will consist of an entire historical epoch. It will have its concrete stages, its succession of tasks, and its timing.'[78] That statement was Chernenko's first public endorsement of the thesis that developed socialism would include a series of separate stages of movement towards the higher phase of communism, a position which has gained official acceptance in Soviet ideology since the 26th Party Congress.[79]

Since 1982, there has been a noticeable increase in emphasis on the improvement and perfection (*sovershenstvovanie*) of mature socialism. The term *sovershenstvovanie* always occupied a key role in the ideology of developed socialism, referring to the type of change carried out in the current period, distinguishing that process of change from the transformation of socialism into communism. However, now the concept of *sovershenstvovanie* has become so central that the current stage is defined as an epoch of improvement of developed socialism.[80] The increase in emphasis on improvement and perfection may be traced to Andropov's statement of April 1982 that 'the tasks facing Soviet society in the final decades of the twentieth century . . . boil down to what one might call the improvement of developed socialism'.[81] What has been involved in the shift in Soviet ideology since Brezhnev's death, a shift which in many ways has been an extension of trends of thought during Brezhnev's last years, has been a rethinking of the nature of the tasks facing Soviet society today. In the early 1970s, discussions of developed socialism emphasised the progress that had been made by Soviet society since the first Five Year Plans and described the Soviet system as being on the verge of advances demonstrating the advantages of a high degree of development of socialism and drawing on the assets which had been accumulated through decades of painstaking labour. The use of the term *sovershenstvovanie* implied that what was imminent for Soviet society was the realisation, not of the communist ideal, but of the full potential of socialism. However, Brezhnev's successors have been willing to admit that the USSR is still quite far from thoroughly translating the principles of socialism into reality. The realism of their pronouncements has signified the sober realisation of the seriousness of the problems that remain unresolved in their society at the present time.

Soviet ideological theorists in the early and middle 1970s saw developed socialism as the stage of overcoming the unevenness of development that was the legacy of earlier Soviet (and Russian) history, and achieving the greater integration of all spheres of society into a single whole. A maturing Soviet society was passing from the last stage of systemic transformation into a state of systemic equilibrium. However, those who have followed Brezhnev have acknowledged that the nature of the current period is conditioned to a large extent by conflicts that remain within Soviet society. Andropov warned in April 1982 that 'progress from one stage to another is a highly complex process that inevitably involves the overcoming of the contradictions and difficulties that are linked with any kind of development. Some things will come easier, others harder. We will be able to advance faster in some fields than others. This is the real picture of social progress. It can't be smoothed into a straight line'.[82] Andropov seemed indeed to be arguing that inconsistency was an inherent characteristic of progressive change in any stage of development of socialism. In February 1983 he offered a formula to summarise the unevenness of change in developed socialism: 'In it are convincingly shown the dialectical unity both of real successes in socialist construction . . . and of the strengthening shoots of the communist future, and of still unresolved problems left for us from the past'.[83]

The nature of contemporary Soviet society has been regarded by recent leaders as mixed, including some attainments reflecting a high degree of industrial growth, technological progress and socialist social transformation, and also some features which seem archaic in an advanced stage of socialism. Chernenko made the point in December 1984 that 'the reality of a society which has entered the stage of developed socialism is a contradictory combination both of major, genuinely historical successes in socialist creation . . . and of unresolved tasks of the present, and also of problems conveyed to us by the heritage of the past, those which in principle might have been resolved earlier, in the preceding stages of our development'.[84] The words of recent Soviet leaders have implied that in the 1960s and 1970s, not only did the Soviet regime not eliminate all the forms of unevenness inherited from the decades of Stalin's rule, but it allowed the building of new contradictions generated by the higher level of development of the Soviet system in the post-Stalin era. Andropov urged Soviet social scientists to devote more attention to the study of non-antagonistic contradictions in socialist society, and warned that the neglect of such contradictions by the leaders of a socialist state could lead to the emergence of disruptive conflicts.[85] One of Chernenko's favourite themes was that not all the 'negative phenomena' in Soviet society that were alien to the principles of socialist morality could be explained as vestiges of the influences of pre-socialist social formations ('survivals of the past').[86] In short, as Chernenko admitted in his last essay, not everything in developed socialism is highly developed; 'not all our tasks and problems have been resolved at the level of the demands of developed socialism'.[87]

5.6 GORBACHEV AND THE NEW PARTY PROGRAMME

It fell to Gorbachev to preside over the adoption of a new Party Programme outlining a course of improvement of Soviet socialism. Gorbachev had given advance notice of the main themes of the new Programme, even before becoming General Secretary of the Communist Party, in a speech to an ideological conference in December 1984. At that time he argued that the main task facing the Soviet Union was the acceleration (*uskorenie*) of the country's social and economic development, and promised that the resolution of that task would raise Soviet society to a 'new, higher level'.[88] Gorbachev made it clear that realism in expectations for the future did not excuse complacency towards problems of the present. In his December 1984 address, in speeches he delivered after succeeding Chernenko and in the new version of the Party Programme there were repeated criticisms of the neglect of problems and the postponement of change during the 1970s and early 1980s, which were said to have allowed stagnation in the Soviet economy. Gorbachev complained that 'a peculiar psychology – how to improve things without changing anything – took the upper hand.'[89] He also insistently attacked inertia and conservatism in the attitudes of party and state officials, making apparent his impatience with unwillingness to adapt methods of administration to new conditions.

Under Gorbachev, the critical assessment of problems in the contemporary Soviet system has undermined the position of developed socialism as the core concept in the analysis of that system. Unlike Andropov and Chernenko, Gorbachev did not mention developed socialism in his remarks to the Central Committee meeting in March 1985 which selected him as the new General Secretary of the CPSU.[90] He referred to that concept only once in his speech in April 1985 setting the agenda for the next Party Congress, and ignored it altogether in his address in October 1985 on the publication of the draft version of the new Party Programme.[91] The term 'developed socialism' occurred only once in the Programme in its final form, as adopted by the 27th Party Congress in March 1986.[92] Gorbachev's major address to the Congress also avoided touching on the concept of mature socialism except in his summary of the results of discussion of the new Programme. The expectation that developed socialism would be the source of the central, organising principles of the new statement of the party's aims, which had been firmly established by Brezhnev, Andropov, and Chernenko, was unceremoniously overturned by Gorbachev.

The new Party Programme did repeat the claim that after 1961 the Soviet Union had entered the stage of developed socialism.[93] In his review of the discussion of the new Programme Gorbachev indicated that a decision had been made to reject, on the one hand, suggestions that references to developed socialism be removed entirely from that document and, on the other hand, proposals that the meaning of developed socialism be elaborated more fully. Gorbachev's words and the text of the new Programme demonstrated continuing agreement with some of the premises of the theory of developed socialism. Gorbachev reaffirmed the necessity of avoiding the error of promising the simple and easy resolution of the tasks involved in building communism in the USSR, while the new Programme, rather than treating Soviet society as being in a stage of transition to communism, described the work facing the Soviet people as 'the systematic and all-round improvement of socialism' through the 'fuller and more effective utilisation of its possibilities'.[94] However, Gorbachev argued that interpretations of developed socialism had often been limited only to statements about success, while many 'burning problems' of the Soviet system had been neglected.[95] His complaint was that the concept of developed socialism had been tarnished by its association with the complacency and self-congratulation of Soviet ideology in the Brezhnev period.

In accordance with Gorbachev's pronouncements, the new Programme regarded the key to the future prosperity and security of the USSR as '*the acceleration of the country's social and economic development*', primarily by the more rapid and thorough introduction of advanced technology in production.[96] The Programme stressed that the fundamental renovation of productive technology and a sharp increase in the productivity of labour in the USSR would require significant changes in the style of economic management. Yet the new Programme seemed to reflect the position taken by Gorbachev in December 1984, to the effect that 'a qualitative transformation of productive forces and the improvement of productive relations determine the essence, the main content of all our activity in the contemporary stage'.[97] While Gorbachev called for the *transformation* of productive forces, including machinery and labour, he only demanded the *improvement* of relations of production, involving administrative structures and social relations.

The core of Gorbachev's Programme was the promise that through the acceleration of social and economic development, Soviet society would in the fairly near future experience a series of interrelated changes in a number of different areas. The Programme predicted that the Soviet economy would make the transition to 'intensive' development, relying on more efficient use of capital, labour and natural resources, rather than on continued increases in the investment of such inputs into production, and as a result of that transition would achieve the highest level of labour productivity and output quality in the entire world.[98] In addition, the differences between collective farm and state ownership of property would be reduced, with the prospect of merging those forms of ownership at some time in the future. Among the social changes of the period of accelerated development would be the attainment of a qualitatively higher standard of living, the creation of a basically classless society, and the elimination of the major differences between urban and rural society in the USSR. Thus the thesis that a classless society would be realised within the framework of socialism was officially approved by the 27th Party Congress.

The main trend projected for the political sphere was the further enhancement of 'socialist self-government' with greater participation by citizens in the life of state and social organisations. As far as culture was concerned, the Programme promised the 'further consolidation of the socialist ideology in the consciousness of Soviet people and the full establishment of the moral principles of socialism'[99], rather than the complete realisation of the precepts of full communism in the values and mores of the people. The Programme did not promise that all those projected changes in economics, society, politics and culture would reach their culmination simultaneously, nor did it specify the particular sequence in which different changes would take place. The result of the processes of change during the period of accelerated social and economic development is to be a 'qualitatively new condition of Soviet society'.[100] What the Gorbachev leadership holds in prospect for the Soviet Union is not a new phase, stage, or even sub-stage of progress, but only a new 'condition' or 'state' (*sostoyanie*) of society. The nature of that new condition will undoubtedly offer Soviet ideological theorists large fields for exploration in the coming months and years. However, it is clear that, however much Gorbachev deplores Brezhnev's failure to achieve effective results in coping with practical problems, the current Soviet leadership has drawn from the ideological theory of the Brezhnev period the conclusions that the dynamic of the current stage is that of the improvement of socialism rather than the transformation of socialism into communism, and that technological and economic development have the potential to contribute to the achievement of a higher level of development of socialist society.

5.7 CONCLUSION

The general trend in Soviet ideology from the Bolshevik Revolution to the present has been the fading of revolutionary optimism, resulting in the gradual postponement of the realisation of the Marxist vision of communism. The institutions and traditions created by the Soviet regime, which have been labelled socialist, have become obstacles not only to the actualisation of the Utopian ideals of communism, but also to the implementation of many of the principles of socialism. The necessary consequence has been the relegation of the transition to communism to the status of a legitimating myth, with little relevance to the Soviet Communist Party's choice of policies to guide the course of change in the near future.

Yet the ideology of Marxism–Leninism has not been discarded in the search for prescriptions for change; every generation of Soviet leaders has struggled to adapt its precepts to the social, economic and political conditions which they have confronted. As evidence that the process we have witnessed has been the adaptation of ideological theory rather than its abandonment, it may be noted that at no time in the past has the ideology failed to furnish a coherent and intelligible overview by political leaders of the decisive factors and emerging tendencies in Soviet society, or to yield a strategy for change intended to reach proximate goals. If the policies prescribed and rationalised by ideological theory have often proved unsuccessful, one reason may be that the theory has not always been accurate in its analyses of existing conditions, and another reason might be that the ideology has been all too accurate in reflecting the values of the Soviet political leadership, even when those values have been mutually incompatible. For instance, there may be a conflict between the preservation of detailed control of economic activity by the Communist Party and state administration and the introduction of more efficient techniques of production. Since Brezhnev's death, Soviet leaders have complained that the neglect of some of the most serious contradictions in the economy and society has led to a widening gap between theory and practice, and between policy pronouncements and their execution. The Gorbachev leadership faces the challenge of carrying out a realistic analysis of the causes of stagnation in the Soviet system without sacrificing the remaining optimism in Soviet Marxism–Leninism that encourages Soviet citizens to hope for steady progress towards a better future.

NOTES

1. Karl Marx and Friedrich Engels, *Selected Works*, vol. 3 (Moscow: Progress Publishers, 1976), pp. 17–19.
2. Ibid., p. 17.
3. Ibid., p. 19.
4. V. I. Lenin, *Selected Works*, vol. 2 (Moscow: Progress Publishers, 1970), p. 358.
5. Ibid., pp. 348, 353, 357.
6. 'O proekte Konstitutsii Soyuza SSR', in I. V. Stalin, *Sochineniya*, vols. 14–16 (Stanford, Cal.: Hoover Institution, 1967), vol. 14, pp. 140–1.
7. Ibid., pp. 149–50.
8. 'Otchetnyi doklad na XVIII s"ezde partii', ibid., pp. 347, 352.
9. *Current Digest of the Soviet Press*, vol. 4, no. 38 (1 Nov. 1952), p. 30.
10. Stalin, *Sochineniya*, vol. 16, pp. 268–9.
11. Ibid., p. 269.
12. Ibid.
13. Ibid., p. 271.
14. Ibid., p. 268.
15. Ibid.
16. 'Ekonomicheskie problemy sotsializma v SSSR', ibid., p. 215.
17. In his report to the 18th Congress in 1939, Stalin had said it would be

necessary for the Soviet Union to outstrip the principal capitalist countries economically in order to make the transition to the higher phase of communism (ibid., pp. 351–2). After the Second World War, Stalin reasserted the importance of the growth of Soviet industry with his call in February 1946 for a 'new mighty upsurge of the economy' ('Rech' na predvybornom sobranii', ibid., p. 19).

18. 'Ekonomicheskie problemy sotsializma v SSSR', ibid., pp. 206–7.
19. Ibid., p. 220.
20. Ibid., p. 271.
21. Ibid.
22. Ibid., p. 272.
23. Ibid., p. 220.
24. Ibid., p. 222.
25. Ibid., p. 272.
26. Robert C. Tucker, *The Soviet Political Mind*, rev. edn (New York: Norton, 1971), pp. 89–91.
27. Ibid., p. 91; Herbert Marcuse, *Soviet Marxism* (New York: Vintage, 1961), pp. 114, 168.
28. N.S. Khrushchev, 'Report of the Central Committee of the CPSU to the 20th Party Congress', in Leo Gruliow (ed.), *Current Soviet Policies*, vol. 2 (New York: Praeger, 1957), p. 55.
29. Ibid., p. 61.
30. 'On control figures for development of the USSR national economy in 1959–1965', in Leo Gruliow (ed.), *Current Soviet Policies*, vol. 3 (New York: Columbia University Press, 1960), p. 42. I have translated *razvernutoe stroitel'stvo kommunisticheskogo obshchestva* as 'full-scale construction of communist society' rather than 'extensive building of communist society'.
31. Ibid., pp. 41, 55.
32. Ibid., p. 64.
33. Some scholars argue that contending forces in the Soviet political leadership forced the moderation of Khrushchev's optimism and transformism in the drafting of the 1961 Party Programme. See for instance George W. Breslauer, *Khrushchev and Brezhnev as Leaders: Building Authority in Soviet Politics* (London: Allen and Unwin, 1982), p. 82. Nevertheless, in historical perspective the Programme clearly bears the stamp of Khrushchev's distinctive influence.
34. 'The Program of the Communist Party of the Soviet Union', in Charlotte Saikowski and Leo Gruliow (eds), *Current Soviet Policies*, vol. 4 (New York: Columbia University Press, 1962), p. 33.
35. 'On the Program of the Communist Party of the Soviet Union', ibid., p. 88.
36. 'On control figures', *Current Soviet Policies*, vol. 3, p. 64.
37. 'On the Program', *Current Soviet Policies*, vol. 4, p. 89.
38. Ibid.
39. However, after the 22nd Party Congress, Khrushchev commented that the Party Programme was a bit too conservative. 'Our party has worked out a programme of construction of communism in twenty years. But I am convinced that if we used our possibilities better we could significantly shorten that time, much more rapidly develop the Soviet economy, and

create an abundance of material goods for the people'. See his *Kazhdaya sovetskaya respublika dolzhna vnesti dostoinyi vklad v stroitel'stvo kommunizma* (Moscow: Gospolitizdat, 1962), p. 7.
40. 'Pyat'desyat let velikikh pobed sotsializma', in L. I. Brezhnev, *Leninskim kursom*, 9 vols. (Moscow: Politizdat, 1970–82), vol. 2, pp. 134–5.
41. Ibid., pp. 92, 99.
42. 'Otchetnyi doklad TsK KPSS XXIV s"ezdu', ibid., vol. 3, pp. 234–5.
43. Robert Sharlet, *The New Soviet Constitution of 1977: Analysis and Text* (Brunswick, Ohio: King's Court Communications, 1978), p. 75.
44. Brezhnev, *Leninskim kursom*, vol. 8, pp. 726–7.
45. See Grigorii Glezerman et al., *Razvitoe sotsialisticheskoe obshchestvo: sushchnost', kriterii zrelosti, kritika revizionistskikh kontseptsii* (Moscow: Mysl', 1973), p. 18.
46. 'Razvitoe sotsialisticheskoe obshchestvo: sushchnost' i problemy', *Voprosy filosofii*, 1976, no. 6, p. 31.
47. Ibid., pp. 33–4.
48. Sharlet, *New Soviet Constitution*, p. 75.
49. 'Otchetnyi doklad XXIV s"ezdu', *Leninskim kursom*, vol. 3, p. 235.
50. 'Obshchestvennye nauki – boevoe oruzhie partii v stroitel'stve kommunizma', *Kommunist*, 1972, no. 1, p. 19.
51. M. A. Suslov, *Na putyakh stroitel'stva kommunizma*, vol. 2 (Moscow: Politizdat, 1977), p. 440.
52. 'O proekte Konstitutsii', *Leninskim kursom*, vol. 6, p. 537.
53. 'Otchetnyi doklad XXIV s"ezdu', ibid., vol. 3, p. 235.
54. Butenko, 'Razvitoe sotsialisticheskoe obshchestvo', p. 41; see also p. 37.
55. Richard Kosolapov, 'The approach to the study of developed socialism', *World Marxist Review*, vol. 17, no. 9 (September 1974), pp. 60–70; Kosolapov, *Socialism: Questions of Theory* (Moscow: Progress Publishers, 1979), p. 464.
56. Glezerman et al., *Razvitoe sotsialisticheskoe obshchestvo*, 3rd ed. (Moscow: Mysl', 1979), p. 25.
57. Maksim P. Kim, 'O periodizatsii protsessa stroitel'stva sotsializma v SSSR', *Kommunist*, 1981, no. 7, pp. 31–40, at p. 40.
58. Yuri V. Andropov, 'Rech' na plenume TsK KPSS', in Andropov, *Izbrannye rechi i stat'i* (Moscow: Politizdat, 1983), p. 286.
59. *Pravda*, 14 February 1984.
60. 'Vystuplenie tovarishcha K. U. Chernenko na zasedanii Komissii TsK KPSS po podgotovke novoi redaktsii Programmy KPSS 25 aprelya 1984 goda', *Kommunist*, 1984, no. 7, pp. 4–8, presents Chernenko's suggestions for the content of the new Programme. Chernenko referred to the prospect of the adoption of a new Programme at the 27th Party Congress in ibid., no. 9, p. 6, and elsewhere.
61. M. S. Gorbachev, *Zhivoe tvorchestvo naroda* (Moscow: Politizdat, 1984), p. 7; 'Rech' general'nogo sekretarya TsK KPSS M. S. Gorbacheva na plenume TsK KPSS 11 marta 1985 goda', *Pravda*, 12 March 1985.
62. The document approved by the 27th Congress is considered by Soviet sources to be a new 'version' of the Third Programme of the CPSU, since the main objectives of the Third Programme, adopted in 1961, have not yet been attained.

63. 'Rech' na plenume', in Andropov, *Izbrannye rechi*, p. 286.
64. 'Aktual'nye voprosy ideologicheskoi, massovo-politicheskoi raboty partii', *Kommunist*, 1983, no. 9, pp. 17–38, at p. 21.
65. 'Vystuplenie tavarishcha K. U. Chernenko', p. 4.
66. Ibid., p. 5
67. 'Leninizm–neischerpaemyi istochnik revolyutsionnoi energii i tvorchestva mass', in Andropov, *Izbrannye rechi*, p. 195.
68. 'Uchenie Karla Marksa i nekotorye voprosy sotsialisticheskogo stroitel'stva v SSSR', ibid., pp. 238, 245.
69. 'Rech' na plenume', ibid., p. 286.
70. 'Aktual'nye voprosy', p. 20.
71. 'Vystuplenie tovarishcha K. U. Chernenko', pp. 4–5.
72. *Zhivoe tvorchestvo naroda* p. 7. However,Gorbachev immediately added that such an approach must not be allowed to delay the solution of urgent problems or the overcoming of shortcomings.
73. The theme of realism has also been associated with a less optimistic assessment of the prospects for rapid improvements in living standards in the USSR. On this point, see Alfred B. Evans, Jr., 'The decline of developed socialism? Some trends in recent Soviet ideology', *Soviet Studies*, vol. 38, no. 1 (January 1986), pp. 1–23.
74. 'Leninizm–neischerpaemyi istochnik', p. 196.
75. 'Uchenie Karla Marksa', p. 245.
76. 'Rech' na plenume', p. 289.
77. 'Aktual'nye voprosy', p. 19.
78. 'Na uroven' trebovanii razvitogo sotsializma', *Kommunist*, 1984, no. 18, pp. 3–21, at p. 8.
79. Gorbachev seemed to express agreement with this thesis in his speech of December 1984. See Gorbachev, *Zhivoe tvorchestvo naroda*.
80. See the statement cited in n. 78 above.
81. 'Leninizm–neischerpaemyi istochnik', p. 196.
82. Ibid.
83. 'Uchenie Karla Marksa', p. 245.
84. 'Na uroven' trebovanii', p. 4.
85. 'Uchenie Karla Marksa', p. 21.
86. See for instance 'Delo vsei partii, dolg kazhdogo kommunista', *Kommunist*, 1983, no. 15, pp. 18–35, at p. 30; 'Avangardnaya rol' kommunistov', ibid., 1982, no. 6, pp. 25–43, at p. 30.
87. 'Na uroven' trebovanii', p. 4.
88. *Zhivoe tvorchestvo naroda*, pp. 8, 46.
89. 'Politicheskii doklad TsK KPSS XXVII s"ezdu Kommunisticheskoi partii Sovetskogo Soyuza', *Pravda*, 26 February 1986, p. 2.
90. 'Rech' general'nogo sekretarya TsK KPSS M. S. Gorbacheva'.
91. 'O sozyve ocherednogo XXVI s"ezda KPSS', *Kommunist*, 1985, no. 7, pp. 4–20; 'Doklad general'nogo sekretarya TsK KPSS M. S. Gorbacheva', ibid., no. 15, pp. 4–11.
92. 'Programma Kommunisticheskoi partii Sovetskogo Soyuza (novaya redaktsiya)', *Pravda*, 7 March 1986.
93. Ibid.
94. Ibid.

95. Gorbachev, 'Politicheskii doklad TsK'.
96. 'Programma'.
97. *Zhivoe tvorchestvo naroda*, p. 19.
98. 'Programma'.
99. Ibid.
100. Ibid.

6 Ideology and Soviet Economic Policy

DAVID A. DYKER

6.1 INTRODUCTION

> Any attempt to evaluate the impact of Marxism–Leninism on policy response must recognise that ideological and pragmatic concerns need not be distinct, but may overlap and intertwine with one another, often in subtle ways . . . To label alternatives and arguments as either ideological or pragmatic is usually a gross over-simplification, for values are rarely, if ever, neatly separated from practical responses to problematic situations.[1]

This is surely a universal proposition, in no way limited in application to Marxist–Leninist or Soviet milieux. The cause of neatness in our present enquiry suffers an additional blow when we turn to consider Joseph Berliner's dictum that 'Marxism is rich in propositions explaining the behaviour of economic variables that are determined by objective social processes, but is not concerned with the problem of finding optimal solutions and choosing among alternatives'.[2] In a word, Marxism is all about the inevitable collapse of capitalism, while the Soviet authorities are trying to run socialism. In so doing they can find only minimal guidance in Marx's elliptical *Critique of the Gotha Programme*, Engels' lugubrious *Anti-Dühring*, or Lenin's hurriedly written and superficial *State and Revolution*. But Berliner, in his classic article, is equally incisive when he remarks that 'the policy *goals* of a Marxist party are influence by its Marxist heritage. The nature of the influence, however, is socio-psychological, rather than scientific. A party that professes to be Marxist will accept as its own certain ends which are implicitly defined as good within the context of the Marxian system, such as social ownership of the means of production, industrialization, welfare of the masses, elimination of urban–rural differences, and the eventual withering away of the state'.[13] From the standpoint of the mid-1980s we can probably take industrialisation as given in the Soviet context, but Berliner's other items form a useful checklist of teleological focal points. We should surely add to that list a strong commitment to centralisation.

But while it is the social welfare function of Soviet Marxism that must primarily concern us, we cannot embark on policy assessment without devoting some space to Soviet efforts at evolving a set of objective laws of socialism. What, for instance, can we make of the 'Basic Economic Law of Socialism', which posits the 'steady expansion and improvement of production on the basis of advanced technique with the aim of the fullest satisfaction of the steadily increasing requirements and the many-sided development of the members of society'? This is certainly no law in the ordinary causal sense of the word, but Berliner attempts to save it by giving it the status of a teleological or functional law. On that interpretation, the Basic Law could be understood to mean that if such a steady expansion and improvement did not take place, then the Soviet system would collapse. But the ups and downs of Soviet history hardly bear out such an interpretation, and Berliner can only conclude that the Basic Economic Law of Socialism is, again, simply 'a statement of the economic goals that a Marxist party ought to pursue'.[4] He comes to a similar conclusion on the 'Law of the Planned, Proportional Development of the National Economy'. In dismissing these formulations as laws, however, we should perhaps be a little careful about consigning them exclusively to the category of goals. Nove suggests that Planned, Proportional Development may, indeed, sometimes come through almost in the role of a guide to action, to the extent that 'one comes across this "law" in the course of arguments against excessive reliance on "automatic" economic forces; in this guise, it amounts to emphasising the primacy of conscious political control of the "proportions" (i.e. primarily over investment)'.[5] Beyond that, both Laws are redolent of an interpretation of socialism which excludes the possibility of antagonistic contradictions, of what in Western parlance would be called the 'balanced growth approach' to developmental problems. What is interesting in that connection is that the reality of Soviet economic history, dominated as it has been by priorities, campaigns and tautness, is much better interpreted in terms of the rival 'unbalanced growth approach'.[6] Thus the interaction between pragmatism and ideology may in some cases actually cloud perception of intra-system realities.

The Law of Value comes into a different category altogether. Firstly, it is, according to the Marxian classics, in the first instance a law of capitalism. Secondly, it is a genuinely causal formulation, at least as far as market economies are concerned, although in positing that freely formed prices will tend to correspond to labour inputs into the goods concerned, it is almost certainly a mistaken one. The problem for Soviet ideologues has been whether the Law of Value does, in fact, hold under socialism. In his *Economic Problems of Socialism in the USSR* Stalin himself had argued that the Law does indeed operate under Soviet conditions, although only in respect of transactions between the state and collective sectors and between the state sector and the worker/consumer. The *categories* of the Law of Value – prices, costs, profits – are consequently quite properly used within the state sector for planning and accounting purposes because the 'external relations' of that sector are dominated by the Law, even though it does not operate as a causal law within state industry. After Stalin's death and in the run-up to the first wave of economic reforms in the Soviet Union this distinction was effectively dropped, and commodity relations were allowed to exist between state sector organisations.[7] The use of a form of the rate of interest, the 'coefficient of relative effectiveness' (CRE), in the assessment of alternative variants of investment projects was formally blessed in 1960, though it had been used informally in some sectors from a much earlier date.[8] There is, however, nothing very specifically Marxian about this formulation.

The CRE apart, none of this has any very great functional significance. No one has ever shown how the Marxian Law of Value can form a basis for operational price-setting. In practice, prices have been set throughout Soviet history on the basis of administrative rules of thumb. Furthermore, the Law of Value cannot even in principle provide a formula for the calculation of *scarcity* prices, which is what a planner needs to make his decisions. What the Law of Value has provided is a language, perhaps to some extent a coded language, for the discussion of the role of the market in putative alternative planning scenarios. At the end of the day, therefore, its significance may not be very different from that of the more vacuous 'laws' discussed above. Yet some commentators have found this use of the Law of Value as a flag of convenience to be deeply insidious for the status of Marxist–Leninist ideology in the Soviet Union. Jack Miller, for instance, argues that

> if adequate revisions are not made, such mutilations of the theory as the admission of intrastate commodities will kill it. From the point of view of elementary internal logical consistency, ideological tidying up after the practical reforms now commencing had better not be done at

> all. On the other hand, to do nothing would kill the ideology in another way, by totally severing it from its tenuous connection with reality.[9]

At the very least, we have to accept that conservatives in the Soviet Union may view playing around with market concepts, whether Marxian or bourgeois, as a dangerous game for a Marxist–Leninist society.

Finally, there is the law of the faster growth of department A of industry (production of the means of production) than of department B (production of the means of consumption). Like the Law of Value, this law was formulated by Marx as a scientific law of capitalism. Soviet ideologues have in the past chosen to adopt it as equally a law of socialism. Now because of the obscurity of its formulation ('production of the means of production' is not a very useful statistical concept in National Income terms, since its summation involves a great deal of double-counting) this law ties in only indirectly with basic, strategic economic policy decisions like the proportion between investment and consumption in National Income. In practice, however, Stalin used assertion of the law as a way of insisting on the need for a rising ratio of investment to National Income, while in more recent years, policy decisions in favour of consumption have been formulated in terms of suspension of the law. Once again we are suggesting that the main function of a Soviet economic law may simply be to provide the language in which policy options are thrashed out. Let us see how far we get with that approach in assessing economic policy trends in the Soviet Union over the past twenty years or so.

6.2 THE 1965 ECONOMIC REFORM AND AFTER

It was in 1962 that Yevsei Liberman published his famous article, 'The plan, profits and bonuses'. Diplomatically vague on the crucial question of the role of market forces, Liberman simply argued that many of the irrationalities of the traditional planning system, which was heavily based on physical planning and crude output indicators,[10] could be obviated by introducing profit as a key success-indicator and as a source for bonus funds. 'What is profitable for society should be profitable for the enterprise', he suggested – a slogan much more in the tradition of Adam Smith than of Karl Marx. Other distinguished Soviet economists like Nemchinov, Novozhilov and Kantorovich set out similar arguments, backed up by proposals for reforming the pricing system. These were often couched in the terminology of the Law of Value, although they had moved a long way from the spirit of the labour theory of value. And when the Brezhnev/Kosygin government did indeed introduce profit as a key planning indicator in the 1965 industrial planning reform, it looked as if convergence was actually happening: as if the technological and organisational imperatives of a complex industrial economy were forcing the Soviet leadership to abandon direct physical planning through the gross output planning indicator in favour of an indicator which would reflect demand and cost-efficiency factors. When, in 1970, they 'repealed' the law of the faster growth of the production of the means of production and embodied the opposite principle in the new Five Year Plan, they seemed to be making some gesture in the direction of the consumer revolution. Implicitly, it was argued by many, this would inevitably condition a shift in political power towards the technostructure.

Twenty years on, the picture looks much less clear. The Galbraithian conventional wisdom on the managerial revolution has failed to throw much light on a Soviet system which remains dominated, at the political level, by a uniquely Soviet Communist Party apparatus. Thus, when we study the evolution of ideological standpoints on economic issues during the 1970s and indeed the 1980s, we must do so, first and foremost, through the prism of *apparatchik* attitudes. At the same time, we cannot ignore what the professional economists and planners think, particularly in a period when the rapid evolution of computer science may appear to have changed fundamentally the balance of feasibility of rationalised central planning. Finally there are the men in the firing line – the industrial and agricultural managers themselves. Managerial revolution or no, experienced captains of industry have their own ideas about how best to organise a socialist economy, and while what they publish is largely limited to the sphere of very specific technical problems, it does give us some inkling of what those ideas may be.

In practice, the 1965 planning reform was a disappointment. The introduction of a capital charge payable by enterprises on their entire fixed capital stock, and of the principle of interest-bearing loans for investment, continued the process of rehabilitation of the rate of interest. It forced enterprises to unload equipment hoards, and thus gave a significant, but short-lived boost to the economy. Profit, however, did not prove to be an effective planning indicator under the given conditions, and attempts to introduce partial decentralisation in limited areas tended to destabilise the whole economy. By the early 1970s the whole issue of how best to organise the planning system had been thrown open again. But while there was now a body of experience of attempted planning reform, there was no consensus at all on how that body of experience should be interpreted. The profit success-indicator proved problematic because it turned out to be too easy to increase profits by using inferior materials, or by distorting product mix towards products with above-average rates of profitability. The party apparatus and some economists interpreted this as evidence that the transplant had been rejected, that you cannot take a capitalist category like profit and simply slot it into a socialist system. Socialism is about planning production directly in relation to need, and as soon as you try to impose value categories on it you are back with the mystifications of the capitalist market. Thus they implicitly identified proper planning with ideological purity, formulating their arguments in terms very similar to those used by Jack Miller, quoted above.

The 'marketisers' among the economists, by contrast, insisted that the profit indicator had not worked properly because the appropriate conditions had not been created. It was, they argued, because the central planners refused to allow prices any leeway to find their natural level, or to allow dissatisfied industrial clients to 'shop around' for the best deal, that profit tended to produce distorted results. In this interpretation, the experience of the 1965 planning reform had merely proved the incompatibility of profit and central planning, and thereby made the case for a movement towards market socialism where the forces of *competition* would ensure that the quest for profit did not turn into profiteering. On one thing, however, the two factions may have been in agreement: that once you start playing around with the Law of Value, it may be difficult to stop very far short of Hungarian–Yugoslav-type revisionism. That proposition clearly creates a lot of problems for an ideology as strongly committed as theirs to the principle of centralisation, yet seeking to accommodate some degree of functional flexibility.

The more conservative elements were also worried about the side-effects of the introduction of a degree of enterprise autonomy in relation to small-scale investments (decentralised investment) and a degree of farm autonomy on subsidiary industrial activity in the countryside. They noted that by the early 1970s decentralised investment was effectively bidding resources away from the centralised investment programme, and that in 1971 the aggregate centralised investment plan was substantially underfulfilled. They observed that the development of subsidiary industrial production on farms was being accompanied by a blossoming of semi-legal and illegal procurement operations. Their response to these threats to state priorities and socialist legality was perhaps predictable, and by the mid-1970s the effective independence of enterprises and farms in these areas had been sharply curtailed. By the last year of the 1971–75 Five Year Plan the primacy of department A of industry had been *de facto* re-established. Meanwhile, more radically-minded economists could point out that the ultimate cause of the difficulties lay in the failure of the 1965 planning reform to decentralise the supply system sufficiently to create a regular basis on which small-scale investment and industrial supplies could simply be bought across the counter. Otherwise, the only way for 'unplanned' operations to secure the supplies was to 'steal' them from the allocations for planned operations through the grey economy and the pusher network. So on this reading, the threat to state priorities and socialist legality comes not from the misapplication of a capitalist principle, but from the failure of the planning reform to make any significant impact on one of the major weaknesses of the traditional system: the clumsiness and inflexibility of the material supply network. Once again, the conclusion is that you must go forward to a system of state trading, a system with substantial elements of market socialism within the industrial sphere. Once again you are in trouble with the principle of centralisation.

Now, from the strictly economic point of view, it is surely obvious that the interpretation of the marketisers was right, that of the conservatives wrong. But the conservatives were not short of practical arguments. The Party apparatus had learned their lessons from the Prague Spring as well as from the history of their own reform. The Czech experience had shown just how difficult it might be to contain the political implications of a radical economic reform, and while Kadar in Hungary had shown that it was not impossible, Soviet *apparatchiki* seemed more impressed by the Czechoslovak lesson. What was apparent from the experience of all the attempts to develop market socialism, from Yugoslavia through to Czechoslovakia and Hungary, was that once the lumbering imprecision of bureaucratic supply planning is cleared away, there is much less work for the Party *apparatchiki*, the professional trouble-shooters of the system, to do. The apparatus men were surely perfectly clear about their own vested interest in the very weaknesses of the centralised approach. This introduces an important new element into our analysis. *A priori* reasoning suggests that ideology may play a key role in providing the grammar of argument and rationalisation. The historical record, however, suggests that these arguments may often, in the last analysis, be about the politics of control and sectional interest.

But that is not the whole story. The reaction of the early and middle

1970s also affected developments which had never looked like threatening the stability of the Soviet economy as a whole, and which indeed had seemed to promise it nothing but good. The most striking example of this is the history of the link (*zveno*) system in agriculture. The normless (*beznaryadnoe*) link is a small, often family-based group of peasants which is allocated a piece of land and is left to get on with fulfilment of the plan on an autonomous basis. Link members share in profits from over-plan sales on the basis of stable norms. Despite the constraints imposed by predictable supply problems, the link system reported excellent results in the late 1960s and early 1970s. One might imagine that Communist Party functionaries, anxious to save the form of the collective and state farm, while revolutionising their content in the direction of flexibility and high labour productivity, would have viewed the system as a godsend.

Not a bit of it. The link system had had its brief moments of glory under Stalin and Khrushchev, and the same cycle repeated itself on this occasion. The authorities suddenly went sour on the whole thing, and by 1971 one could end up in prison for being too radical in that connection.[11] Certainly, Soviet agricultural performance was rather good during the years 1966–73, and conservative leaders and apparatus men may well have felt that they could now dispense with such dangerous ideas. But why consider them dangerous in the first place? There seem to have been three basic reasons. First, local apparatus men were accustomed to the notion that peasants are so stupid that they need to be told what to do. There is an element of traditional Bolshevik psychology here, which has little to do with ideology in any higher sense, but which we ignore at our peril. Secondly, the authorities feared that the link might be *too* successful, that it might serve as a basis for *peasant enrichment*. Certainly it was the policy of the Brezhnev–Kosygin government to improve peasant remuneration, in line with the principle of removing urban–rural differences. But because it removed farm-level control over wages-fund and wage and bonus rates, the normless link system meant that the authorities were no longer able to control the *distribution* of income. It is surely a mark of the Soviet socialist tradition, in relation to the 'welfare of the masses' theme, that the distribution of incomes should be *planned*. Finally, there must have been some uneasiness that behind the fair face of the link system might lurk the beast of privatisation.

Another mark of the Soviet socialist tradition is the principle that there should be full employment, and Soviet directors have traditionally had very limited powers of dismissal. Under the Shchekino system, first introduced experimentally in 1967, managers were given the right to create redundancies, and to use part of the monies thus economised to pay increased bonuses to the remaining workers. The experiment showed good results, and was extended steadily through the 1970s. But by 1980 only about ten per cent of the Soviet industrial labour force was working under full Shchekino conditions.[12] A number of factors constrained the development of the system during the Brezhnev era. Managers were often reluctant to part with surplus labour because it provided them with a cushion against the vagaries of the material supply network. Planners, in turn, showed themselves rather too eager to claw back Shchekino supplements after a few years, leaving the workers wondering what was in it for them.

Perhaps most important, the government balked at the risk of creating substantial pockets of unemployment. It is one thing to develop the Shchekino system in particular areas with an extreme labour shortage, or in specific, highly dynamic sectors like chemicals, where redundant workers can largely be reabsorbed within the same association. Development on a national scale would clearly put extreme pressure on the fairly rudimentary Soviet system of labour placement, and introduce the possibility of substantial sectoral and regional pockets of unemployment. There are socialist societies, like Yugoslavia, which have learned to live with unemployment, and there can be no doubt that it was increasingly recognised in the Soviet Union through the Brezhnev period that full employment was simply the other side of the coin of over-manning, feather-bedding, poor labour discipline and therefore low labour productivity. With the labour shortage becoming increasingly acute, that was, of course, very bad news for the overall economic performance. But the political commitment to full employment held firm, perhaps strengthened by the spectacle of the capitalist West falling down so badly on precisely that variable. Here, again, we can see the ideological theme of 'welfare of the masses' coming through strongly.

6.3 ANDROPOV'S NEW BROOM

Brezhnev's successor was concerned primarily with getting things done, with counteracting the tendency to policy drift that had characterised the last years of the old General Secretary, particularly in the industrial field. Yet he chose to write his one major work from his brief period in power on the theme of 'The teaching of Karl Marx and some questions of socialist construction in the USSR'. Summing up the essence of the Soviet system, he argued that

> the system functions and is perfected through the process of continually finding new forms and methods of developing democracy, extending the economic rights and opportunities of the working man on the production floor, and in all dimensions of socio-political activity. . . . This is real socialist self-management of the people, which develops in the course of construction of full communism.[13]

The most significant thing about this statement is the use of the word self-management, *samoupravlenie*, the same word as the Yugoslavs use. In the past, this word has been anathema in the Soviet Union, and while Aliev assures us that the Soviet concept of self-management 'differs fundamentally from its anarcho-syndicalist interpretation',[14] Andropov's treatment does seem to mark a change in the interpretation of the meaning of authority and *edinonachalie* ('one-man management') under Soviet socialism. The Law on Working Collectives and Increasing their Role in Management,[15] passed in 1983, sought to concretise and operationalise this new interpretation.

Yu. Tikhomirov, an Academy of Sciences jurist, sums up the spirit of the law in terms of a series of dialectical unities: the unity of rights and obligations, the unity of one-man management and participation, the unity of discipline and democracy.[16] Another scholarly writer is more down to earth when he posits that 'working collectives . . . elaborate and adopt counterpart plans, confirm measures to raise labour productivity and socialist competition arrangements . . . apply social incentive measures . . . and impose penalties for infringements of labour discipline'.[17] Thus, in practical terms, Andropov's self-management involves at least two specific elements which represent pressure on, rather than pressure off, the workers: labour discipline and taut planning. Let us look at these in turn.

One of Brezhnev's last major economic enactments was the law on labour discipline, promulgated in 1980,[18] but it was left to Andropov to mount a veritable campaign to eradicate the easy-going working practices which had become so widespread under his predecessor. The basic principle of the new approach was that workers who did not toe the line should be punished by a reduction of their labour coefficient (*koeffitsient trudovogo uchastiya*, KTU), which determines their wage rate, or by dismissal. Andropov's accession marked a renewed readiness to extend the principle of the Shchekino system, in particular through a variant of it called the Leningrad system, which has developed as a way of reducing over-manning among design workers. The difference between the Shchekino and Leningrad systems seems to be that whereas the former is concerned primarily with the technical issue of rationalising and automating production lines, the latter evinces a much stronger 'moral' tone. At the Elektrosila factory in Leningrad, 220 people from the design-constructor department were made redundant over the period July 1983 – November 1984, or rather, strictly speaking, they resigned. Each individual was subjected to a fairly terrifying process of personal 'attestation'. The unfortunate 220 did not even stay for the attestation, but simply fled. At the Leningrad Metal Factory, the principle has been introduced that only the best 70 per cent of design workers receive bonuses, so that nearly one third of the personnel are always feeling the noose around their necks.[19] There is an element of technical rationalisation here, as design work becomes increasingly computerised and, therefore, less labour-intensive. More fundamentally, however, they are simply trying to clear out dead wood. Thus Andropov seems to have worried rather less than Brezhnev about unemployment.

The problem with the Shchekino – Leningrad approach to the labour productivity problem is that it tends to move in abstraction from the general planning problem. Just as the Shchekino system gets stuck because, *inter alia*, with the uncertainty of supplies, only a fool gets rid of 'surplus' labour, so improved labour discipline may get stuck for precisely the same reason. But it would be unfair to suggest that Andropov did not realise this. On the contrary, a decree of August 1983 explicitly recognised the link between the discipline problem on the one hand and the supply problem, indeed the planning problem as a whole, on the other:

> Ministries and departments and business leaders fail to create at some enterprises, building sites and farms the necessary organisational and economic conditions for normal, high-productivity work. Inadequacies in planning, material–technical supply and the organisation of production leads to lay-offs, storming, excessive overtime, and to non-fulfilment of plan targets and commitments. This in turn affects discipline and, in the last analysis, rates of growth of productivity.[20]

So Andropov's concept of self-management takes us through the work discipline theme to the essential problems of the Soviet planning system. It offers some comfort in relation to the 'withering away of the state', but its implications for the 'welfare of the masses' are at best ambivalent.

Chernenko insisted at the April 1984 Plenum of the CPSU Central Committee that 'we cannot possibly get by without a further increase in the level of tautness of our work in the economy'.[21] This is fair enough in the sense that there is a great deal of scope in the Soviet economy for people to work more efficiently. But the term 'taut planning' has historically meant something rather more specific in the Soviet Union. It has implied, among other things, the tactic of trying to maximise performance by putting the maximum direct pressure for high performance on the people concerned. The relationship of this to the spirit of Bolshevism hardly needs to be spelt out. (What it has to do with planned, proportional development is, of course, another question.) The trouble is that while taut planning may be good for short-term output results, it tends to induce managers and workers to play safe, especially in relation to new technologies or anything else that disturbs steady work patterns. In Andropov's reading, this problem is solved if the tautness is imposed by the workers themselves, rather than by an extraneous planning authority. This is where self-management comes in, and this is why Andropov placed so much emphasis upon the autonomous brigade system in industry and construction. With work-teams receiving just an aggregate sales or output target for a period of, say, three months, a wage and bonus fund and the necessary material supplies, they would in principle have substantial freedom to pay themselves more for working harder, especially since under Andropov brigades were increasingly given the right to make low-calibre brigade members redundant. But two fundamental problems remain. First, the system will only work if the brigades can count on the necessary supplies actually coming through. Secondly, the central planners have to respect the principle of stable norms, and not, as they have so often done in the past, claw back extra payments by reducing the wages fund after a couple of years. Once again, then, we are back with the general planning problem, and therefore with the problem of over-centralisation. So let us turn now to a consideration of the outstanding piece of legislation on the industrial planning system produced during the Andropov period.

6.4 THE INDUSTRIAL PLANNING EXPERIMENT

In one very important respect Andropov's planning experiment, which went into operation in selected ministries on 1 January 1984 and was extended in coverage on 1 January 1985 and again on 1 January 1986, showed complete continuity with Brezhnev's very conservative planning decree of 1979. The process of downgrading the keystone of the Kosygin planning reform, the profit success-indicator, continues. Profit does, indeed, gain in importance as a source of finance for bonus funds, decentralised investment funds and so on, but loses its special role in relation to fund-forming coefficients. Under the experiment, enterprises face a battery of planning indicators, of which sales/deliveries in accordance with contracts is the most important. Thus, while under the old system it was usually enough to fulfil *aggregate* sales or output targets to receive bonuses, the experimental system predicates that each individual delivery has to be completed before any incentive payments are made. But the *pattern* of contracts continues to be determined by the central planners. At this general level, the experimental decree is clearly dominated by conservative apparatus and 'perfect computationist' thinking. The way to solve supply problems is to punish bad suppliers with the utmost harshness, safe in the knowledge that with contemporary computational hardware the standard of coordination of basic plans is improving all the time.

What happens if things go wrong? Well that, of course, is where the party man comes in. If managers are not sufficiently motivated by the threat of losing all their bonuses, if there are supply breakdowns upstream, it is the duty of the party secretary to come in and sort out the trouble in the name of fulfilment of contracts, just as in the past he has done so in the name of gross output.[22] Now, in practice, computerisation of Soviet planning is proceeding very slowly, and progress reports on the experiment indicate extreme problems with coordination, which means that enterprises often find themselves in danger of losing bonuses through no fault of their own.[23] Regarding the long-term prospects for full communism, this may be bad news for the party, because it reflects Soviet technological backwardness *vis-à-vis* the capitalist West *and* the improbability of the eschatological propositions which form an important element in the Soviet Communist Party's claim to legitimate power. In terms of the present, it does at least keep the apparatus in a job. We shall return to this key dilemma when we look at the new Party Programme.

The other major thrust of the industrial planning experiment relates to autonomous enterprise funds. Legislation lays down that there should be a return to the 1965 principle of decentralised investment really being put into practice. Re-equipment investments, up to a value of four million rubles in heavy industry, and 2.5 million rubles elsewhere, are now to be left to the independent decision-making of the enterprise.[24] In addition, enterprises are to be allowed more freedom in allocating their socio-cultural and housing funds and amortisation allowances. Finally, the overall rate of retention of profits, for investment and incentive purposes, is increased. Now, there is nothing wrong with any of that, except that just as in 1965 no provisions are made to ensure orderly material supply to enterprises wishing to make use of their new rights of disposition. We should not be surprised, then, to discover that many directors of enterprises on the experiment are complaining that they have the money, but can find no one to sell them the bricks, mortar and machines they need to put their decentralised plans into action.[25] If the experiment were generalised throughout Soviet industry, we should surely discover a widespread increase in the vigour of the grey economy, of the incidence of unofficial procurement through the pusher network, just as we did in the late 1960s and early 1970s. Now, where would that leave one of Andropov's other favourite slogans, 'socialist legality'? It is not difficult to see why beleaguered *apparatchiki* are anxious to see salvation in a pragmatic 'mixed-economy' approach, which would introduce some of the flexibility of the market without calling into question their own 'leading role' in the economy. But if the mixture is not right in a technical sense there is a very real danger of the whole system degenerating into a battle between first and second economies, in which the party men would have to compete with the pushers in breaking the rules so as to retain their control over the basic priorities of the system. Of course, the Soviet system is, in any case, shot through with rule-bending and corruption, and everyone knows that it is. But there may be a critical level at which the notion of 'social ownership of the means of production' becomes so blatantly compromised as to create a problem of political credibility.

Finally, the experimental decree features the principle of stable norms. As we saw earlier, this principle is of crucial importance for the Andropov concepts of self-management and brigade autonomy. But the decree's provision that no bonuses at all should be paid unless sales/deliveries plans are met is in flat contradiction to that principle since it implies centrally-imposed tautness, which in turn implies that the relationship between incentives and performance should be continually modified to maintain maximum pressure on producers. Some enterprises on the experiment have even reintroduced the Stalinist principle that top bonuses should be paid for *over*fulfilment of plans.[26] There must be some doubt as to whether enterprise managers working under that kind of pressure can avoid putting the same kind of pressure on their workers. In any case, the failure of the experiment to institute any kind of substantial overall decentralisation means that hard-pressed planners are forced to continue to rely on 'planning from the achieved level', whereby plan targets are adjusted in response to past performance trends. That means that even when planners are not going for maximum tautness, they still tend to chop and change plans, which destroys stable norms. Thus the realities of an over-centralised system, can, in practice, permit only a very limited form of self-management.

6.5 AGRICULTURE: THE LINK, THE 'COLLECTIVE CONTRACT' AND THE PRIVATE SECTOR

The 1970s were a bad decade for the cause of intra-farm decentralisation, but, under the pressure of consistently bad performance in the period after 1973, the Soviet authorities had been forced back to a more pragmatic policy stance by the early 1980s. Brezhnev himself called for more personal initiative and responsibility and less 'petty tutelage' in his speech on the Food Programme for the period up to 1990,[27] and more genuinely autonomous interpretations of the link system soon started to appear in the Soviet press again. Under the rubric of the 'collective contract', the principle was established that members of autonomous links or brigades should be paid on the basis of pre-contracted prices, while they should at the same time be bound to deliver pre-contracted quantity and quality. After the 1982 change in leadership, the collective contract idea was pushed as the central feature of policy for the grass-roots level in agriculture, with Gorbachev, of course, firmly in charge.[28]

Neither Andropov nor Gorbachev ever insisted on a uniform interpretation of the precise content of the collective contract system, and farm managements have come up with widely varying applications. Under the most common system, work-team members are remunerated on the basis of KTUs (see above), with the coefficient of each member being decided by the work-team as a whole. But the farm decides the *monetary* value of each KTU. We can, however, find cases where the collective contract was being interpreted in a much more genuinely normless way during the Andropov and Chernenko periods. In the crisis areas of beef and fodder production, and also in market gardening, a number of reports featured work-teams being paid a standard price for as much as they could deliver, and being left to distribute the proceeds as they saw fit.[29] But the trend through the Chernenko period was away from the genuinely autonomous towards a much more *dirigiste* interpretation of the collective contract, and there was a general movement towards much closer monitoring of rates of remuneration.

If we can believe that the centre really has left these matters to the farms to decide then we must suppose that local party officials have been giving forceful advice, and that advice has surely been much concerned with distributional matters. There can, indeed, be no doubt that the institutional barriers which stop peasants drifting from poor farms to rich ones may create a vicious circle of poor incentives and poor performance in the less well-off farms, which the normless link system can only exacerbate. It is equally true that the principle of voluntariness in the formation of links has meant that the best workers tend to club together, leaving weaker ones to do the best they can – much in the spirit of the Leningrad system. This, again, has tended to create uncomfortably large differentials in performance and income between the best and the worst links.[30] None of this, of course, amounts to a valid criticism of the link system itself. Rather, it argues powerfully for a proper system of land rent, greater farm autonomy in relation to overall manning levels, and more investment in basic training for all agricultural workers. There can be no doubt in this connection that the Law of Value is one of the things which has inhibited the development of a proper land rent system in the Soviet Union, and that the tradition of centralisation has been especially damaging in the countryside. Thus, ideology certainly has a lot to answer for in the socialist sector of agriculture.

Policy on the private sector in agriculture, which in 1979 still produced as much as 26.5 per cent of total agricultural output,[31] has been rather more consistent in recent years. In his speech on the Food Programme, Brezhnev called for 'obligatory and systematic aid' from the state and collective sectors to the private, and there has been substantial continuity of policy here through to the present day. The crux of the matter is, of course, the aid that the private sector can give the state and collective sectors, particularly in relation to that most difficult bottleneck, fodder. The sorts of deals that farms have been negotiating with their peasants in their private capacity have involved farming out livestock – pigs and cattle – to the peasants to fatten on their private plots. In return for guaranteed supplies of some fodder at reduced prices, the peasants deliver a proportion of the resultant fatstock to the farm. This is obviously a good idea, but we can once again cite instances where bureaucracy and red tape breed self-fulfilling prophecies. In the past, peasants have not been allowed to sell their 'share' directly to the farm, but have had to take it to the local agricultural procurement centre. As well as inhibiting the development of cooperation, this has let in speculators who go around farms offering high prices,[32] which must offer plenty of grist to the mill of a local party secretary looking for spivs and kulaks under the bed. Nevertheless, for the time being, the non-combative interpretation of the role of the private sector within state and collective agriculture continues to predominate. There is, indeed, no *ideological* reason to suppress subsidiary private agriculture. Sheer political prejudice is a problem, but the ideological dimension may be genuinely helpful in explaining why the private sector in agriculture is a less tortured issue than the link system within the socialism farm.

6.6 WHICH WAY GORBACHEV?

It is early days yet for the new leader. In any case, he was very closely associated with both industrial and agricultural policy-making under his two predecessors. In a *Pravda* leader published soon after Gorbachev's accession, Andropov's favourite combination of labour discipline and planning discipline was heavily featured.[33] Poor workers, the leader stated, should be sacked. It did not go so far as to prescribe the same for poor planners, but the message was clear enough, and there is apparently still a good deal of confidence, probably misplaced, in the scope for more rational forms of centralisation. The same emphases were apparent in Gorbachev's speech to the 27th Party Congress in 1986. The dominant theme, then, is one of continuity, but if we look at specific developments in industry and agriculture we can pick up some subsidiary themes.

In his opening speech to a Central Committee round table in mid-1985, on the subject 'Initiative, Organisation and Effectiveness', Gorbachev was clearly keeping all his options open when he declared that 'while strengthening the main features of centralised planning, we propose to broaden further the rights of enterprises, to introduce genuine business accountability, and on this basis to increase responsibility for, and material interest in, the final results of work, at the level of the collective and of the individual worker. That is the purpose of the economic experiment'.[34] Other participants at the round table were rather more forthright. In particular, the director of the Noril'sk mining combine stated plainly that the degree of centralisation in the planning system 'is to a certain extent actually having a negative effect on the development of the national economy', very much echoing the theme of Novosibirsk economist Tatyana Zaslavskaya's celebrated 'secret report' of April 1983.[35]

Subsequent experience has now confirmed that a kind of 'experiment within an experiment' is taking place in the management of light industrial enterprises. The key feature of this experiment is that enterprises are given some freedom to negotiate prices and contracts with suppliers and the retail network by themselves.[36] The experience of the Volga Auto and the Sumy Engineering Works, which have been able to expand and retool production on the basis of retained profits, was commented upon favourably by Gorbachev in his report to the 27th Party Congress.[37] If Gorbachev really does want to push the Soviet planning system in the direction of a GDR – Bulgarian-type compromise, or indeed towards Hungarian-style market socialism, all he has to do is to extend such experiments to their logical conclusion. We should certainly not assume that just because Mr Gorbachev is young he is a radical; after all, he got the job because of his impeccable apparatus background. Experiments of the kind that have been mentioned do, however, remind us that the marketising tendency among Soviet economists and industrial managers is still vigorous, as do the recurrent, if non-committal, references to the virtues of 'wholesale trade in the means of production' in official decrees. Wholesale trade in the means of production is, indeed, like 'acceleration' and 'reconstruction', a key code word in the semiotics of the current planning reform debate. And if such an obscure Marxian formulation makes it easier to talk about the market, who is to say that ideology is always a constraint?

In agriculture, the trend since Chernenko's death has so far been a cautious one. Reports on the collective contract, for instance, have tended to emphasise more limited versions of this practice, although there was a definite rise in the temperature of the debate in early 1986 with the publication of a number of articles praising more radical arrangements.[38] Gorbachev's speech to the Party Congress called for the wider diffusion of contract and other job-by-job systems of payment at the levels of teams, groups and families, although the main emphasis of his speech was upon improved soil fertility, better storage and transport and improved machinery construction.[39] On this, as on other matters, Gorbachev seems to be keeping his options open.

Perhaps the most significant statement on agriculture in the period before the Congress was made by a *kolkhoz* brigade leader at the 1985 Central Committee round table:

> We often discuss with our workmates the question of whether we have really earned our standard of living through our labour. There are many cases in our region where people in the *kolkhozy* making the heaviest losses live well, even better than in our highly profitable *kolkhoz*. When people live on credit rather than income the whole attitude to work of the worker himself changes for the worse. Discipline and organisation deteriorate, and there is no real concern with final results. That's why we need real *khozraschet* [business accountability].[40]

Thus the brigade leader raises nearly all the issues that have exercised the Soviet leadership over the past few years, but frames them in a novel way. The golden rule should be that all emoluments are earned. This is the basis of good work discipline, just as handouts will always encourage slackness and poor management. So if discipline and efficiency are the first priorities of the party leaders, they have to be prepared to forget about controlling the distribution of income. Last but not least, *profits matter*. Where that leaves the welfare of the masses and the principle of centralisation, not to mention the Law of Value, is anybody's guess. But nothing could better illustrate the way in which 'ideological and pragmatic concerns . . . may overlap and intertwine with one another'.[41]

We have seen the appearance of one major ideological document since Gorbachev took over: the new Party Programme.[42] Various aspects of the Programme are discussed elsewhere in this volume and we limit ourselves here to a consideration of those parts that relate to economic policy. The Programme, as approved by the 27th Congress in March 1986, commits the party to the goal of 'accelerated socio-economic development' which has so far served as the leitmotiv of the Gorbachev general secretaryship. Although the ultimate aim remains full communism, the Programme breaks new ground in admitting that a slow-down in economic growth occurred during the 1970s and early 1980s and that this was due in part to a 'lack of firmness in the implementation of policies'. Particular emphasis is placed upon the 'human factor', upon the application of science and technology, upon the re-equipment of industry, and upon economy in the use of natural resources. References to the importance of the guidance of economic activity, albeit upon 'Leninist principles', suggest that official Marxism–Leninism has at least been persuaded that management matters, that it may, indeed, constitute a factor of production as important as labour itself. If Gorbachev really wants to turn the Soviet planning system upside down he will find references of this kind very convenient indeed.

Let us conclude by trying to sum up what ideology may mean to Gorbachev in the context of his present policy preoccupations. Economic 'laws' as such need cause him little embarrassment. The Basic Law of Socialism and the Law of Planned, Proportional Development may not help him to understand his own economic system, but they can hardly hinder him. While the law of the faster growth of department A was re-established, *de facto*, for the period 1975–80, it was ditched again for the subsequent quinquennium, and the ratio of investment to National Income has, indeed, fallen slightly in recent years. The new Five Year Plan suggests, but does not commit itself to, faster growth in production of the means of consumption. Thus the law of the primacy of department A is as dead as a dodo, though the rates of growth of the two departments are still used as a vehicle for serious policy discussion. The Law of Value remains a nuisance in relation to land rent, but beyond that it seems to impose few constraints on the leadership. In fact, by dipping into a different part of the Marxian treasure-house, and using the term 'wholesale trade in the means of production' to divert attention away from price problems towards inter-sectoral problems, the contemporary Soviet leadership is again demonstrating its capacity to handle ideology with some flexibility.[43]

Turning to more general ideological considerations, the formulations of the new Party Programme in relation to 'commodity–money relations', cost accounting and the 'improvement' of price formation are clearly designed to give the authorities maximum freedom of manoeuvre in policy terms, while retaining the idea of the inherent superiority of socialism and the ultimate transition to full communism. But there is still the most awkward issue of the 'welfare of the masses'. Current trends on discipline, employment and distribution of income all seem to fly in the face of this principle, and the Party Programme confirms that those trends will continue in the long term.

While we may interpret the discipline drive as to some extent a *substitute* for economic reform, we should be under no illusions that more economic reform would do anything else but strengthen the tendency to greater inequality. One only has to look at the experience of the West over the past decade or so to confirm that point. Here, then, is an ideological issue, and ultimately an issue in political legitimacy. But there is no evidence that worries over this are going to stop Mr Gorbachev continuing on his chosen course.

Turning to the other points on our checklist, the commitment to elimination of urban–rural differences will continue to prove an embarrassment as long as the commitment to centralisation in agricultural management and social ownership of the agricultural means of production continues to prove stronger. The principle of social ownership need not impose any serious constraints in the industrial area, but the problem of over-centralisation is only a degree less grave here than it is in agriculture. However ingenious is the wholesale trade in the means of production formulation, no official document gives any promises on when, or in what form, such wholesale trade may be introduced. For the time being, and despite the industrial planning reform, the Soviet planning system remains as over-centralised as ever, and that is one of the most suffocating constraints that Gorbachev labours under. If we are prepared to interpret that constraint as primarily in ideological one, then we must, in the last analysis, assess the net impact of ideology on Soviet economic decision-taking as strongly negative.

NOTES

1. Joan DeBardeleben, 'Marxism–Leninism and economic policy: natural resource pricing in the USSR and the GDR', *Soviet Studies*, vol. 35, no. 1 (January 1983), pp. 36–52, at p. 37.
2. Joseph S. Berliner, 'Marxism and the Soviet economy', in Morris Bornstein and Daniel R. Fusfeld, eds., *The Soviet Economy. A Book of Readings*, revised edition (Homewood, Illinois: Irwin, 1966), pp. 18–33, at pp. 20–21.
3. Ibid, p. 20.
4. Ibid, pp. 24–25.
5. Alec Nove, *The Soviet Economy*, 3rd edition (London: Allen and Unwin, 1968), p. 321.
6. See D. A. Dyker, *The Soviet Economy* (London: Crosby Lockwood Staples, 1976), chapter 8.
7. Jack Miller, 'Marxist economic theory in the USSR', in Vladimir G. Treml, (ed.), *The Development of the Soviet Economy: Plan and Performance* (New York, Washington and London: Praeger, 1968), pp. 181–96, at pp. 194–5.
8. D. A. Dyker, *The Process of Investment in the Soviet Union* (Cambridge: Cambridge University Press, 1983), pp. 103–9.
9. Miller, 'Marxist economic theory', p. 195.
10. For a discussion of these irrationalities see D. A. Dyker, *The Future of the Soviet Economic Planning System* (London: Croom Helm, 1985).
11. Aron Katsenelinboigen, *Studies in Soviet Economic Planning* (New York: M. E. Sharpe, 1978), p. 66.
12. V. Fil'ev, 'Shchekinskii metod i perspektivy ego dal'neishego razvitiya', *Voprosy Ekonomiki*, 1983, no. 2, p. 59.
13. Yu. Andropov, 'Uchenie Karla Marksa i nekotorye voprosy sotsialisticheskogo stroitel'stva v SSSR', *Voprosy Ekonomiki*, 1983, no. 3, pp. 3–17, at p. 12.
14. G. Aliev, Speech on the draft law on working collectives, *Pravda*, 18 June 1984, p. 2.
16. 'V Politburo TsK KPSS' and 'Zasedanie Prezidiuma Verkhovnogo Soveta SSSR', *Ekonomicheskaya Gazeta*, 1983, no. 25, p. 2.
16. Yu. Tikhomirov, 'Edinstvo prav i obyazannostei', *Ekonomicheskaya Gazeta*, 1983, no. 38, p. 15.
17. I. Samoshchenko, 'Kollektiv v sisteme upravleniya', *Ekonomicheskaya Gazeta*, 1983, no. 35, p. 10.
18. 'O dal'neishem ukreplenii trudovoi distsipliny i sokrashchenii tekuchesti kadrov v narodnom khozyaistve', *Ekonomicheskaya Gazeta*, 1980, no. 3, p. 4.
19. A. Strugach, 'Inzhenery i novaya tekhnika', *Pravda*, 2 December 1984, p. 2.
20. 'V TsK KPSS, Sovete Ministrov i VTsSPS', *Ekonomicheskaya Gazeta*, 1983, no. 33, pp. 3–4.
21. K. Chernenko, Speech reported in *Ekonomicheskaya Gazeta*, 1984, no. 16, pp. 3–4, at p. 3.

22. See A. Berezin, 'Vospitanie kollektivizma', *Ekonomicheskaya Gazeta*, 1984, no. 15, p. 5; P. P. Grishkyavichus, 'Otvetstvennost' za dogovor', *Ekonomicheskaya Gazeta*, 1984, no. 22, p. 5.
23. See A. Gnidenko and I. Divnogortsev, 'Bol'she prav – vysshe otvetstvennost'', *Ekonomicheskaya Gazeta*, 1984, no. 30, p. 8; M. Rudoi, 'K eksperimentu gotovy', *Ekonomicheskaya Gazeta*, 1984, no. 51, p. 8.
24. 'O shirokom rasprostranenii novykh metodov khozyaistvovaniya i usilenii ikh vozdeistviya na uskorenie nauchno-tekhnicheskogo progressa', *Ekonomicheskaya Gazeta*, 1985, no. 32, special supplement, p. 3.
25. See B. Ural'tsev, 'Otvetstvennost' vo vsekh zven'yakh', *Ekonomicheskaya Gazeta*, 1984, no. 35, p. 8; S. Tsagaraev, 'Eksperiment i vstrechnyi', *Ekonomicheskaya Gazeta*, 1984, no. 28, p. 8.
26. A. Kulenis, 'Vysokoe kachestvo obuslovleno dogovorom', *Ekonomicheskaya Gazeta*, 1984, no. 13, p. 6.
27. L. I. Brezhnev, 'O Prodovol'stvennoi programme SSSR na period do 1990 goda i merakh po ee realizatsii', *Ekonomicheskaya Gazeta*, 1982, no. 22, p. 5.
28. Dyker, *The Future*, p. 93.
29. Ibid., pp. 93–4.
30. I. Meshcheryakova and I. Zub, 'Zadacha byla nelegkoi', *Ekonomicheskaya Gazeta*, 1984, no. 33, p. 13.
31. I. Shmelev, 'Obshchestvennoe proizvodstvo i lichnoe podsobnoe khozyaistvo', *Voprosy Ekonomiki*, 1981, no. 5, p. 69.
32. V. Gomanov, 'Kolkhozu podspor'e', *Pravda*, 29 April 1981, p. 3.
33. 'Ukreplyat' planovuyu distsiplinu', *Pravda*, 20 March 1985, p. 1.
34. 'Initsiativa, organizovannost', effektivnost'', *Ekonomicheskaya Gazeta*, 1985, no. 16, p. 3.
35. Ibid., p. 4. For the 'secret report' see T. Zaslavskaya, 'Doklad o neobkhodimosti bolee uglublennogo izucheniya v SSSR sotsial'nogo mekhanizma razvitiya ekonomiki', *Materialy Samizdata*, AS 5042, 26 August 1983.
36. A. Matulyavichus, 'Kak trebuet eksperiment', *Ekonomicheskaya Gazeta*, 1984, no. 21, p. 13; A. Bionchuk, 'Mnogoe prishlos' menyat' . . .', *Ekonomicheskaya Gazeta*, 1985, no. 8, p. 7.
37. *Pravda*, 26 February 1986, p. 5.
38. F. Bogomolov and Ya. Glezer, 'Otlazhivat' mekhanizm podryada', *Ekonomicheskaya Gazeta*, 1985, no. 14, p. 17; I. Kostenko, 'Osnova zarabotka – rastsenka za produktsiyu', *Ekonomicheskaya Gazeta*, 1985, no. 19, p. 17.
39. *Pravda*, 26 February 1986, pp. 4–5.
40. *Ekonomicheskaya Gazeta*, 1985, no. 16, p. 4.
41. De Bardeleben, 'Marxism–Leninism and economic policy', p. 37.
42. For the full text, see *Programma Kommunisticheskoi partii Sovetskogo Soyuza. Novaya redaktsiya* (Moscow: Politizdat, 1986).
43. But note that Nemchinov was using similar terminology 25 years ago! See Nove, *The Soviet Economy*, p. 262.

7 Local Soviets and Popular Needs: Where the Official Ideology Meets Everyday Life

MICHAEL E. URBAN

Well-removed from the clash of opposing social systems on the grand stage of history, the relentless progress of 'developed socialism' towards the communist future and the other epic themes of official Soviet ideology is an identifiable component in the creed of the party-state which is confined to much more modest matters. Its project involves immediate, palpable improvements in the everyday lives of Soviet citizens: its concern is more with the availability of such things as kitchen utensils or housing space than with the millenarian visions associated with 'the construction of communism'.

Although the focus of this chapter falls upon mundane matters of this kind, we should note that this discourse does not exist in complete isolation from the epic themes of Soviet ideology. In fact, the official version claims a close connection between communist eschatology and advances in the sphere of popular consumption. The latter provides, as it were, a visible manifestation of the progress made by Soviet society in realising the chiliastic goals contained in the former. For example, Chernenko's last public statement, his address to constituents during the elections to republican and local Soviets (February, 1985) and Gorbachev's first speech as party leader made this point in standard Soviet style. Chernenko's statement put it thus: 'We know, comrades, that the ultimate goal of all our efforts in the economic sphere is improving the wellbeing of the people. And here we are unswervingly going forward.'[1] Gorbachev's address referred to 'subordinating all economic growth . . . to the interests of the Soviet people' and coupled this desideratum with what has by now become the officially prescribed process by which living standards are to improve: popular participation in local soviets.[2]

In the official view, then, there is a direct link between process and result. Hence, as we shall see below, an enlarged scope of authority for, greater 'visibility' in, and increased access to those institutions charged with identifying and responding to popular needs is regarded as the *conditio sine qua non* for 'improving the wellbeing of the people.' Inasmuch as there is no place in the official scheme of things for paternalistic forms of needs satisfaction, it is important to underline this participatory dimension in the ideology. Higher levels of mass consumption depend on an expansion of the democratic aspects of the political system. Nowhere is this more evident than in the standard slogans that pepper the daily press: 'goods for all – the affair of everyone', 'goods are the concern of the deputies [of soviets]', and the manifold references, following Brezhnev's speech to the 26th Party Congress, to Soviet democracy as 'a concrete concern for the concrete individual'.[3]

What is the meaning of this attention in official Soviet discourse to the satisfaction of popular needs? On first inspection, one might think that it signals the regime's resolve to raise living standards and, perhaps, to secure thereby a greater measure of popular support. Indeed, the Soviet leadership itself sees improvements in consumption as indispensable to the provision of material incentives required to boost labour productivity.[4] While not necessarily wrong, such a view would quickly run into difficulties; the emphasis placed on upgrading the level of popular consumption would raise expectations among the populace who, if disappointed by the performance of the system, could hardly be expected to offer enthusiastic support to a regime which ceaselessly promised improvements but failed to deliver them. In this respect, there are strong grounds to suggest that the rhetoric on improved living standards has in fact contributed to a state of chronic disappointment. As Antonio Carlo has shown, both the Eighth and Ninth Five Year Plans provided for higher growth rates in the consumer goods sector than in producer goods, and in neither case did such growth rates materialise.[5] The Tenth Five Year Plan (1976–81) abandoned this preference for consumer goods growth, but the Eleventh and Twelfth restored it.[6] Recent official statements indicate continued disappointment in this area.[7]

How can we account for this apparent paradox: a regime which continually solicits popular support by means of promises of improved living standards and then routinely breaks its promises? What is worse (or, for lovers of the paradoxical, 'better'), we find in the official discourse both an acknowledgement of the reason why living standards have not improved – the soviets on which all depends have not performed as expected – and a reaffirmation of the original policy which entrusts the matter to these same soviets.[8]

This study takes, in some respects, an unconventional approach to this problem: I argue that the significance of the matter of popular needs satisfaction in Soviet ideology does not exist on the surface level of official discourse (that is, what the discourse seems to be about on first inspection). I wish to show that within this sphere of Soviet ideology something else occurs at other, deeper, levels. Its meaning is not disclosed in pragmatic terms – 'we are doing such and such in the world in order to bring about certain results' – but in noological ones which are congruent with political relations extant in the USSR. In order to develop these ideas, I shall have recourse to three methodological approaches which highlight different aspects of this central thesis. These approaches are policy analysis, the theory of the 'dictatorship over needs', and semiotics. As I hope to show, although each proceeds from different assumptions and entertains different questions, the three complement one another. Each sheds light on particular aspects of our object of analysis such that, taken together, they illuminate a picture whose complete outlines would not be visible from the perspective of any one approach operating individually. Before carrying this analysis forward, however, a brief synopsis of the role of soviets in satisfying popular needs, as portrayed in the official ideology, is in order.

7.1 SOVIETS AND POPULAR NEEDS: AN OVERVIEW OF FORMAL POLICY

The difficulty which the political centre has encountered in realising its projected increases in the growth rate for the consumer goods sector involves, in its own view, more than mere postponement of the improvement of the material comforts of the Soviet population. Without increases in the consumer sector, material incentives are not present in sufficient quantity to motivate worker performance across the economy as a whole and, by the simple measure of the time spend queuing for what is available, an enormous number of man-hours is lost to production.[9] Although the cases of this problem, as identified by the regime, are many and varied, the chief culprit which it has singled out is the 'branch principle' in the planning system – that is, centralised direction of the economy through its various branches which run from the centre down to performing units – which has grown to irrational proportions.[10] The branch principle, run amok, is known by the perjorative term 'departmentalism'. It connotes economic behaviour on the basis of narrow self-interest; production, that is, for the sake of meeting the formal indicators set out in the plan, rather than production which yields articles of utility. As such, it is held responsible for any number of the forms of waste, inefficiency and so forth which plague Soviet economic performance.

The antidote identified in policy prescriptions to counteract departmentalism is an upgrading of the 'territorial principle' in Soviet planning. This principle is manifest through a number of mechanisms, but regional and local soviets are regarded as its most important embodiments. It is through the intervention of soviets in the activity of the economic units located on their respective territories that coordination is to replace chaos, irrational production is to give way to the efficient use of resources, and waste is to be curtailed while the quality of products is improved. As G. V. Barabashev has put it, the intention of the party and the government is to strike 'an optimal balance of centralism and decentralism, defining the authority of the soviets at various levels'. This policy 'is directed toward strengthening the leading role of these organs [soviets] in meeting the task of harmoniously joining the branch and territorial bases of administration in the localities'.[11]

Since 1957, an ongoing cycle of legislation in the Soviet Union has directed itself to upgrading the role of local soviets and, ostensibly at least, to promoting the territorial principle in the economy.[12] This legislation, particularly certain articles in the 1977 Constitution[13], national laws on the status of district[14] and regional[15] soviets as well as certain reiterations of their provisions by the republics,[16] and, from time to time, by the centre itself,[17] has equipped local soviets with an impressive array of formal powers and greatly expanded their legal authority in economic matters. Schematically, the main features of this legislation can be grouped into the following four policy areas[18]:

1. *Planning*. Soviets are to compose comprehensive plans for the social and economic development of their respective territories. These plans not only govern enterprises or institutions subordinate to the soviets themselves, but also include those units under the authority of higher bodies, such as republican or all-union ministries. In the latter case, these units are required to submit to the planning commissions of soviets their own planning data. Soviets then assemble these data and attempt to strike 'balances' within their respective territories between such things as producer output and customer demand, labour supply and the types of

quantities of labour required by the local economy, wage levels and the supply of consumer goods, and so forth. In a word, the soviets are called on to enforce the 'territorial principle' by coordinating all the varied economic activity in the localities.

In order to accomplish this task, a number of formal powers have been awarded to soviets. With respect to the planning function *per se*, the most important of these would be the right to communicate to centrally directed enterprises located on their territories, as well as to the ministerial and department authorities which direct these enterprises, and to suggest alterations in their production plans. Such alterations have as their *raison d'être* the advantages which should accrue to all units when the proper territorial balances are struck. Units not subordinated to local soviets are required to study the planning suggestions which soviets make, to incorporate them into their own plans or to provide the soviets with written explanations when they do not.

2. *Implementation and control.* As enterprise plans are being carried out and as changes in these plans are introduced as a result of unanticipated occurences, soviets are to be supplied by the enterprise and their superiors with all data relevant to the fulfilment of, and alterations in, the plans themselves. In monitoring economic activity, the finance departments of local soviets and their counterparts in all enterprises and institutions located on their respective territories are legislatively scripted for the leading role. Auditing and financial supervision are viewed as crucial to the project of rationalising economic performance and uncovering 'hidden reserves'. On the one hand, all enterprises have been required to designate budget officers, freed from all other administrative responsibilities, who report directly to top management or, in cases involving apparently improper action on the part of top management, to management's superiors at the next level.[19] On the other, finance departments of local soviets, especially those at the regional level, are expected to play, in conjunction with their counterparts in economic enterprises, a larger part in rationalising economic performance by altering both their 'vertical' superiors (ultimately, the ministries) and the soviets to which they are attached to cases of unauthorised transfers of resources, poor or irrational economic activity and improper use of economic inputs.[20]

Of direct relevance to our concern with the satisfaction of popular needs is the function which local soviets are to perform in both the planning and monitoring phases of their activities, which ensure that consumer demands are met. For instance, enterprises producing in both the producer and consumer goods sectors typically transfer resources from the latter to the former during the course of the plan, either because they experience input shortages or have identified higher rewards for over-fulfilling their plans for producer goods.[21] Through the monitoring of enterprise activity, local soviets are expected to detect such resource transfers and, by means of a number of expanded legal powers, to prevent the ensuing injuries to consumer welfare.

3. *Expansion of legal powers and technical capabilities*. Although the more ambitious phases of the legislative corpus under consideration here have projected the idea of placing the production of articles for local consumption and, perhaps even more importantly, all state housing[22] under the direct authority of local soviets, current practice suggests a much more modest role for soviets in these areas. Some four fifths of consumer goods production remains the preserve of enterprises whose predominant activities are in the producer goods sector.[23] Similarly, although enterprises have been required by law to transfer their housing stock to local soviets (a process which, in the RSFSR, was to have been completed by 1985[24]) the great majority of housing is still controlled by economic enterprises.[25]

It seems that the current strategy in these areas is for local soviets to exert their influence on enterprises not subordinated to them, in order to secure more beneficial results for local consumers. A number of expansions in soviet authority come into play here. First, all title papers for new construction are the property of the respective regional soviets or agents designated by these soviets. This control over building permits is claimed as a direct tool, or as bargaining leverage, by means of which soviets can enforce their comprehensive development plans for the locality on reluctant enterprises.[26] Second, the budgets of regional soviets are supplemented by a transfer of ten per cent of the above plan profits of enterprises located on their territories. Third, the staffs of local soviets, particularly individuals working in planning and finance, are being enlarged and better prepared through education and technical training.[27] Finally, as we shall see in more detail in the following section, local soviets are to be assisted in promoting consumer welfare by their deputies who work in local enterprises.[28]

4. *Popular participation*. A number of provisions in Soviet law are ostensibly designed to facilitate the articulation of demands by citizens and to encourage popular representatives and the state machinery to respond effectively to these demands. So far as the anticulation of

demands is concerned, considerable attention in the Soviet literature[29] has been devoted to the institution of the *nakaz izbiratelei* ('mandate of the voters'), whereby deputies, usually during the election campaign, receive formal charges from their constituents to see to it that the state administration fulfils some specific demand related to their everyday needs, say, the improvement of a city park or the construction of a new department store. Once received and ratified by the soviet, a *nakaz* is incorporated into the soviet's economic and social plan and acquires the force of law. It becomes, that is, the legal responsibility of the soviet and related institutions to fulfil it.[30]

Concomitantly, the authority of soviet deputies and their responsibilities to their constituents have been expanded. The 'Law on Deputies to Soviets' (1972)[31] specifies the responsibility of the deputy in helping to meet 'the needs of the population of his electoral district' and, towards that end, establishes the deputy's right to submit inquiries both to the executive committee of his or her soviet and to economic enterprises in the locality which are subordinated to higher organs. Moreover, the deputy is entitled to replies from these administrative bodies within a specific period of time. Finally, each deputy is required to report back to his or her constituents and to the nominating organisation at regular intervals.[32] At such meetings the public has an opportunity to inquire into the progress made in fulfilling *nakazy* or to ask questions and offer suggestions on any other aspects of the soviet's work.

7.2 THE PERSPECTIVE OF POLICY ANALYSIS

The first question which the perspective of policy analysis might put – what is/are the objective(s) of the policy? – has been addressed in the preceding section. In brief, the policy manifestly intends to raise the standard of living of the Soviet population by allocating more resources to the consumer sector and by enlisting the energies of the soviets to see to it that legislative intentions are carried out in practice. The next question to be addressed would be: has the policy succeeded? Chernenko's speech to the April 1984 Plenum of the Central Committee, which was primarily devoted to the matter of soviets and their role in the economy, answered this question both authoritatively and concisely. 'In general', he remarked, 'a definite contradiction exists between the enriched potentials of the soviets and how they utilise these in practice'.[33] In fact, Soviet research on this topic has for some years been drawing the conclusion that the policy in practice bears little, if any, resemblance to the way in which it appears on paper. An extended discussion of this policy research would, of course, take us too far afield. Our concern, after all, is with ideology rather than with the mechanics of policy implementation in the USSR. None the less, a consideration of a sample of this research will tell us something not only about the policy itself but, I think, why it should be regarded principally as an ideology requiring other methods to unlock its inner meanings.

As early as 1976, the Institute of State and Law in Moscow published the results of its empirical study of local soviet reform in the Latvian republic.[34] The findings were devastating. Soviets were not carrying out the function of comprehensive planning assigned to them; enterprises and their superior organs were not supplying soviets with the requisite planning data; 'protocols of agreement', which authorise the transfer of housing and social services from industrial enterprises to local soviets, would be concluded between enterprises and soviets but were subject to routine violation by the enterprises. Soviets had not the political clout to enforce the law or the protocols.

The difference between formal authority and real power in the case of local soviets seems sufficient to support Stephen Sternheimer's generalisation that since Stalin local autonomy has, in fact, declined.[35] G. B. Polyak's study of city budgets, for instance, documents a reduced percentage of indigenous revenues, budgetary means and social expenditures by city soviets over the period 1950–75.[36] The generation of revenues and control of investment is more and more concentrated toward the centre. Take, by way of illustration, the budget for the City of Moscow in 1982. In the category of capital investment, the City Soviet controls only two fifths of its 'own' budget. The majority of the funds belong to ministries and departments and are merely channelled through the city budget.[37] The City Soviet, moreover, depends for 91 per cent of its revenues on enterprises not subordinated to it; about a quarter of these funds are channelled directly back to such enterprises.[38] Like other local governments in the USSR, the Moscow City Soviet is also obligated to assist local industry in fulfilling its plans.[39] Combining this obligation with the financial dependence of local soviets on economic enterprises located on their territories, it would be surprising to find vigorous enforcement of the territorial principle when the forces of departmentalism are inclined to resist.[40]

We are already discussing a third question which is common to the enterprise of policy analysis, namely, the question 'why?' Why, that is, have the manifest objectives of the legislation on soviets and the consumer economy not been achieved in practice? The reply found in the Soviet literature is essentially that, although a few things have improved, most have not,[41] and the blame goes to individuals. This personalisation of culpability is worth underlining. It serves the purpose of deflecting attention away from structural factors in the Soviet system which militate against the ostensible objectives of the policy.[42] In place of an analysis which would seek to uncover those conditions extant in the political order which have so stubbornly resisted the changes announced in the legislation, it substitutes accusation and exhortation. Consequently, the policy is itself always regarded as 'correct' (never mind that it does not work) and is therefore regularly reiterated as a reminder of what should be occurring. The fact that what should be occurring is not is attributed to shortcomings among individuals – they are not behaving as they are supposed to[43] – rather than to the policy itself.

This phase of policy analysis under Soviet conditions resembles a morality play. Loath to identify social relations themselves as the target for change, reluctant to undertake measures which would address themselves to inducing change by altering the incentive systems under which individuals and organisations operate, the regime seems content to moralise. In so doing, it tries to account for what in the end can only be regarded as its own failure to realise its stated objectives as the deplorable work of various villains, whom the regime, of course, constantly combats. We have already met one such malevolent actor, 'departmentalism'. Others will be familiar to readers of the Soviet literature in this or related areas. 'Formalism' – a pattern of merely going through the motions – is regarded as the reason why soviets have done so little to formulate and implement plans for the social and economic development of their territories.[44] 'Bureaucratism' and 'red tape' are said to account for situations in which queries, complaints and suggestions sent by Soviet citizens to the appropriate authorities are simply filed and forgotten.[45] And for cases such as those of soviet deputies who fail to represent the grievances of their constituents before local administrators for fear of being made to feel 'uncomfortable,'[46] we might have recourse to the category 'inertness and rigidity of the forms and methods of management' which Gorbachev employed in his address to the 27th Party Congress to explain away essentially all socio-economic shortcomings in the USSR.[47]

It bears mention that none of these terms for the opprobrious – 'departmentalism', 'formalism', and so on – actually explains anything, although each might be taken as a topic for investigation itself. But the Soviet authorities seem little inclined to promote studies of this type.

Rather, the preference goes to affixing names to phenomena. In the absence of any analysis of these phenomena and the conditions under which they thrive, the names have a purely noological significance. It is at this point that conventional Soviet policy analysis has exhausted its ability to account for the regime's performance regarding local soviets as fulfillers of popular needs. Although it can identify the objectives of the policy and chart the performance of the policy in practice, it can offer no response to what seems now the major question: Why has the policy failed? Of course, Western analysts, unencumbered by the constraints which the Soviet state places on its own social scientists, are able to address this question. Even so, another, and for our purpose more significant, problem would remain; namely, how can we explain a long-standing policy which has failed, is recognised by the Soviet regime as a failure, *yet is repeatedly reaffirmed by this same regime*? This question lies outside the scope of conventional policy analysis. Other conceptual tools, a fundamentally different attitude, are required to address it. Our orientation is shifting here from a concern for the instrumental to an interest in the symbolic.

7.3 THE PERSPECTIVE OF 'DICTATORSHIP OVER NEEDS'

In order to address the question which has just been put, I want first to draw upon a body of recently emerging social theory which has been developed in the main by scholars from East Europe. Differences among these theorists are many, but a central problematic seems to unite them into a more or less identifiable intellectual current in Soviet studies. This problematic, in simple terms, concerns the nature of authority in state socialist systems, of which the Soviet Union is the leading example. Given this interest and, perhaps, because of the pronounced 'bureaucratic' features of the Soviet state, it should not be surprising that the ideas of Max Weber[48] have exercised a strong influence on these thinkers. The work of three of their number, Ferenc Feher, Agnes Heller and Gyorgy Markus, will serve here as the principal variant of this theoretical orientation which I shall apply to our topic of local soviets and popular needs.

Feher, Heller and Markus define Soviet state socialism with the phase 'dictatorship over needs'.[49] As former students of Georg Lukács, they seem especially sensitive to the matter of how human needs are structured by the particular social formation within which concrete individuals come to a consciousness of, and are able to express, their needs.[50] In this respect, any social formation would constitute a 'dictatorship over needs'; but the forcefulness of this phrase as applied to state socialist systems derives from their thesis that in such societies the dictatorship is immediate and 'brutal'. As a pure type, it involves a direct connection between the recognised existence of a human need (never mind its satisfaction) and the will of the state. In this way, the state defines its subjects as the bearers of the needs which it alone recognises. The state likewise reserves for itself a monopoly on the means by which these needs will be met.[51]

This central thesis sets up a particular authority relation between party-state officials, on the one hand, and subjects on the other. Officials, those occupying party and state offices, perform two sets of functions. They engage in instrumental activity related to the specific tasks associated with their respective positions *and* they bear political responsibility for pacifying the particular domain which they manage.[52] This second function also has two sides. On the one hand, it means that individual officials personify the dictatorship for those whom they superintend. On the other, it involves them in transmitting popular demands into the arena of decision-making. Yet, mediated by the dictatorship in this way, popular demands are transformed in the very process of their transmission. Feher, Heller and Markus use the example of the President of the Academy of Sciences and his relations with those in his domain to illustrate this transmission/transformation of needs within the dictatorship. The President 'will fight tooth and nail to get central funds committed to the founding of some new research institute . . . he will constantly lament the insufficiency of finances for the upkeep of resort homes, nurseries, etc. for workers of the Academy . . . [but] . . . he will never raise a single question about the principle of censorship of scientific publications'. The irony here, these authors feel, goes deeper, for the President himself is probably an elder scientist who 'personally considers the further proliferation of academic institutes to be a mere folly, while deeply detesting the power which formal or informal censorship gives to the young and semi-educated headhunters in the cultural apparatus'.[53]

For our purposes, a particularly important insight in this theory involves the status of citizens in state socialist societies. Inasmuch as the dictatorship defines and satisfies all needs, the bearers of needs can only appear before it as supplicants. 'The good subject is one who asks for favours, for this is a sign of trust in the state, but it is important to know what the proper requests are'.[54] And, of course, 'proper' ones express some need (on the part of an individual) which has the approval of the dictatorship. Consequently, the dictatorship takes on the character of paternalism.[55] At any point in time some tacitly recognised arrangement exists between the regime and its subjects which guarantees to the latter a socially acceptable minimum of needs satisfaction in return for submission to the dictatorship or, what amounts to the same thing, the restriction of all expression of need to a request for what the dictatorship has sanctioned.[56]

From this perspective, the official ideology of the Soviet state is not an ideology at all. It is a set of empty phrases, endlessly repeated, but believed by no one. It is an ossified dogma which occludes political discussion.[57] What counts in such a society is the paternal relation between regime and subjects which de-politicises all questions of human needs and transforms them into requests which individual subjects present to officials of the party-state.[58]

What light do the (ideal–typical) relationships as set out in this theory shed on our topic of local soviets as satisfier of popular needs? The answer may already be obvious. Beginning with citizens (subjects), we find that their role is to present petitions (*nakazy*) to those designated by the authorities to receive them, namely, deputies of soviets. Those petitions which are validated and become thereby a matter of state responsibility are selected by neither the citizens (subjects) nor the representatives (deputies) which the dictatorship has selected for them, but by representatives of the dictatorship.[59] It remains the right of individual citizens (subjects) to appear before these authorities with other personal requests for assistance.[60]

Taking, next, the deputies of soviets, it appears that their activity, too, is stamped with the mark of the dictatorship. On the one hand, they aggregate those demands that the dictatorship has agreed to meet. On the other, they explain on the behalf of the dictatorship to the bearers of needs why certain of their requests cannot and/or should not be met.[61] It is then symptomatic of the status of deputies of soviets within the dictatorship that the upgrading of their role involves above all the right to ask questions and to receive replies.

The case is somewhat similar for the executive officers of a soviet, although the character of their position is Janus-like. On the one hand, they act as agents of the dictatorship in certifying which needs will receive attention. On the other, they themselves appear as supplicants before more senior officials when they articulate popular needs and carry these forward towards the centre of the dictatorship. Hence, they request such things as economic data from enterprises, departments and ministries in order to formulate development plans for their territories.

They sign 'protocols of agreement' with these same officials to relocate more of the means of consumption within the authority of their respective soviets. But these protocols, too, bear the character of petitions which senior officials, as we have seen, usually choose not to honour. Equally, as we noted above, the financial relationship which exists between the soviet and the higher officials resembles an allowance which paternal authority grants to its subjects with specifications as to its proper use.

The paternal character of the dictatorships is, of course, most sharply expressed at the apex of the party-state hierarchy. The policy on local soviets and popular needs satisfaction can be taken as an excellent illustration of just this. Paternal authority decrees benefits and responsibilities for its subjects. Neither the benefits nor the responsibilities materialise much, but this is of small import for paternal authority *per se*. In fact, this result provides the dictatorship with the opportunity to display anew its paternal concerns by scolding those it holds responsible for the shortcomings and by again instructing all subjects to behave in the proper way. When they do so, it tells them, all will be well. Consequently, from this perspective the policy in question cannot be regarded as a failed one at all. Its very reiteration is proof of its success.

7.4 THE PERSPECTIVE OF SEMIOTICS

The validity of the thesis suggested by the perspective of the theory of 'dictatorship over needs' – that is, viewing the legislation on local soviets and popular needs as a medium for the ongoing reproduction of the dictatorship, rather than as an instrumentally oriented strategy designed to induce change in the social order – would largely depend on the justifiability of altering our reference point by shifting attention from the ostensibly pragmatic intent of legislation to its mythic dimension. Can the legislation be read as a variant of mythic discourse? Some recent studies of Soviet political communication which employ a semiotic approach indicate that it can.

Semiotics is a method for analysing human communications which derives from the larger intellectual current of structuralism. Its proper object might be defined as 'the unconscious value system or system of representation which orders social life'.[62] That is, it regards the meaning of any statement, text, and so on as ultimately grounded in a code or 'deep structure' which enables the production of meaningful statements, texts, and so on. Meaning, then, does not reside in the individual elements of communication but in the structure which binds the elements into a system of meaning.[63]

The structural study of myth and folklore can be dated from the appearance in 1928 of Vladimir Propp's *Morphology of the Folktale*.[64] In this classic work, Propp showed that all Russian folktales were in fact variations on a single tale and that the meaning of its various manifestations (the individual tales themselves) was not be found on the level of character (appearances) but on the level of plot (structure). A. J. Greimas has refined Propp's work and has reduced the structure of narrative to an 'actantial model' which he regards as basic to the generation of meaning in folktales and certain other forms of narrative.[65] According to Greimas, relationships are conducted among six 'actants' (characters, split characters, groups of characters, and so on, depending on the text) which are basic to the narrative. Narrative is initiated by some need on the part of the Receiver which is identified by the Sender who commissions a Hero/Subject to engage in a quest for that Object which will fulfil the need. In so doing, the Sender marks the Subject as Hero and, in the course of his quest, the Subject is equipped with the capacity to secure the Object through the assistance afforded him by the Helper. This assistance (and his own desire) enables him to overcome the negative force of the Opponent (or villain).

Studies along these lines have been especially fruitful in isolating the structure or code of Soviet political discourse. A full exegesis of these works is beyond the scope of the present analysis, but a few of the central points can be indicated. These should bring into relief how the legislation on soviets and popular needs can be read as a code bearing certain specific meanings which are not readily apparent on the level of 'first inspection'.

Employing Greimas' model, Alexandre Bourmeyster has argued that the structure for all political discourse in the Soviet Union can be regarded as the *Skaz* (the 'Tale') which amounts to 'a mythic history of the Soviet Union from October 1917 to our times, the permanent confirmation of the scientific truth of Marxism–Leninism. It is the identity card of the collective Soviet people, with a biography, a curriculum vitae, a programme for the future. It . . . enables the authorities to communicate with their subjects . . . [It] is the generative model of Soviet political discourse, the reason for the existence of each of the narrative programmes'.[66] The *Skaz* functions in such a way as to confine all ostensibly political discussion to the mythic level. It seals off meaning from events in the world, it eschews practical analysis and pragmatically-oriented activity. In demonstrating his point, Bourmeyster examines an extreme case in Soviet political discourse, conversations held between the then recently elected General Secretary of the party, Yuri Andropov, and workers and managers at the Ordzhonikidze machine-building works in Moscow. Interestingly, Andropov's statements, in an apparent attempt to communicate on the practical level, often shifted the format of the discussion away from the *Skaz*, while all others in the dialogue closed ranks against his efforts and repeatedly returned the discussion to the familiar level of the mythic. Communication in this episode was simply impossible outside of the framework of the code[67] (perhaps confirming Frederic Jameson's point that the actantial model proves its utility precisely in those instances involving apparent departures from it),[68] yet within the code itself comment on the 'real' situation in the plant was equally impossible.

Soviet legislation of the kind we have been considering may also be analysed in terms of the actantial model. Here I might summarise the main points highlighted by the model and draw on the findings of a previous semiological study[69] of this legislation. First, there is an imbalance in the structure in favour of the Sender (party-state). The Subject (local soviets) has the power neither to accept nor refuse the mission which the Sender entrusts to him. Rather, his situation is one of being unable to refuse.[70] Hence, the Subject cannot even be counted as a reluctant hero, much less a robust battler for the well-being of the Soviet people. From the onset he is flawed. He is unable to display the *desire* to act as Subject. Second, it will be noticed that the Sender, the Helper and the Opponent are all the party-state (or its products) appearing under different forms. This conflation has the effect of inducing considerable confusion and ambivalence into the communication system. For instance, is the Subject, a local soviet, to regard an industrial enterprise located on its territory as Helper or Opponent when this enterprise generates revenue for the soviet by increasing its profits at the expense of cutting short its consumer goods production? Third, the Subject is equipped with abstract rights in order to do battle with a concrete Opponent who, moveover, is the Sender in another guise. A previous analysis of this legislation, employing in part Claude Lévi-Strauss's formula for the mythic mind, showed that within this structure of relationships, the Subject functions so as to equilibrate, rather than overcome, the lack of well-being itself.[71] Rather than change, the structure of the legislation functions so as to induce stasis.

Semiotics can be used to tap another, 'deeper' level of meaning in Soviet ideology which is analogous to the 'arrangement' or 'social contract' between regime and society alluded to by theorists discussed in the preceding section. As Bourmeyster puts it: 'The pledge of the *Skaz* would be a safe-keeping accepted by a population systematically disinformed and conscious of being so, but anxious above all to maintain the status quo'.[72] Another recent semiological analysis (using Greimas' qualificative method)[73] found that a speech by Chernenko on local soviets and popular needs was structured in such a way as internally to cancel the practical force of the dozens of manifest injunctions which it contained. Simultaneously, this structuration displaced the meaning of the speech onto the noological plane where it functioned as an appeal to appreciate what presently exists (the 'social contract') and to have patience with things as they are.[74]

Although much remains to be done before it is possible to speak with full confidence about the deep structure of Soviet political discourse, this method seems a promising one for the analysis of ideology, Soviet or otherwise. Its strength lies in the fact that it is able to carry out a concrete analysis of political texts and test through an elucidation of their *internal* structures those interpretations which other approaches (say, either policy analysis or the theory of 'dictatorship over needs') supply from their respective vantage points outside of the ideology itself.

7.5 CONCLUSIONS AND PROSPECTS

Each of the three methods employed in this study contributes to an understanding of Soviet ideology in the area of popular needs satisfaction. Conventional policy analysis adjusts our focus to the apparently instrumental features of the legislation on local soviets and their role in meeting popular needs. It enables us to specify the objectives of the policy and to inquire into the matter of whether these objects are being realised in practice. Using primarily Soviet sources, we found a sharp contrast between the stated goals of the policy and its actual implementation. Such a disjunction between intentions and results prompts the question 'why'? That is, how can the failure of this policy be explained? We might respond to this question by assembling concepts, drawing on or constructing a theory. But given our concern with ideology, we should be alert to two other considerations which emerged during our policy analytic exercise. These suggest that the answer to the question does not lie on the plane of the instrumental, the plane to which conventional policy analysis is confined.

We noticed, first, that although Soviet research on the role of soviets in the economy reports the failure of the policy, it makes no effort to explain it. We might then infer that this is no mere oversight. Rather, explanation of the failure would probably be an intrusion upon some 'already existing' rationale maintained by the party-state. As we saw, this rationale amounts to a collection of names – 'departmentalism', 'bureaucratism' and so on – which the authorities attach to opprobrious phenomena. It seems unlikely that the extant rationale would fare well in a contest of ideas waged from the other side by alternative explanations derived from social science theory. Hence, it also seems unlikely that such alternative explanations would be much welcomed by the authorities. The official ideology, therefore, might be regarded as a blockage or distortion in the communications system which inhibits certain reports about the world.[75] In order to pursue the study of policy, one should, therefore, confront this blockage and entertain the possibility that the meaning of the policy is not contained in its apparently instrumental prescriptions but resides at another level.

A second consideration whch surfaced at the stage of policy analysis was the regime's recognition that indeed the policy had failed to meet its objectives and that this recognition yielded renewed emphasis on the same policy, unaltered. Should someone, on encountering a locked door, take a key from his pocket, attempt to insert the key into the lock, discover that the key did not fit and then continue in attempts to unlock the door with this same key while proclaiming that, despite the results, it was the correct key, we would have difficulty in maintaining that such a person was engaged in instrumental behaviour. Of course, the issues which we are examining in this study are considerably more complex than unlocking doors. What is of importance, however, in the analogy just offered is the attitude taken by the subject in either case, an attitude which displays small regard for success on the instrumental level.

The theory of 'dictatorship over needs' radically alters our perception of local soviets and popular needs. The categories which it provides allow us to detect aspects of the phenomenon which would remain obscure to conventional policy analysis. Moreover, the theory immediately suggests answers to questions which policy analysis, without a theory to guide it, would find impossible to address. How valuable are these answers? Should we regard this theory as having explained once and for all the issues which we have been discussing? I think not. My hesitation results not so much from shortcomings in the theory, but from the fact that it is a theory applied by human observers to human actors. In the present case, for instance, the actors claim that needs satisfaction occurs through democratic and participatory mechanisms (soviets) while the observers (theorists) argue that such claims are false and that needs satisfaction is unthinkable outside of the dictatorship. Why should we accept one version over the other? This is where semiotics, it seems to me, makes its contribution.

Skipping over a number of methodological issues in order to make this point as directly as possible, the semiotic approach can be regarded as offering essentially the following advice: 'Listen to what the actors are saying. Take it seriously. Find out what it means'. The studies reported in this paper indicate that the meaning of local soviets as satisfiers of popular needs is ideological (in the broad sense of the term). What is more, this meaning emerges from *within* the structure of the official discourse.

In analysing this structure, we are able to settle at least some of the conflicting claims put forward by the actors, on the one hand, and the theorists on the other. It would be wrong-headed, in terms of the structure of the communication, to regard, say, 'paternalism' and 'democracy' as mutually exclusive categories. More accurate, I think, would be a view that sees each category as occupying a different space, a different level of communication. Of course Soviet citizens participate in the democratic institutions of their society and, thereby, define and attend to their needs. But they do so in a particular way, namely, through the medium designated by the official ideology or *Skaz*. Inasmuch as reality is defined by the Soviet regime and this definition brooks no rivals, how could things be otherwise? But an examination of this definition tells us that it has little if any practical import. The structure, as we say, functions in such a way that soviets equilibrate the forces associated with a lack of needs satisfaction. On the practical level, the lack is not overcome.[76] *As a practice*, blaming the officially established culprits in the officially established ways takes the place of and prevents social communication oriented toward asking the obvious questions: What is going wrong here? How can we fix it?

We would do well to conclude this chapter by recalling the fact that ideologies are not things-in-themselves leading lives of their own. Rather, they are conditioned by, and in turn condition, social practices. Should such practices be undergoing change, we might expect concomitant alterations in ideology; conversely, ideological changes may anticipate and engender new social practices. The ideology analysed here is, of course, no exception to this rule, and the analysis itself would be incomplete without some consideration of the prospects for change.

Ideological change is not, at this point, visible with respect to the elements in the official discourse on popular needs satisfaction through the system of soviets. This discourse has already come to exhibit the quality of a more or less static system. Over the past twenty years or so, one would be hard-pressed to identify any new additions of signs commonly employed. Yet there are indications at the moment that these same signs may be recombined into another structure which would open the discourse to practical considerations. Such restructuration would amount to a profound change in ideology, but this change would be difficult to detect owing to the continued presence, the repetition, of the established elements in the discourse. The Programme adopted at the 27th Congress of the CPSU includes the collection of signs associated with the conventional ideology on the role of soviets in satisfying popular needs, while the interpretation of the Programme by some of the high officials in the party-state can be read as an attempt at pouring new wine into old bottles.

On the surface, the text of the new Programme seems fully congruent with the ideology discussed in this chapter. On the one hand, it reiterates the party's paternal concern for the well-being of the Soviet people and notes the improvements to come in the areas of consumer goods and services (see Part II section 3 of the Programme). On the other, it speaks in some detail of those negative forces which have thwarted the development of popular involvement in the soviets and have, thereby, retarded both Soviet democracy and its expected product, namely, higher levels of needs satisfaction. In this respect, the Programme (Part II section 4) numbers among the vices plaguing soviets: 'bureaucratism and formalism, departmentalism and localism . . . incompetent workers and those lacking initiative, unconscientiousness, abuse of office, careerism, striving for personal enrichment, nepotism and protectionism'. The text, then, highlights the misbehaviour of individuals, moralising that all would be well if only individuals would do the right thing.

How might individuals be induced to do the 'right thing'? It is this practical question which bears some examination, inasmuch as some signs of change are evident here. Specifically, the changes in the structure of political discourse inaugurated by Gorbachev during the early months of his tenure as General Secretary of the party can be regarded as something of a restoration of the practical dimension to the official ideology.[77] It remains to be seen whether this practical orientation initiated at the top will take root below, whether it in fact signals the development of a more democratic style in soviet work (something quite prominent in Gorbachev's rhetoric) and, indeed, whether Gorbachev himself will sustain this practical orientation. What can be said at this point is that recent press coverage of soviet activities has tended to reflect the Gorbachev approach[78] and that other politicians seem to be following suit.[79] A continuation and amplification of these trends would seem to be necessary conditions for overcoming the inertia of current power relations wherein soviets count for so little and the 'dictatorship over needs' for so much.

NOTES

1. *Izvestiya*, 23 February 1985.
2. *Izvestiya*, 12 March 1985.
3. *Materialy XXVI s"ezda KPSS* (Moscow: Politizdat, 1981), p. 49.
4. See, for instance, Gorbachev's report to the 27th Congress, *Pravda*, 26 February 1986, p. 6.
5. Antonio Carlo, 'The crisis of bureaucratic collectivism', *Telos*, no. 43 (summer 1980), pp. 3–10.
6. See Ryzhkov's speech to the 27th Party Congress, *Pravda*, 4 March 1986, and the basic directives of the Twelfth Five Year Plan in *Pravda*, 9 March 1986.
7. See, for instance, Chernenko's address to the CPSU Central Committee as printed in *Izvestiya*, 11 April 1984.
8. Ibid.
9. See for instance Ryzhkov's speech to the 27th Party Congress, *Pravda*, 4 March 1986.
10. See for instance *Sovety narodnykh deputatov*, April 1981, pp. 16, 39–41.
11. 'Na novom etape', ibid., June 1981, pp. 9, 12.
12. Some of this legislation is outlined by Ronald J. Hill in his 'Party–state relations and Soviet political development', *British Journal of Political Science*, vol. 10 no. 2 (April 1980), pp. 149–65, and in the same author's 'The development of local government since Stalin's death', in Everett M. Jacobs, ed., *Soviet Local Politics and Government* (London: Allen and Unwin, 1983), pp. 18–33. See also Michael E. Urban, 'State socialist administration in the USSR', in K. Tummala (ed.), *Administrative Systems Abroad*, 2nd edn (Washington DC: University Press of America, 1984), esp. pp. 378–82.
13. The articles in question are numbers 146–8.
14. See *Vedomosti Verkhovnogo Soveta SSSR*, no. 12 (24 March 1971), arts 132–3.
15. Reprinted in *Sovety narodnykh deputatov*, August 1980.
16. See, for instance, *Sobranie postanovlenii pravitel'stva SSSR*, no. 15 (1978), art. 99.
17. See *Izvestiya*, 2 April 1981 and 15 May 1983.
18. More extended discussions of the legislation concerning the role of local soviets in the economy may be found in V. A. Perttsik, *Realizatsiya zakonodatel'stva mestnymi sovetami* (Moscow: Yuridicheskaya literatura, 1985); V. S. Martemyanov, *Khozyaistvennye prava mestnykh sovetov* (Moscow: Yuridicheskaya literatura, 1981); and other works.

19. See *Sobranie postanovlenii pravitel'stva RSFSR* (1980), item 66.
20. See, for instance, *Sovety narodnykh deputatov*, February 1981, pp. 86–7.
21. Barabashev, 'Na novom etape', pp. 15–16; P. Shamanov, 'Rastut etazhi Sverdlovska', *Izvestiya*, 17 June 1981.
22. See particularly 'Osnovy zhilishchnogo zakonodatel'stva Soyuza SSR i soyuznykh respublik', *Izvestiya*, 25 June 1981.
23. *Izvestiya*, 20 November 1984.
24. *Sobranie postanovlenii pravitel'stva RSFSR*, no. 4 (1979), art. 28.
25. See B. V. Konoplev's co-report to the USSR Supreme Soviet as reported in *Izvestiya*, 24 June 1981.
26. Interview with M. Shchetinina, secretary of Moscow Regional Soviet, Moscow, 15 November 1979.
27. Interview with G. V. Barabashev, head of the Department of State Law and Soviet Construction at Moscow State University and member of the Methods Council of Moscow Regional Soviet, Moscow, 28 May 1982.
28. See *Sovety narodnykh deputatov*, February 1981, pp. 23–32.
29. See, for instance, G. V. Barabashev, 'Organy narodnogo predstavitel'stva', *Sovety narodnykh deputatov*, June 1978, pp. 9–16; B. Osipchik, 'Vypolnenie nakazov – delo otvetstvennoe', ibid., March 1978, pp. 29–36.
30. Ukaz Prezidiuma Verkhovnogo Soveta SSSR, 'Ob organizatsii raboty s nakazami izbiratelei', in *Izvestiya*, 3 September 1980.
31. *Vedomosti Verkhovnogo Soveta SSSR*, no. 36 (1972), art. 347.
32. Barabashev, 'Organy', p. 14.
33. *Izvestiya*, 11 April 1984.
34. *Sovetskoe gosudarstvo i pravo*, January 1976, pp. 23–31.
35. Stephen Sternheimer, 'Running Soviet cities: bureaucratic degeneration, bureaucratic politics, or urban management?', in G. B. Smith (ed.), *Public Policy and Administration in the Soviet Union* (New York: Praeger, 1980), p. 87.
36. G. B. Polyak, *Byudzhet goroda* (Moscow: Finansy, 1978).
37. *Spravka o plane ekonomicheskogo–sotsial'nogo razvitiya Moskvy 1980 i 1981 gg. Materialy* (Moscow: Mossovet, 1980), p. 38.
38. *Byudzhet goroda Moskvy na 1982 god; otchet ob ispolnenii byudzheta goroda Moskvy za 1980 god* (Moscow: Mossovet, 1981), pp. 6–7.
39. See S. A. Avak'yan and L.A. Sobolev, *Metodicheskie rekomendatsii po sovershenstvovaniyu otnoshenii ob''edinenii, predpriyatii i organizatsii Ministerstva elektrotekhnicheskoi promyshlennosti s mestnymi sovetami, ikh organami i deputatami* (Moscow: Informelektro, 1981), pp. 5–19.
40. For an interesting discussion of the financial dependence of local soviets and how this relates to their inability to enforce their formal powers, see the article by the chairman of L'vov City Soviet in *Izvestiya*, 13 August 1984.
41. Compare, for instance, D. Kartvelishvili, 'K vysokim konechnym rezul'tatam', *Sovety narodnykh deputatov*, October 1985, pp. 7–14, with G. Gubanov, 'Pustyr': vybrannye mesta iz perepiski so vedomstvami', *Izvestiya*, 9 July 1985.
42. I have discussed some of these in 'Technical assistance and political control: a research note on the Organization–instruction department of local soviets', *Comparative Politics*, vol. 17 (April 1985), pp. 337–50, and in 'Conceptualising political power in the USSR: patterns of binding and bending', *Studies in Comparative Communism*, vol. 18 (Winter 1985),

pp. 207–26.
43. A rare, although by no means revolutionary, exception to this pattern is an article by O. Latsis advocating competition among firms in retail trade: see his 'Dlya pokazatelya ili dlya pokupatelya', *Izvestiya*, 2 November 1984.
44. See, for instance, the editorial 'Sovety i ekonomika' in *Izvestiya*, 15 May 1983.
45. See, for instance, V. Surkov, 'A gde zhe otpoved' byurokratam', *Izvestiya*, 21 September 1982.
46. See for instance *Sovety narodnykh deputatov*, April 1981, pp. 45–8.
47. *Pravda*, 27 February 1986, p. 2.
48. See, for instance, his *Theory of Social and Economic Organizations* (New York: Free Press, 1947).
49. Ferenc Feher, Agnes Heller and Gyorgy Markus, *Dictatorship over Needs* (New York: St Martin's Press, 1983).
50. The seminal work of Lukacs on this subject is his essay, 'Reification and the consciousness of the proletariat', in his *History and Class Consciousness* (Cambridge, Mass.: MIT Press, 1971).
51. Feher, Heller and Markus, *Dictatorship*, pp. 89–90.
52. Cf. George Konrad and Ivan Szelenyi's argument that the ruling class in state socialist societies stakes its claim to authority on the basis of both technical and 'teleological' knowledge in their *Intellectuals on the Road to Class Power* (New York: Harcourt, Brace and Janovich, 1979).
53. Feher, Heller and Markus, *Dictatorship*, p. 111.
54. Ibid., p. 176.
55. Paternalism has been a pronounced attribute of Russian authority relations in the pre-Soviet period as well: see, for instance, Walker McKechnie and Don Karl Rowney, eds, *Russian Officialdom* (Chapel Hill: University of North Carolina Press, 1980).
56. Feher, Heller and Markus, *Dictatorship*, p. 76.
57. Ibid., pp. 185–92.
58. Empirical accounts of this process may be found in Theodore Friedgut, 'Citizens and Soviets: can Ivan Ivanovich fight City Hall?', *Comparative Politics*, vol. 10 (July 1978), pp. 461–77 and Vladimir Voinovich, *The Ivankiad* (New York: Farrar, Straus and Giroux, 1977).
59. See Michael E. Urban, 'Information and participation in Soviet local government', *Journal of Politics*, vol. 44 (February 1982), pp. 79–80.
60. See for instance M. Shimansky, 'Po lichnomu voprosu', *Izvestiya*, 11 January 1985.
61. Urban, 'Information and participation', pp. 81–2.
62. Frederic Jameson, *The Prison-House of Language* (Princeton NJ: Princeton University Press, 1972), p. 101.
63. See for instance Umberto Eco, *A Theory of Semiotics* (Bloomington: University of Indiana Press, 1976); Terence Hawkes, *Structuralism and Semiotics* (Berkeley: University of California Press, 1977); and Roland Barthes, *Elements of Semiology* (New York: Hill and Wang, 1968).
64. Vladimir Propp, *Morphology of the Folktale*, 2nd edn (Austin: University of Texas Press, 1968).
65. A. J. Greimas, *Structural Semantics* (Lincoln: University of Nebraska Press, 1983).
66. Alexandre Bourmeyster, 'Iouri Andropov dialogue avec les ouvriers

soviétiques', *Essais sur le dialogue*, vol. 2 (1984), p. 317; idem, 'L'Enonciateur, l'enonciataire et l'autre', *Essais sur le discours soviétique*, vol. 2 (1982), pp. 61–98.
67. Bourmeyster, 'Iouri Andropov'.
68. Frederic Jameson, *The Political Unconscious* (Ithaca, NY: Cornell University Press, 1981), p. 126.
69. Michael E. Urban and John McClure, 'The folklore of state socialism: semiotics and the study of the Soviet state', *Soviet Studies*, vol. 35 (October 1983), pp. 471–86.
70. See Bourmeyster, 'Iouri Andropov', p. 318.
71. Urban and McClure, 'Folklore', esp. p. 481.
72. Alexandre Bourmeyster, 'Utopie, ideologie et skaz', *Essais sur le discours soviétique*, vol. 3 (1983), p. 44.
73. A. J. Greimas and F. Rastier, 'The interaction of semiotic constraints', *Yale French Studies*, vol. 41 (1968), pp. 86–105.
74. Michael E. Urban, 'The structure of signification in the General Secretary's address: a semiotic approach to Soviet political discourse', *Coexistence*, vol. 24, no. 3 (December 1987).
75. See, for instance, Jurgen Habermas, 'On systematically distorted communication', *Inquiry*, vol. 13 (Autumn 1970), pp. 184–219, and the same author's *Theory of Communicative Action* (Boston: Beacon, 1984).
76. For a stimulating discussion of structure and its functioning in the area of practical pursuits, see Lucien Goldmann, 'Structure: human realities and methodological concept', in his *The Languages of Criticism and the Sciences of Man* (Baltimore, Md: Johns Hopkins Press, 1970), pp. 98–124.
77. For a discussion of this question, see Michael E. Urban, 'From Chernenko to Gorbachev: a repoliticization of official Soviet discourse?' (Paper presented to the III World Congress for Soviet and East European Studies, Washington DC, 30 October– 4 October 1985).
78. See, for instance, the editorial in *Izvestiya*, 3 May 1985.
79. A. A. Gromyko's address to the Gorky Regional Soviet is one illustration of this: see *Izvestiya*, 14 November 1985.

8 Soviet Ideology and Female Roles

MARY BUCKLEY

Several assumptions about ideology underpin the discussion that follows. Ideology is here viewed as one aspect of politics; and so to understand the political we must grasp the significance of ideology to it.[1] This significance may vary according to historical context, political system, leadership, level of economic development, issue and situation. I do not assume that ideology is either constantly shaped by, or reducible to, external determinants, but rather that ideology interacts with other factors. Thus ideology can inspire policy, be ignored by policy, be seriously modified itself by policy or serve to qualify policy. Its impact on society is not constant over time and neither is its role necessarily homogeneous across issues.

Some strands of ideology, moreover, may be more durable than others. Certain arguments may be championed with consistency across historical periods, while others may fall fallow, never to be cultivated further. Completely new strains may be incorporated into the existing corpus of ideas, thereby serving to graft fresh notions onto more established ones. Charges may be made that in the USSR the true spirit of Marxism is either violated by these additions and subtractions or creatively extended by them. Either way, I suggest, the content of ideology matters. It matters because arguments put forward by Soviet official ideology are not only promoted through propaganda, but have implications for policy and discussions about policy. Just as policy priorities may shape ideology, so the emphasis of ideology at any given time may set the parameters of discourse and debate.

In keeping with this, Soviet ideology's view of women has been inspired by far more than the Marxist classics. Ideology has been affected by historical context, political and economic priorities, societal values and demographic policy, as well as by developments in Soviet theory. So the Marxist arguments on women and society that the

Bolsheviks inherited have since been extended, adapted, qualified and variously packaged to suit the perceived needs of the Soviet state as defined by its successive leaderships. In short, Soviet ideology has taken different approaches to the position of women, tailored to the priorities of different periods of Soviet history. Whilst allowing that each period may have its shifts in emphasis and may not necessarily offer neat coherent arguments and conceding that certain positions persist over time, five analytically distinct periods can nevertheless be distinguished: from the revolution to about 1930; from 1930 to the death of Stalin; the Khrushchev years; the Brezhnev years; and the period from 1981 up to the present day. I shall deal briefly with the first three of these, directing more of my attention to the 1970s and 1980s.[2]

8.1 1917 TO THE 1960s: FROM REVOLUTION, EMANCIPATION AND DEBATE TO ECONOMIC AND POLITICAL ROLES

The revolutionary situation of 1917 and the following decade provided a catalyst for lively discussions of women's emancipation which had their roots in earlier Russian political ideas. The rupture with Tsarism now offered a context for the pursuit of equality. Hence, practical possibilities fired ideology and vice-versa. True to Marxist ideology, equality of the sexes was proclaimed in law, along with the principle of equal pay for equal work. The patriarchal family, enshrined in the 1836 code of Russian Law, was challenged. Divorce was made simple, marriage was declared a civil, not a religious affair, maternity pay was granted to working women and abortion was legalised. Ideology clearly inspired policy, and arguments in favour of changes in female roles were voiced by Alexandra Kollontai, Inessa Armand and others. Discussions centred on the topics of domestic labour, maternity, the family, sexual relations and women's organisations.[3]

Different pressures, however, were exerted in the 1920s. Traditional attitudes and values about woman's place pulled one way and ideas about emancipation the other. Many members of the party, male and female alike, found the notion of sudden changes in gender roles difficult to grasp in their entirety and certainly hard to practise in what was a conservative and predominantly peasant society. Traditional attitudes, coupled with the Marxist aversion to special institutions for women on the grounds that they divided the working class, detracted from class struggle and ran the risk of fostering bourgeois feminism, accorded the new Women's Department of the Party or Zhenotdel (*zhenskii otdel*) the status of a precarious and much criticised institution. Yet despite this fragility of the woman question, extensions to Marxist theory were made in these years. Armand, for example, asserted that the success of both women's liberation, and indeed socialism itself, was connected to the socialisation of domestic labour and child care.[4] In a similar vein, Kollontai's theoretical discussions of the family offered a preliminary analysis of domestic labour and sexuality.[5] The argument that socialism would not be constructed without the socialisation of domestic life, and that women could not be liberated without it, widened the boundaries of discourse. Socialist economic relations were viewed as necessary, but not sufficient, in this context.

As the historical context changed, the woman question took a new form, subordinate to the practical requirements of forced industrialisation, collectivisation and war. These were far more pressing priorities than analysing or promoting equality of the sexes. The political survival of socialism in one country through the forced construction of an industrial state necessitated discipline and order in daily life, with no place for the luxury of pondering the woman question. Furthermore, the prevalence of traditional attitudes about women, despite women's newly won legal emancipation, meant that the shelving of debate about women's lives was not seriously challenged.

Soviet ideology on women was adapted to fit these circumstances. Women were persistently portrayed as 'a great army of labour' and 'a colossal reserve of labour power'.[6] On International Women's Day, women were invariably praised for sitting confidently at the wheels of tractors, cars and planes and simultaneously encouraged to work 'much harder' to fulfil and exceed the economic plan.[7] Woman's place in productive labour was paramount. The importance of economic acitivity for women did, indeed, have ideological roots in the Marxist classics where participation in the labour force was seen as a prerequisite for emancipation and an end to economic and social dependence on men. However, the heavy emphasis on woman's economic roles was due to economic policy rather than concern for female liberation.

Equality, nevertheless, was mentioned. It was argued that the economic roles of women, coupled with early Soviet legislation, illustrated how equality existed. There were still problems, Karl Radek regretted in 1933, such as inadequate childcare facilities and too few dining rooms, but what was important was that socialism was developing services which capitalism could not offer.[8] And in rural areas, according to Stalin, collective farms rendered rural women equal to rural men. As he put it: 'without collective farms – inequality. With collective farms – equal rights'.[9] Rural women, in Nadezhda Krupskaya's estimation, 'already stand in earnest before the factual equality of which Il'ich spoke'.[10] It was argued that 'the complete liberation of women' was already an 'outstanding achievement'.[11]

The woman question remained officially closed until the second half of the 1960s. This, however, did not stop Khrushchev from raising questions about female roles as early as 1956. One of Khrushchev's central concerns was to breathe fresh life into the party. Addressing the 20th Party Congress on this theme, he remarked:

> It should not be overlooked that many party and state organs put women forward for leadership posts with timidity. Very few women hold leading posts in the party and soviets, particularly among party committee secretaries, chairpersons of soviet executive committees, and among directors of industrial enterprises, collective farms, machine tractor stations and state farms.[12]

Yet again policy priorities of the Soviet leadership affected which female roles were selected for scrutiny and how they were to be treated. Khrushchev's attempt to instil democracy into Soviet politics and to step up political mobilisation almost inevitably led to the question: who is active in politics and who is not? Observation revealed that although women constituted over half of the population, their profile in high politics was still a low one.

So, as the 1950s drew to a close, references to the political role of women increased. A Central Committee resolution of March 1959 stressed that a 'differentiated approach' to political agitation among the population should be adopted, taking into account 'different characteristics of various groups'.[13] Women constituted one such group thought to be a distinct category. Another resolution of January 1960 called for propaganda work geared firstly to drawing the remaining housewives into the economy and political activity and secondly to combatting feudal attitudes towards women.[14] Lectures, conferences and discussion groups for women were encouraged and the women's councils (*zhensovety*) were active in sponsoring them. Prior to these resolutions, the 21st Party Congress of 1959 and the June 1959 plenum of the Central Committee championed the 'further development of democracy in every way' and the greater involvement of the people in administration.[15] Thus, new life was officially given to social organisations and in keeping with this, the *zhensovety* were revived and extended.

Although the late 1950s and early 1960s witnessed these official efforts to move female roles onto the agenda where relevant to other prominent issues, the woman question was still cast not as a goal of Soviet socialism, but as a success already achieved. According to Vera Bil'shai: 'the experience of the Communist Party and Soviet state in implementing the factual equality of women and men in social production and in all spheres of state and social activity is of great world historic significance'.[16] Bil'shai argued that the new Soviet state had not only granted women formal equality in law, but 'had done everything' for securing equality in production and administration.[17] Indeed, she claimed that just as the national question and peasant question had been solved, so too had the woman question.

Nevertheless, the early post-Stalin years opened up the possibility of delving further into inequalities and at the last party congress over which Khrushchev presided in 1961 'remnants of inequality' tiptoed in. It was declared at this 22nd Congress that:

> Remnants of inequality in the position of women in everday life must be completely eliminated. Conditions must be created for the harmonious combination of motherhood with a more active participation of women in the labour force, society, science and the arts. Women must be given lighter work, which is at the same time adequately paid.[18]

Longer maternity leave was also granted, more household appliances were called for and attention was directed at the need for more public dining rooms. The woman question was not declared unsolved, but the hardships of the double burden were implicitly defined as problems.

8.2 THE BREZHNEV YEARS: DECLINING BIRTH RATES, LABOUR SHORTAGES AND DEVELOPED SOCIALISM

Where Khrushchev's priority of reinvigorating the party had shone a spotlight on women's political roles, concern about economic productivity, combined with consternation about declining birth rates and labour shortages, led the Brezhnev leadership to scrutinise the relationship between women's domestic and economic roles.[19] A very serious requirement of the economy – labour – was not only in inadequate supply, but becoming scarcer. The practical difficulty was that, as a vital 51 per cent of the Soviet labour force, women were needed both at work and in maternity wards. For the requirements of the Soviet economy to be met, an answer had to be provided to the question of how women could combine their roles in production and reproduction without neglecting either role, simultaneously increase their efficiency in the workforce and also bear more children. How women could fulfil the roles of worker and mother with high productivity in each was of increasing importance to the Soviet state.

Just as Khrushchev had expressed his views about the lack of women in top jobs at the 20th Party Congress, so the new collective leadership used party congresses to indicate anxiety about female roles. While the 23rd Party Congress in 1966 paid little attention to issues directly affecting women, the 24th Congress of 1971 made the official party position clear:

> In the past five year period a series of important measures were taken on party initiative with the aim of improving the working conditions of women and simultaneously easing their domestic work . . . It is well known, comrades, that in the forthcoming five year plan several further steps in this direction are envisaged.
> The goal of party policy is for Soviet woman to have new opportunities regarding childrearing, participation in society, recreation and study.[20]

In the same spirit, the 25th Party Congress of 1976 announced that: 'the party considers it its duty continually to protect women, to improve their position as workers, mothers, childrearers and housewives'.[21] Herein were enshrined four female roles. Much subsequent Soviet social science research has been predicated on the assumption that women have these four roles to perform.

The clear message that researchers transmitted to policy makers was that not only did the roles of mother and worker conflict, since women in the labour force found it hard to have large families, but also that the tension between them was made acute by the female 'double burden' or 'double shift'. Unlike men, working women performed two main roles: one in the paid workforce, followed by a 'second shift' of domestic labour at home. This obtained whether or not children entered the picture. Already bearing a double burden, working women began to think twice about reproduction, especially when it came to having second and third children. Examination of the double burden was just one focus of research conducted in the 1960s and 1970s, and invariably fed into debates on other themes which included: the reorganisation and rationalisation of female labour in the workforce and in households; inequalities between the sexes; the seriousness of the decline in the birth rate; and the nature of family life. Scrutiny of the way in which the main arguments were couched shows how the main focus of enquiry was often not the double burden itself, but its relevance to other problems.

Economists such as Shishkan, Kotlyar, Turchaninova, Sonin, Tatarinova, Yuk, Panova, Kozachenko and Eremina, for instance, organised their research around the topic of how best to promote a more rational and efficient use of labour resources.[22] This was in response to pressures to make the economy more productive. They contended that female labour had to be studied carefully since women constituted half the Soviet labour force. The workforce, therefore, could not be made more productive without reorganising female labour. Moreover, the sheer size of the female work force was not the only reason for studying it. Important improvements in the economy, argued Samokhina, were dependent upon changes in female labour since it was the least qualified.[23] Thus, the direction of the economy was seriously tied to improvements in what Eremina described as the 'quality' of female labour.[24] Not only was this 'quality' now subject to scrutiny, but investigations into the 'special interests' of women as a group were declared timely, if not overdue.

General agreement existed that the female organism should be protected from harmful working conditions such as dust, chemicals, noise and wide temperature fluctuations. It was lamented that poor working conditions had indeed persisted under socialism and that they harmed woman's health.[25] Various recommendations were put forward to help combat this situation, including special commissions for examining women's working conditions, a department of women's work to be attached to local soviets to monitor and control the conditions of female labour and a year off work after childbirth, rather than an immediate return to the workplace. In fact, in 1976 the newly named State Committee on Labour and Social Questions, previously known as the USSR State Committee on Questions of Labour and Wages, broadened its scope to pay greater attention to problems faced by working women. In addition, Commissions for Questions Concerning the Work and Daily Life of Women and For the Protection of Mothers and Children were set up in both the USSR Supreme Soviet and in the legislatures of each union republic. Similarly, trade union commissions began to inspect women's working conditions and to offer recommendations for improvement.[26]

Many economists reached the conclusion that one clear improvement would be to shorten women's working hours. Shishkan, for instance, suggested that: 'one of the ways of solving problems of the effective use of female labour is to grant women the opportunity to work a part-time day, or a part of the working week'.[27] Shishkan construed the rationalisation of female labour to take domestic and non-domestic roles into account. He did not limit the scope of rationalisation to the workplace. In his view, this was quite appropriate, given that female roles at home affected those at work and did not exist in isolation. The advantages of part-time labour would not only secure greater harmony between these roles, but also mean a higher output when women were performing their economic roles. In defence of part-shifts, Shishkan cited evidence suggesting that the productivity of those working part-time was higher than those in full-time jobs. He also pointed out how some workers would prefer part-time jobs. And surveys backed this conclusion up.[28]

Yet despite his support for part-time labour, Shishkan maintained that it had 'only subsidiary significance for solving questions of female labour'.[29] More attention should be directed at mechanising production and increasing the levels of technical skills since 'the solution of these very problems will provide the opportunity not only to raise the effectiveness of female labour, but also bring about factual social equality of the sexes'.[30] Attaining factual equality was thus explicitly tied to mechanisation and an increase in skills.

The aspect of Shishkan's thesis that became controversial was the desirability of part-time labour for women. Against those who argued that it constituted a lowering of the status of women's work and was therefore a step backwards, Panova claimed that equality of the sexes should not necessarily mean equal time in the workforce for men and women if this meant a heavier overall burden for women.[31] Disagreements became lively and were openly acknowledged to exist in interviews and in printed materials.

The party made its position on part-time labour clear at the 25th Congress in 1976 by declaring its commitment to 'create greater opportunities for women with children to work a part-day or part-week and also to work at home'.[32] Now, interestingly, the debate about the desirability of part-time work had raged in the 1960s and continued throughout the 1970s. An explicit party policy appeared after discussion had been going on for ten years among social scientists. Furthermore, discussion did not cease immediately after the party line was declared. Official commitment to part-time labour for women was reasserted by Gorbachev at the 27th Party Congress in 1986. He promised wider adoption of flexible working hours on the grounds that they allowed women more successfully to combine motherhood with activities outside the home.[33]

Whilst open debate prevailed over the desirability of part-time labour and also the gravity of the decline in the birth rate, there was at the same time general agreement that women workers constituted a 'special category' of labour, because of their roles in production and reproduction. Debate about the problems of this special category was possible because ideology characterised developed socialist society as one confronting unsolved difficulties.

Despite the recognition of unsolved problems, there were many questions about female roles that Soviet social scientists did not investigate in these years, particularly women's political roles. Ideological and political constraints still precluded many channels of enquiry. For example, social scientists did not raise the possibility of structures of inequality in the Soviet political system or explore mechanisms of excluding women from important political posts. No analysis was conducted of the informal networks of Soviet city administration which serve to screen women out through what Stephen Sternheimer describes as their 'male bias'.[34] The relationships between sex, hiring, promotion and party control of appoinments were not explored. Ideology allowed no theoretical space for discourse on discrimination through institutional restraints. Therefore Soviet social science has not examined why the female presence is higher in local party politics, but falls off dramatically at higher levels. Neither has the relevance to political mobilisation of skills practised in the *zhensovety*, such as sewing, been queried.[35]

Nevertheless, debate about female roles was much wider in the 1960s and 1970s than had been the case for almost forty years. The woman question was not only reopened and reinvigorated, but in comparison with the silence of the years that preceded this period, some probing questions were posed by an enlivened Soviet social science. The recognition of the existence of inequalities at home and at work may have been overdue, but when it came it was extremely refreshing. Furthermore, the espousal of the concepts of developed socialism and non-antagonistic contradictions rendered the existence of inequalities theoretically plausible and thus gave legitimacy to research into them. Yankova, Gruzdeva and many others could now all proclaim the woman question 'unsolved' and be guaranteed ideological protection. Slotting the woman question into the logic of developed socialism, Nagiev argued, 'the attainment of factual equality, as distinct from obtaining political rights, is a protracted, complicated and many-sided social process'.[36] Like all protracted complicated processes, attaining equality demanded grappling with and resolving non-antagonistic contradictions. Their persistence was responsible for 'vestiges of the past' and their resolution was the key to solving the woman question.

So, whereas the liberation of women had been declared a great achievement of socialism as early as the 1930s, by the late 1960s the definition of this 'achievement' had been considerably narrowed. The 'social task' of 'great historic significance' that had been solved was legal equality of the sexes. The woman question in its entirety had not been answered after all, but just one aspect of it.

The distinction between equal rights (*ravnopravie*) and equality (*ravenstvo*) was increasingly stressed. *Ravnopravie* amounted to formal equality (*formal'noe ravenstvo*) before the law. *Ravnopravie* as *formal'noe ravenstvo* was therefore legal equality (*yuridicheskoe ravenstvo* or *pravovoe ravenstvo*). But *ravenstvo* itself was much broader embracing 'political, economic and everyday life'. *Ravenstvo* was synonymous with equality in practice and viewed as factual equality, referred to as *fakticheskoe ravenstvo* or sometimes as factual social equality, or *fakticheskoe sotsial'noe ravenstvo*.[37] Whereas formal equality entails no more than legislation, factual equality demands changes in behaviour and attitudes.

Soviet ideology now held that factual equality was not won immediately after the revolution. On the contrary, 'vestiges of inequality' or 'remnants of factual inequality' still remained. While solving the woman question was only possible under socialism, it did 'not come easily' and was a complex and protracted process. The new line, as stated by Tatarinova, was that while the Soviet state had made great strides towards promoting equality, 'it would be incorrect to think that all questions were solved, that difficulties needing to be overcome did not exist, and that new problems would not arise'.[38] Moreover, the nature of the woman question altered over time. As Gruzdeva put it, 'solving the woman question passes through different stages at different levels of the development of socialism'.[39] The task of social scientists was to identify these stages and discuss their significance for women.

8.3 FROM BREZHNEV TO GORBACHEV: DEMOGRAPHIC POLICY, THE WOMAN QUESTION AND MALE ROLES

While many of the arguments rehearsed in the 1960s and 1970s were reiterated in the 1980s, evaluation of female roles has shifted somewhat.

Over the past few years, this particular question has been proclaimed of growing importance to the Soviet state, and significant in ways different from the past. Its fresh topicality is linked directly to 'the problems of encouraging a growth in the birth rate and rearing the future generations'.[40] Since the USSR is suffering from a fall in the birth rate, then all problems concerning female labour, motherhood and children, asserts Rzhanitsina, are linked to the further development of the main productive force: labour.[41] It is currently argued that the woman question has taken on a new content which cannot be isolated from other concerns for socialist society, in particular, demography. Small family size is the problem in terms of which the woman question is now stated.

This explicit linking of the woman question to the 'population problem' is consistent with the message of the 26th Party Congress of 1981, which revealed that:

> In accordance with the instructions of the 25th Party Congress the Central Committee has given serious attention to the drawing up and implementation of an effective *demographic policy*, aggravated in recent years by the population problem. The main way to solve it is through greater concern for the family, newlyweds and above all women (applause). It is surely clear to everyone how at times it is not easy to combine the duties of motherhood with active participation in production and society.[42]

After having declared strong support for a demographic policy, the Congress went on to caution that despite all the measures already taken by the party to ease the female double burden, 'a noticeable turning point has not yet come about. Wider and more effective measures are needed'.[43] So continued backing was given to more kindergartens, part-time labour for women and up to a year off work after childbirth. More explicitly than ever before, party policy was committed to boosting the birth rate and more wholeheartedly than hitherto to alleviating the double burden.

In keeping with this official connection between the woman question and the population problem, demographers' contributions to discussions carry greater legitimacy and weight. The theme that Viktor Perevedentsev plugged after the 26th Party Congress was that unless the birth rate rose considerably in the 1990s, there could be a serious strain on labour resources during the second decade of the twenty first century when the generation born in the 1950s reached retirement age. Although it was too late for policy to have any substantial effect on the economic aspect of the demographic situation before the end of the century, Perevedentsev argued that it was 'important to act now' in order to prevent negative population trends intensifying and if possible 'to optimize the process of population reproduction'.[44] This could be done, he suggested, through a special programme for developing marriage and family relations. Similar arguments are voiced with increasing regularity in Soviet academic journals and newspapers. And by 1985 the notion of women as a 'socio-demographic group' had entered the sociological literature on women in developed socialist society.[45]

Accompanying the recent spate of academic publications on the population problem are books which offer advice on marriage, contraception and sex. One such 1981 publication carried a chapter entitled 'Soon a Child in the Family', which propagandised: 'pregnancy and birth are necessary for the female organism. It is well known that after childbirth woman blossoms for a second time, and starts to live a full life. Women who have many children usually look younger than their age and younger than those without children'.[46] The special programme for developing marriage that Perevedentsev called for appears to be going ahead. This is because small family size in Russia, Belorussia, the Ukraine and Baltic states is now viewed by policy-makers as a serious problem in need of rectification.

The reason behind it, Valentei stresses, is nothing to do with socialism *per se*. Rather,

> There are several objective factors why there are fewer children in the family. However, it is hardly a permanent process natural to socialism. Rather the present trend toward a declining birth rate stems from the specific contradictions of the moment, a certain period in Soviet society's economic development, when the best possible balance between all fields of material production and the non-productive sphere has not yet been secured.[47]

The lag in the development of the non-productive sphere is seen as all-important. In particular, insufficient kindergarten facilities, inadequate pre-school education, not enough new flats and shortcomings in the service sphere deter working women from having more than one child. Some, like Valentei, depict these lags as non-antagonistic contradictions. Ryabushkin, however, characterises them as 'difficulties' associated with 'a number of objective circumstances' which are not 'serious contradictions'.[48]

Alongside these objective reasons for small families are subjective ones. Ryabushkin laments that the position of women in the family 'does not always correspond to their social status'.[49] While respected by co-workers in the labour force, women were 'overburdened' at home. While the 1960s and 1970s were rather silent about the need for male roles to change even though the double burden was amply documented, writers of the 1980s are rather gingerly edging the issue further onto the agenda.

One catalyst for further discussion of male roles was provided by Brezhnev's speech to the Trade Union Congress of March 1977. It was here that he thanked women for their 'self-sacrificing work' and declared, 'to speak plainly: we men are indebted to them (applause). We have still done far from everything to ease the double burden'.[50] Where Yankova had hesitated to develop this theme very far in the 1970s, Novikova, Sidorova and Turchaninova in the 1980s have come out firmly in favour of husbands and children actively participating in housework. They maintain that many trade unions 'are striving to overcome the tenacious tradition of shifting all the housework onto the shoulders of women and are propagandising the structure of families where men and children actively participate in housework'.[51] Rzhanitsina, too, cautions that the unfair distribution of household responsibilities leads to female discontent in marriage. Since the stability of the family life is a Soviet goal and is seen as a prerequisite of larger families, the possible link between female overwork in the home and divorce and the definite link between a heavy domestic load and smaller families have finally forced male roles into the picture. If men assumed domestic roles, not only would the female double burden be alleviated, but marriage might be more stable, divorce less likely and more children a possibility. Consistent with this, at the 27th Party Congress Gorbachev reaffirmed the party's goal of strengthening the family with a view to achieving new stable socialist families whose members did not quarrel. Despite the slight fall in the divorce rate, Gorbachev regretted that the number of divorces was still large.[52]

Like Yankova before her, Rzhanitsina hesitates to prescribe the boundaries of the male role in domestic labour and qualifies her support for changing male roles as follows:

> Of course we are not embarking on an itemised distribution of absolutely every household responsibility and chores between husband and wife and other members of the family, but are speaking about a rational distribution of work and the creation of the best possible situation for each member of the family.[53]

Greater mechanisation of housework, she feels, would create opportunities for 'restructuring' the traditional distribution of household chores, allowing men to 'help out' with the arduous tasks. Where restructuring domestic labour may mean for Rzhanitsina no more than lending a hand, it means participation for Novikova, Sidorova and Turchaninova and has become a propaganda issue. Linking the male domestic role to the decline in the birth rate has given it the status of a legitimate problem deserving to be tackled. It has not been raised because of a concern with sexual equality *per se*, but because of its relevance to Soviet demographic policy. Nevertheless, while it is framed in terms of the economic requirement of a 'rational distribution' of work and in keeping with the moral goal of family stability, interviews which I conducted in 1979, 1980, 1984 and 1985 with female social scientists made it clear that its relevance to equality was in their minds, even if they did not necessarily express it in quite this way on paper.

Going further than others, Gruzdeva and Chertikhina devote a whole section of their recent book to 'Children, Husbands, Free Time'.[54] Here they neatly illustrate how men spend more time than women watching television; walking in the park; meeting friends; reading books, newspapers and journals; going to dances, the cinema, theatre, concerts and museums; studying; and pursuing hobbies such as photography, painting, sport, hunting and fishing. While teenage women spend more time reading than men, as soon as they marry, and before children are born, their reading time falls substantially. Once married, men read more. Interestingly the great drop for women does not take place after children are born, when only a small reduction occurs, but before. While not developing their findings into a coherent critique of traditional gender roles and the attitudes that go with them, Gruzdeva and Chertikhina, quoting Gorky, end their book with a gentle appeal to men to recall that 'the height of culture is defined by relations towards women'.[55]

Soviet writings of the 1980s portray developed socialist society as one in which 'ever greater opportunities for the solution to problems'[56] exist due to greater 'scientific control' of socio-economic processes than was possible before.[57] Control follows the analysis of social phenomena, which involves exposure of society's shortcomings and a search for ways to overcome them. As far as the woman question is concerned, it is acknowledged that thorough enquiry into the position of women in society has only very recently been undertaken.[58] This is because solutions were just not possible in the past and hence it would have been premature to investigate what could not have been solved. This is consistent with Marx's observation that human beings only set themselves those problems which they can solve. As Novikova, Sidorova and Turchaninova put it, 'before, mainly for economic reasons, it was not possible to solve many problems at once, therefore at each stage of socialist construction priority was given to the most urgent'.[59] Under developed socialism, problems can be solved through sensitivity to their complexity and awareness of their relationships to other problems. 'Complexity' is the key buzz word. While the existence of several such 'complexities' was noted in the 1960s and 1970s, specification of the intricacies of processes of social change is the task of the 1980s.

The complexity of solving the woman question is now connected in the abstract to processes of social integration, attaining social homogeneity, achieving equality, developing democracy and pursuing communist morality. Furthermore, these processes are all interrelated because the stage of developed socialism, described by Chernenko as 'a whole historical epoch',[60] heralds 'the turning of the socialist system into a totality'.[61] As an organic whole, developed socialism faces interrelated tasks of broadening scope.

Attaining equality is thus just one of its tasks. Furthermore, the process of attaining complete social equality between the sexes is now cast as part of two distinct, albeit related, general processes of constructing a socially homogeneous society and a classless one.[62] Social homogeneity here refers to a complete abolition of the old division of labour and a classless society is viewed as one in which an approximation or fusion of 'class forming' characteristics takes place. Processes which in the past made the working class and collective farm peasantry different from each other are now on the wane. The general trend of developed socialism is, therefore, social integration, which leads to 'the increasingly greater assertion of social equality'.[63] Here equality for everyone becomes the main focus, rather than equality according to sex, which is subsumed under 'social equality' as just one aspect of it.

Alongside social integration is a growth in the role of non-class or inter-class distinctions in everyday life. Harking back to a theme popularised by Khrushchev, differences between social groups such as women, pensioners, young workers, young farmers, students and pupils are being underlined. Distinctions between these groups are emphasised, together with the desirability of a differentiated approach to cope with their various needs.[64] These non-class distinctions do not clash with social integration, insist theorists, since they are not divisive in the way that class antagonisms are.

A differentiated approach to the distinct needs of social groups is connected to the development of democracy, the role of trade unions, and an increase in forms of collective agreement (*kollektivnye dogovory*).[65] As part of the growth of democracy, the role of the trade unions in solving social problems increases under developed socialism. In recognising women as a distinct social group, trade union commissions can analyse the difficulties they face and offer policy recommendations to the party to alleviate them. Policy making is thereby broadened through collective agreement. Brezhnev reasserted the relevance of trade unions to the development of democracy at the 17th Trade Union Congress in 1982 and also severely scolded them, along with three ministries, for not paying sufficient attention to issues affecting women.[66]

Just as the role of the trade unions is one aspect of developing democracy, so, too, is an increase in female participation in leadership roles. At the 26th Party Congress it was regretted that 'the opportunities for the promotion of women into responsible posts have still not been fully realised. Such a situation ought to be rectified'.[67] Then, in the draft Party Programme released in 1985, it was noted that the party would be more active in promoting women to positions of leadership.[68] Soon after at the 27th Party Congress, Gorbachev declared that 'women are being moved into leadership posts more actively. They have become more numerous in the composition of the organs of the party and the soviets'.[69] And he was right. It was at this Congress that Alexandra Biryukova was appointed to the Secretariat of the Central Committee of the CPSU. Promotions of women had also taken place in the congresses held in the union republics in the run up to the 27th Congress. Svetlana Kasumova, for example, was appointed in early 1986 to both the Bureau and the Secretariat of the Central Committee of the Soviet republic of Azerbaidzhan.[70]

Whilst the promotion of women is officially supported by the party, success is still gradual and limited. Some Soviet social scientists argue that, although socialism creates the conditions for an increase in the number of women in top jobs, 'due to a number of reasons women do not always take full advantage of this'.[71] And in one recent work, the prevalence of unfair attitudes towards women in the workplace was mentioned. It was pointed out that owing to 'psychological barriers', women's performance at work was generally undervalued, whereas overgenerous estimates were made of male contributions.[72]

In keeping with the spirit of the differentiated approach, Gorbachev appealed at the 27th Party Congress for a revival of the women's councils, or *zhensovety*, in the workplace and in residential areas.[73]

However, the differentiated approach to political mobilisation entails not simply access to management posts, but broader processes such as 'the growth of creative activity' and 'the many-sided harmonious development of the identity' (*lichnost'*) of women.[74] More spare time for women is conducive to developing *lichnost'*, which is in turn made possible by more kindergartens, more new flats, part-time labour, skilled labour and male participation in domestic work. These are policies to which the Soviet leadership is committed. And an expansion of skilled work is part of the general goal of ending all manual, unskilled and heavy labour as proclaimed at the 26th Party Congress and the 17th Trade Union Congress. One dimension to this process of transforming labour is the definitive freeing of women from heavy physical work, night shifts and work in dangerous conditions.[75] This will not only contribute to the resolution of the non-antagonistic contradiction between mental and manual labour, but will also reduce the social division of labour according to sex, diminish skill and wage disparities, promote the rational organisation of labour, ease the double burden, create more free time for women and render motherhood more attractive. In short, 'wide and effective measures' for facilitating a combination of female roles are characteristic of the organic totality of developed socialist society.

8.4 CONCLUSION

From the revolutionary situation of the 1920s we have moved to the stability of the organic totality of developed socialism of the 1960s, 1970s and 1980s. Ideology has been relevant at every stage of Soviet development and the desirability of female activity in the workplace and politics are themes that have always been present. However, the emphasis of Soviet ideology on women has varied. Different female roles have been highlighted at different times, first, consistent with economic, political and demographic priorities, and secondly in keeping with developments in ideology, themselves frequently tied to political concerns. Evidence does, indeed, suggest that ideological statements about female roles are flexibly adapted to meet the priorities of different periods.

Furthermore, Soviet ideology on women, once formulated, itself carries implications for policy and debate. At a very general level, the significance of a declaration that the woman question has been solved is that no special policies for promoting equality of the sexes are needed, since equality already exists or is guaranteed to come about. There is no need to conduct investigations into the problems that women face in the economy, politics and home, since by implication they either confront none or have only to cope with difficulties which will cease through solutions to other problems. Conversely, an unsolved woman question not only warrants investigations into female roles, but also requires an analysis of the position of women in society for informed policy recommendations to be made. How extensive this analysis becomes depends upon how the solution to the woman question is conceived. How equality of the sexes is viewed will affect which questions about female roles are posed, what sort of data are gathered and the kinds of policy proposals that are drawn up.

But simultaneously, the very concepts used, and the nature of the relationship between these concepts, affects the sorts of analyses that are promoted. Concepts not only set the boundaries of enquiry, but also point theoretical discourse in a particular direction. In short, depending upon the extent of the theoretical space generated by a specific interrelationship of concepts, the latitude of debate may vary. In this sense, the parameters of ideology may shape the diversity of issues that come onto the agenda and the limits to the divergence of conclusions. Developed socialism, with its non-antagonistic contradictions, prised open problem areas too long sealed, and gave breadth to debate. And, despite the recent linkage of the woman question to the population problem, broad scope for discussion remains. The continued presence of the concept of 'non-antagonistic contradiction' will ensure at the theoretical level that a return to the strait-jacket of the Stalin years with their numerous 'solved' problems will not take place.

As Soviet concepts generate more and more possible space for discussion, we cannot refrain from indulging in speculation about the probability of ideological developments outstripping policy priorities. Policy makers, after all, do not always have complete control over the direction that the logic of concepts takes, the questions they inspire, or the range of replies. A political leadership may indeed desire debate, but may not anticipate or approve of all of the contributions to it. Reflections upon male roles, once begun, may open up a Pandora's box of non-antagonistic contradictions between the sexes. The theoretical space is there, even if political aversion to the topic remains. And perhaps, under a General Secretary such as Gorbachev, the aversion will be less than before.

NOTES

Some of the information drawn upon in this chapter was gathered in the USSR. I would like to thank the British Council and the Soviet Ministry of Higher and Special Education for trips to Kiev and Moscow in 1979, 1980 and 1985. I am also grateful to the Society for Cultural Relations with the USSR for making possible a visit to Moscow in August 1984.

1. Ideology is here defined as a political belief system which is composed of interrelated ideas. Together these ideas furnish a doctrine which offers a theoretical explanation of reality and defends a preferred political order, either past, present or future. Pursuit of these ideas gives rise to an action programme or strategy to bring about their implementation through political and social action. This definition of ideology is not restricted to Marxist ideology, but is conceived to embrace all ideologies, be they Marxist, anarchist, social democratic, fascist or other.
2. More detailed discussion of the arguments of these periods may be found in Mary Buckley, *Women and Ideology in the Soviet Union* (Hassocks, Sussex: Wheatsheaf, forthcoming).
3. See Richard Stites, *The Women's Liberation Movement in Russia* (Princeton University Press, 1978); and Rudolf Schlesinger, *The Family in the USSR* (London: Routledge, 1949).
4. Inessa F. Armand, *Stat'i, rechi, pis'ma* (Moscow: Politizdat, 1975). For further elaboration see Alix Holt, 'Marxism and women's oppression: Bolshevik theory and practice in the 1920s', in T. Yedlin (ed.), *Women in Eastern Europe and the Soviet Union* (New York: Praeger, 1980), p. 87.
5. Alexandra Kollontai, *Selected Writings*, trans. Alix Holt (New York: Norton, 1977).
6. *Pravda*, 8 March 1939, p. 1.
7. *Pravda*, 8 March 1941, p. 4.
8. *Izvestiya*, 8 March 1933, p. 2.
9. Ibid., p. 3.
10. Ibid.
11. *Izvestiya*, 8 March 1949, p. 3.
12. *Pravda*, 15 February 1956, p. 10.
13. See *KPSS v rezolyutsiyakh i resheniyakh s"ezdov, konferentsii i plenumov TsK*, 8th edn, 14 vols (Moscow: Politizdat, 1970–82), vol. 7, p. 516.
14. Ibid., vol. 8, p. 49.
15. G. Shitarev, 'O novykh formakh partiinoi raboty', *Partiinaya zhizn'*, 1961, no. 11, pp. 10–11.
16. Vera Bil'shai, *Reshenie zhenskogo voprosa v SSSR*, 2nd edn (Moscow: Gospolitizdat, 1959), p. 253.
17. Ibid., pp. 3–4.
18. *Materialy XXII s"ezda KPSS* (Moscow: Gospolitizdat, 1961), p. 393.
19. Some results of this research may be found in Gail Warshofsky Lapidus, *Women in Soviet Society: Equality, Development and Social Change* (Berkeley: University of California Press, 1978). A focus on the relationship between female roles is offered in Mary Buckley, 'Women in the Soviet Union', *Feminist Review*, vol. 8 (summer 1981), pp. 79–106.
20. *Materialy XXIV s"ezda KPSS* (Moscow: Politizdat, 1972), p. 75.
21. *Materialy XXV s"ezda KPSS* (Moscow: Politizdat, 1976), p. 85.

22. N. M. Shishkan, 'Sotsial'no-ekonomicheskie problemy povysheniya effektivnosti obshchestvennogo truda zhenshchin', candidate degree dissertation abstract, Kishinev, 1969; Shishkan, *Trud zhenshchin v usloviyakh razvitogo sotsializma* (Kishinev: Shtiintsa, 1976); A. E. Kotlyar and S. Ya. Turchaninova, *Zanyatost' zhenshchin v proizvodstve* (Moscow: Statistika, 1975); M. Ya. Sonin, 'Ravnye prava, neravnye nagruzki', *Ekonomika i organizatsiya promyshlennogo proizvodstva*, May–June 1978, pp. 5–18; Nadezhda Tatarinova, *Primenenie truda zhenshchin v varodnom khozyaistve SSSR* (Moscow: Nauka, 1979); Z. M. Yuk, 'Voprosy ratsional'nogo ispol'zovaniya truda v Belorusskoi SSR', candidate degree dissertation abstract, Minsk, 1968; N. V. Panova, 'Zhenskii trud v sotsialisticheskom proizvodstve', candidate degree dissertation abstract, Vilnius, 1970; V. I. Kozachenko, 'Sotsial'no-ekonomicheskie problemy ispol'zovaniya zhenskogo truda v kolkhozakh', candidate degree dissertation abstract, Kishinev, 1969; Z. I. Eremina, 'Problemy ispol'zovaniya zhenskogo truda v narodnom khozyaistve SSSR v sovremennykh usloviyakh', candidate degree dissertation abstract, Saratov, 1972.
23. Z. V. Samokhina, 'Puti preodoleniya ostatkov neravenstva zhenshchin i muzhchin v usloviyakh razvitogo sotsialisticheskogo obshchestva', candidate degree dissertation abstract, Moscow, 1972.
24. Eremina, 'Problemy ispol'zovaniya zhenskogo truda', p. 3.
25. Panova, 'Zhenskii trud', p. 16.
26. Joel C. Moses, *The Politics of Female Labor in the Soviet Union* (Ithaca, NY: Cornell University, Western Societies Program Occasional Paper no. 10, 1978), pp. 46–8; Z. A. Volkova et al., *Komissiya po rabote sredi zhenshchin pri FZMK* (Moscow: Profizdat, 1979); Z. A. Volkova et al., *Komissiya profkoma po voprosam truda i byta zhenshchin, okhrany materinstva i detstva* (Moscow: Profizdat, 1984).
27. Shishkan, 'Sotsial'no-ekonomicheskie problemy', p. 17; Shishkan, *Trud*, pp. 163–80.
28. Shishkan, 'Sotsial'no-ekonomicheskie problemy', p. 17; Panova, 'Zhenskii trud', pp. 17–18.
29. Shishkan, 'Sotsial'no-ekonomicheskie problemy', p. 19.
30. Ibid.
31. Panova, 'Zhenskii trud', p. 18. Various views of social scientists on part-time labour for women and other topical issues may be found in Mary Buckley, *Soviet Social Scientists Talking: An Official Debate about Women* (London: Macmillan, 1986).
32. *Materialy XXV s"ezda*, p. 217.
33. *Bakinskii rabochii*, 26 February 1986, p. 6.
34. Stephen Sternheimer, 'Communication and power in Soviet urban politics', in Everett M. Jacobs (ed.), *Soviet Local Politics and Government* (London: Allen and Unwin, 1983), pp. 149–50.
35. Genia Browning, 'Soviet politics – where are the women?', in Barbara Holland (ed.), *Soviet Sisterhood* (London: Fourth Estate Books, 1985), p. 221.
36. N. Kh. Nagiev, 'Kommunizm i sotsial'noe ravenstvo polov', candidate degree dissertation abstract, Baku, 1971, p. 7.
37. S. V. Brova, 'Sotsial'nye problemy zhenskogo truda v promyshlennosti', candidate degree dissertation abstract, Sverdlovsk, 1968, p. 4.

38. Tatarinova, *Primenenie truda zhenshchin*, p. 7.
39. E. B. Gruzdeva, 'Vozrastanie roli zhenshchin–rabotnits v obshchestvennom proizvodstve i sovershenstvovanie ikh byta v usloviyakh razvitogo sotsializma', candidate degree dissertation abstract, Moscow, 1979, p. 1.
40. L. Rzhanitsina, *Female Labour under Socialism: the Socio-Economic Aspects* (Moscow: Progress, 1983), p. 73.
41. Ibid.
42. *Materialy XXVI s"ezda KPSS* (Moscow: Politizdat, 1981), p. 54.
43. Ibid., p.55.
44. *Sotsiologicheskie issledovaniya*, 1982, no. 2, pp. 80–8.
45. E. E. Novikova, *Zhenshchina v razvitom sotsialisticheskom obshchestve* (Moscow: Mysl', 1985), pp. 9–32.
46. N. M. Khodakov, *Molodym suprugam*, 3rd edn (Moscow: Meditsina, 1981), p. 99.
47. D. Valentei, 'Control of demographic processes', in *Demographic Processes* (Moscow: Social Sciences Today, 1983), p. 15.
48. T. Ryabushkin, 'The demographic policy of developed socialist society', ibid., p. 48.
49. Ibid.
50. *Pravda*, 22 March 1977, p. 1.
51. E. E. Novikova, T. N. Sidorova and S. Ya. Turchaninova, *Sovetskie zhenshchiny i profsoyuzy* (Moscow: Profizdat, 1984), p. 162.
52. *Bakinskii rabochii*, 26 February 1986, p. 6.
53. Rzhanitsina, *Female Labour*, p. 168.
54. E. E. Gruzdeva and E. S. Chertikhina, *Trud i byt sovetskikh zhenshchin* (Moscow: Politizdat, 1983), pp. 182–208.
55. Ibid., pp. 220–1.
56. Novikova et al., *Sovetskie zhenshchiny*, p. 8.
57. Valentei, 'Control of demographic processes', p. 11.
58. Novikova et al., *Sovetskie zhenshchiny*, p. 5.
59. Ibid., p. 154.
60. *Bakinskii rabochii*, 5 April 1985, p. 2.
61. R. I. Kosolapov et al., *Developed Socialism: Theory and Practice* (Moscow: Progress, 1983), p. 40.
62. Novikova et al., *Sovetskie zhenshchiny*, p. 4.
63. Kosolapov et al., *Developed Socialism*, p. 133.
64. A. Nelyubin, *Massovo-politicheskaya rabota po mestu zhitel'stva* (Moscow: Moskovskii rabochii, 1983), p. 69.
65. Novikova et al., *Sovetskie zhenshchiny*, pp. 153–249.
66. *Materialy XVII s"ezda professional'nykh soyuzov SSSR* (Moscow: Profizdat, 1982), p. 55.
67. *Materialy XXVI s"ezda*, p. 72.
68. *Bakinskii rabochii*, 26 October 1985.
69. *Bakinskii rabochii*, 26 February 1986.
70. *Bakinskii rabochii*, 2 February 1986.
71. Novikova et al., *Sovetskie zhenshchiny*, p. 55.
72. Novikova, *Zhenshchina v razvitom sotsialisticheskom obshchestve*, p. 69.
73. *Bakinskii rabochii*, 26 February 1986.
74. Novikova et al., *Sovetskie zhenshchiny*, p. 159.
75. Ibid., p. 154.

9 Ideology and the National Question: Marxism–Leninism and the Nationality Policy of the Communist Party of the Soviet Union

PETER DUNCAN

The aim of this chapter is twofold: to outline the development of Soviet Marxism–Leninism in relation to the national question in the USSR; and to consider whether any relationship can be discovered between ideological pronouncements and the actual policies pursued towards national minorities. 'Nationality policy' is not an area that can be fenced off on its own, but is something that forms a part of every field of activity of the Communist Party of the Soviet Union (CPSU): the economy, cadre policy, education and culture, internal security, the armed forces and foreign policy, for example. It would be impossible in a chapter this size to describe, even in outline, the working of nationality policy in all these fields. I shall therefore be highly selective, choosing examples mainly in relation to the questions of federalism, language and cadre policy. With respect to ideology, I shall be especially concerned with references to the flourishing, coming together and fusion of nations.

9.1 BEFORE THE REVOLUTION

A central theme of the *Manifesto of the Communist Party* is the need for the unity of the working classes of all countries. Marx and Engels asserted 'the proletarians have no fatherland', and considered this both a factual and a programmatic statement. Capitalism was depriving the workers of their nationality: 'national differences, and antagonisms between peoples, are daily more and more vanishing'. The emancipation of the proletariat in the leading industrialised states would lead to the still more rapid disappearance of these differences and antagonisms.[1]

It would probably be wrong, however, to conclude that Marx and Engels believed that nations ought to disappear. In *The German Ideology* (1845–6) and again in a letter of 1866, Marx poured scorn on thinkers who expected the workers of the future world to speak a single language, or who believed in the negation of the nationalities. He feared that this would mean in practice the absorption of all nations by one.[2] The founders of Marxism did not expect nationalism to survive capitalism. They considered that the nationalism of their time could be either progressive or reactionary. They proclaimed no general right of nations to self-determination, but viewed each national movement on its own merits in the light of the international struggle of the working class.[3]

Lenin took great pains in his writings on the national question, as on other issues, to show that his views were derived from applying the method and conclusions of Marx and Engels to contemporary problems. In the application of Marxist principles Lenin showed a high degree of flexibility. For example, as a Soviet specialist recently put it, Lenin's views on federalism underwent a 'difficult evolution':[4] from hostility to federalism to acceptance, under the pressure of events, of the need for it. At the same time, Lenin consistently followed the founding fathers in both theory and practice, by emphasising the need for the unity of the workers of all nationalities, and by subordinating the national question to the class struggle. He also shared their belief that the interest of the proletariat were best served by the existence of large states, which offered the maximum potential for economic development.

In Lenin's letter to S. G. Shaumyan of 6 December 1913 he supported regional autonomy, while fiercely opposing federalism. The right to self-determination did not signify a right to federation. Lenin clearly hoped that the minorities would see the economic and political advantages of remaining in a large state, in which they would be guaranteed equality and language rights as citizens, but no particular collective privileges. If a nation wished to secede, however, it could 'go to the devil'. Lenin favoured 'democratic centralism' within the state, together with 'the autonomy of all parts.' The right to secession was an exception to the general preference for centralism, an exception dictated by the need to overcome the minorities' fears of Great-Russian nationalism. Similar motives were behind Lenin's rejection of Shaumyan's belief that Russian should be the state language. It was a progressive step for the minorities to learn Russian, but it would be still more progressive if they chose to do this voluntarily.[5]

Confusion was to arise over Lenin's attitude to the longer-term future of relations between nationalities. In his writings he repeatedly referred to the *sblizhenie* (coming together, convergence) and *sliyanie* (merging, fusion) of nations. Unfortunately he used these words with different meanings in different contexts. Sometimes the process of *sblizhenie* and *sliyanie* of nations was occurring under capitalism; sometimes he used the terms to refer to the unity of the masses against capitalism; at other times he used them to refer to the fusion of nations and the dying out of national distinctions under communism. These differences of meaning account for some of the confusion among Soviet specialists on the nationality question as to whether *sliyanie* is going on today, under 'mature socialism,' or whether it is a phenomenon of the future.

Thus, in late 1913, Lenin wrote of the '*sliyanie* of all nations in a higher unity', which grew with every stretch of railway line, every international trust or trade union.[6] He spoke of class-conscious workers fighting for the '*sliyanie* of workers of all nationalities in the struggle against reaction and every bourgeois nationalism'.[7] In these cases *sliyanie* is a contemporaneous process. In early 1916, he was clearly referring to the future, however: 'An aim of socialism is not only the abolition of the fragmentation of humanity into small states and every national isolation, not only the *sblizhenie* of nations, but also their *sliyanie*'. This *sliyanie* was 'inevitable'[8] and it would come after the disappearance of classes.[9] The *sblizhenie–sliyanie* formula appears seven times in two other works of 1916, referring in each case to a process occurring after the socialist revolution. On one of these occasions it is stated that the process 'will be completed with the withering away of the state'.[10] After the October Revolution, Lenin continued to use the formulation in different senses. Thus, in early 1918, he described the federation of nations as 'a transition to voluntary *sliyanie*'.[11] A year later, however, he called for the '*sblizhenie* and *sliyanie* of the proletarians and working masses of all nations for the revolutionary struggle for the overthrow of the bourgeoisie'.[12]

9.2 FEDERATION AND *KORENIZATSIYA*

In 1916 Lenin wrote that the right of self-determination was not absolute; the liberation of large nations was more important than the self-determination of small nations. Lenin explicitly endorsed Marx's view of the necessity of waging war against reactionary nations; if a few nations began a socialist revolution and others represented bourgeois reaction, the socialist nations would have to crush the latter.[13] After October 1917, the new Soviet government reaffirmed the right of nations to self-determination. Already in December 1917, however, the hostility of the Ukrainian government to the Bolsheviks led Stalin, the People's Commissar for Nationalities, to question this right, and in January 1918 he redefined the principle to be 'a right not of the bourgeoisie, but of the working masses of the given nation'.[14]

Stalin's explicit subordination of national self-determination to the needs of socialism was in line with the position taken by Marx, Engels and Lenin. The idea that self-determination was to be exercised by the toilers appeared in Lenin's draft proposal for the Constituent Assembly, the 'Declaration of the Rights of the Toiling and Exploited People'. This conceded the principle of a 'federation of the Soviet Republics of Russia'. The workers and peasants 'of all the nations of Russia' were to decide at their own Congresses of Soviets whether or not to participate in the federation.[15] During the Civil War the Bolsheviks sought to bring the toilers, as represented by the Russian Communist Party (RCP), to power in as much of the former Russian Empire as possible. Unfortunately, the local nationalities were poorly represented among the industrial workers, and so the dictatorship of the proletariat meant the dictatorship of a Russian minority.

The fact that Lenin was anxious about antagonising the minorities at this time is clear from his remarks during the discussion of the Party Programme, adopted at the 8th Congress in March 1919. 'From the workers of those nations which under capitalism were oppressors', he observed, 'are demanded special care in relation to the national feeling of the oppressed nations . . . and aid to ensure not only the actual equality but also the development of the languages and literatures of the formerly oppressed nations, in order to remove all the traces of the alienation and distrust inherited from the capitalist epoch'.[16] Communists who opposed the use of non-Russian languages were Great-Russian chauvinists.[17] It should be stressed that Lenin made these points on many occasions.[18] In 1920 he reaffirmed that national and state divisions would 'still persist for a very, very long time even after the realisation of the dictatorship of the proletariat on a world scale'.[19]

The 1919 Party Programme incorporated Lenin's ideas on national equality and the right to secede, while emphasising proletarian unity. A 'federal association of states' was envisaged as 'one of the transitional forms' to 'complete unity' (*polnoe edinstvo*).[20] As well as the RSFSR, Communist-ruled soviet republics were established in the Ukraine and Belorussia, and for a time in Estonia, Latvia and Lithuania. But the 8th Congress made it clear that, despite the existence of these independent states, the RCP was to remain a centralised organisation operating within them all. The Ukrainian and other regional committees were subordinated to the RCP Central Committee.[21] Thus, the leaders of the 'independent' republics were subordinated to Moscow.

In 1920–21, the Bolshevik conquest of Azerbaijan, Armenia and Georgia, considered strategically and economically necessary, raised the question of federal links between the soviet republics. Stalin advocated 'autonomisation', the transformation of the republics into autonomous republics of the RSFSR. Lenin had become increasingly worried about the behaviour of Moscow's emissaries in Transcaucasia and the need to respect native opinion. On 26 September 1922, Lenin sent a letter to the Politburo rejecting 'autonomisation' and insisting that the RSFSR and other independent republics should federate as equals in a 'union of Soviet Republics of Europe and Asia'.[22] As a first step the three Transcaucasian republics were federated into one, over Georgian Communist objections; then on 30 December, the RSFSR, the Ukraine, Belorussia and Transcaucasia united in the USSR.[23] On the same day, Lenin was in despair at the brutal treatment of the Georgians by Moscow's representative, G. K. Ordzhonikidze, and the collusion of Stalin and F. E. Dzerzhinsky. He predicted, in one of his last writings, that with the Great-Russian chauvinist domination of the state apparatus, the 'freedom to secede' from the USSR would be 'a mere scrap of paper'. The 'strictest rules' would have to be introduced to guarantee the position of the national languages in the republics, and it might even be necessary to re-devolve to the republics responsibility for all aspects of internal affairs.[24]

In practice, the 1924 USSR Constitution reserved most powers to the centre, reinforcing the already centralised nature of the party. On the other hand, the 12th Party Congress in 1923 adopted the policy of *korenizatsiya*: seeking roots in the minority populations by recruiting 'national' (that is, national minority) cadres to run the national republics, and increasing the role of the national languages. Lenin's goal of *sliyanie* was not abandoned; but national cultures, 'national in form, socialist in content', would be encouraged to blossom for the time being. Instruction in the national languages was rapidly introduced into the schools, and in some cases into higher education as well.[25] Many languages which formerly existed only in the vernacular were given alphabets and literary forms. The Russian language ceased to be a compulsory subject in the schools of the national republics. In the Ukraine, where most of the industrial workers were Russian-speaking, the party leadership was handed over to native Ukrainians. These promoted the Ukrainian language to the point where, in 1933, eight ninths of factory newspapers were in Ukrainian and all university lectures had to be delivered in that language.[26] The 15th Congress in 1926 resolved that particular attention should be devoted to economic development in the formerly backward borderlands.[27] This policy led to the migration of workers, specialists and administrators from the RSFSR to develop industry in the non-Russian republics and train personnel from the native population. At least up to the early 1930s party recruitment of native cadres was pursued energetically. It is difficult to imagine that all these efforts for the well-being of the non-Russians would have emerged had it not been for Lenin's repeated concern for them in his writings, which became transformed into the ideology of his successors.

9.3 STALIN AND RUSSIAN NATIONALISM

In 1930 the party declared that Great-Russian chauvinism was a larger threat than local nationalism.[28] Russian nationalist ideas seem to have been growing within the party, under the impact of 'socialism in one country'.[29] Stalin apparently increasingly saw the blossoming of the nationalities as a threat to the state. Already in the 1920s, 'Muslim communists' led by Sultan Galiev had been purged on charges of nationalism.[30] In the borderlands, collectivisation inevitably took the form of an attack on the national minorities, as the Russian workers from the towns sought to impose change on the non-Russian peasants. The Kirghiz and Kazakhs suffered heavy losses as nomads were forcibly settled. In the Ukraine, it was openly claimed that an aim of collectivisation was to abolish the individual peasant basis of Ukrainian nationalism. Purges within the Ukrainian party in 1930–32 proved to be the prelude to the artificially-induced famine of 1932–33 which killed perhaps seven million people. In 1933 N. A. Skrypnik, the leading official proponent of Ukrainianisation, committed suicide amidst charges of nationalism, and many nationally-minded intellectuals were exiled or shot.[31] From 1934, central party leaders began openly to express and encourage Russian nationalist feeling. Accusations of bourgeois nationalism abounded against non-Russian communist leaders, and the native élites were devastated in the purges. By 1938, many national schools had omitted Russian from the curriculum; in that year, it was made compulsory.[32] It would appear that the regime was seeking to build a political base among the Great-Russian population, as the dominant nation, in order to hold the Soviet Union together.

In 1941, large numbers of Ukrainians and people from the Caucasus and newly-incorporated Baltic nationalities welcomed the Nazi invasion. Some fought with the Germans against Soviet Russia (as did some Russians also). Stalin's accusation that whole nationalities had collaborated with the Nazis was disowned by later Soviet leaders.[33] But the deportation of these groups to Central Asia was a signal to the other nationalities, especially the Muslims, to accept their subordinate place in the increasingly Russian-dominated USSR. Stalin's invocation of Tsarist Russian heroes in the Great Patriotic War and his toast to the Russian People, the 'leading nation'[34] of the Soviet Union, were bids for Russian support.

The final years of Stalin saw a celebration of this ideological innovation, the leading role of the Russian nation. The inventiveness and creativity of the Russians were praised to unheard-of heights, and tsarist colonialism was held to have been of positive benefit to the minorities. Traditional heroes of the non-Russians, such as Imam Shamil who resisted tsarist expansion into the Caucasus, were portrayed as reactionaries.[35]

9.4 KHRUSHCHEV AND THE RESURGENCE OF THE NATIONALITIES

In 1956, Khrushchev denounced Stalin's terror and the deportations of whole nationalities. He published Lenin's last articles, attacking Russian chauvinism and Stalin personally. These actions formed a watershed. They laid the political and ideological basis for the resurgence of the cultures of the national republics and their political cohesion. An early indication of this was the decision by the Azerbaijan Supreme Soviet, within months of Khrushchev's speech, that Azeri would be the sole official language of that republic. Historians from the traditionally Muslim nationalities sought to rehabilitate Shamil fully, while Moscow historians insisted that he was objectively reactionary. Decisions in the late 1950s increased the economic and cultural powers of the union republics.[36]

As the 1959 census was to reveal, native languages were gaining at the expense of Russian. Khrushchev was hostile to Russian nationalism but promoted the Russian language, apparently as a means of accelerating the *sliyanie* of nations in the USSR. It may have been the case that his promotion of *sliyanie* was in response to rising minority nationalism. It seems more likely, though, that it was his utopian claim that communism was around the corner which drove him to try to reduce the significance of national distinctions. The Party Programme of 1961, adopted at the 22nd Congress, attacked nationalism and chauvinism and posited the *rastsvet* (flourishing) of nations under socialism. It laid down that, as communism was built, the nations and national cultures would draw closer together (*sblizhenie*) until complete unity (*polnoe edinstvo*) was achieved. The word *sliyanie* did not appear in the Programme, although it was used at the Congress. The Programme reaffirmed Lenin's view that national distinctions would take considerably longer to disappear than class distinctions. The Russian language was described as having become 'the language of inter-nationality communication and cooperation of all the peoples of the USSR'. The Programme left open the possibility of increasing the rights of the republics; on the other hand, it stated that republican boundaries were 'increasingly losing their former significance'.[37] Scholars such as P. G. Semenov of the Academy of Sciences' Institute of State and Law were more specific in indicating the temporary nature of the federal system. This sounded ominous for the national republics, since Khrushchev was proposing to rewrite the Soviet Constitution.[38]

9.5 BREZHNEV AND THE POSTPONEMENT OF *SLIYANIE*

After the overthrow of Khrushchev, the new leadership of Brezhnev and Kosygin refrained from repeating the promises of an imminent communist society. In the field of nationality relations the talk of *sliyanie* disappeared from Politburo members' speeches. At the 23rd Party Congress in March 1966, while speaking of the Soviet people in the singular, Brezhnev emphasised the *sblizhenie* of the peoples (plural) of the USSR. He promised that the party would care for the interests and national particularities of every people, and raise all Soviet people in the spirit of proletarian internationalism.[39] The Central Committee ideological journal *Kommunist* in 1969 spelt out that *sblizhenie* was not *sliyanie*; the latter, in the sense of the elimination of all national differences, was a long process which would occur only after the achievement of world communism.[40] This position would seem to accord with the views of Lenin as outlined above.

In the meantime, while political leaders were moving towards this position, scholars were being encouraged to debate the dynamics of nationality relations. Since 1959, Semenov had been arguing that national statehood was no longer necessary for the development of Soviet nations. Political and social equality between the nations had been achieved; 'national statehood and federation as a whole have fulfilled their historical mission'. Soviet society was approaching the point where the full state and legal *sliyanie* of nations would 'become a matter of the foreseeable future'.[41] He continued to develop this Khrushchevite line into the Brezhnev period. In 1965, he rejected the view (which he attributed to E. V. Tadevosyan) that Lenin had always favoured the creation of national state units and by 1917 had come to favour federalism on principle. Rather, the Soviet federation had arisen out of the specific circumstances of the Civil War. Semenov characterised the party's aim now as to proceed 'through the strengthening of national sovereignty to the all-round unity of Soviet nations and nationalities, with the final perspective of their complete inevitable *sliyanie*'.[42] Implicitly, *sliyanie* might take place in the USSR alone and not depend on the world victory of communism.

In 1966–67 the journal *Voprosy istorii* hosted a discussion on the theory of the nation. In the first article, two Volgograd professors, P. M. Rogachev and M. A. Sverdlin, spoke of 'certain elements of *sliyanie*' existing among the Soviet nations already. Perhaps they had the USSR in mind when they wrote, ostensibly about Africa: 'ethnic groups of very diverse origin, living within one unitary state, often fuse into one nation'. But they defended the position of the national republics: 'national statehood' was 'already an attribute' of socialist nations.[43] Whereas Rogachev and Sverdlin emphasised the importance of a common territory and integrated economic life as characteristics of a nation, M. S. Dzhunusov of the Academy of Sciences' Institute of Philosophy emphasised the importance of ethnic self-consciousness and culture. 'Ethnic boundaries will still exist for a long time, even after the disappearance of state frontiers'.[44] It seems that scholars who favoured accelerated *sliyanie* saw this as flowing from growing Soviet economic integration and the dispersion of the nationalities around the whole country, whereas those who saw *sliyanie* in the distant future believed that national identification had more subjective causes.

Grey Hodnett has pointed out that both Russians and non-Russians were found on each side in the debate on the need for national statehood.[45] It is not necessarily the case that scholars' views reflect those of a political patron, but academic debates in the USSR are not separate from discussions among policy-makers. In November 1969, the fiftieth anniversary of a letter by Lenin protesting against Great-Russian chauvinism in Soviet Turkestan was marked by the publication of a 'joint issue' of the Russian-language newspapers of the five Central Asian republican parties.[46] This event would seem to be a warning by the Central Asian élites against returning to a Stalinist nationality policy, at a time when the rehabilitation of Stalin was being actively considered in Moscow.

In outline, the Brezhnev leadership in the 1970s settled for an ideological position that defended national statehood, i.e. the need for federalism; postponed *sliyanie* to the indefinite future; but sought increasingly to emphasise the greatness of the Russian people. The last factor was never pursued to the extent that it had been under late Stalinism, and probably could not have been without the use of mass terror against the national minorities and their élites. On the other hand, the view of Russian superiority appeared in party documents (which it had not under Stalin) and thus became enmeshed with the official ideology. At the 24th Congress in 1971, Brezhnev said: 'In the formation, strengthening and development of this powerful union of peoples with equal rights, which have taken the road to socialism, all the nations and nationalities of our country have played their role, above all the great Russian people. (*Applause*). Its revolutionary energy, selflessness, diligence and deep internationalism have rightly won it the sincere respect of all the peoples of our socialist Motherland. (*Prolonged applause*).' But he attacked 'nationalism, chauvinism, national narrowness and conceit in any form' and promised 'profound respect for all nations and nationalities'. Brezhnev made no mention of *sliyanie*, but said that the party was committed to 'the flourishing of socialist nations and their gradual *sblizhenie*'. He continued: 'In the years of socialist construction in our country there arose a *new historical community of people – the Soviet people*'. He also used the phrase 'multinational Soviet people'.[47] These ideological phrases, often repeated, became linked with the idea that the Soviet Union was at a stage of 'mature' or 'developed' socialism.[48] This latter viewpoint, formulated in the Brezhnev era and accepted by his successors, implies that communism is a long way off; so, therefore, is *sliyanie*, and it is not necessary to refer to it continuously.

Brezhnev's speech in 1972, on the fiftieth anniversary of the USSR, essentially repeated the themes of the 24th Congress, singling out the Russian people. The speech has become famous for its claim that 'the national question, in the form in which it reached us from the past, was solved in full, finally and irreversibly'. But Brezhnev went on to say that relations between nationalities continued to throw up new problems and tasks, on top of existing nationalist prejudices.[49] While the General Secretary emphasised the 'all-round *sblizhenie*' and 'cohesion' of the nationalities, it is interesting that republican First Secretaries on this occasion preferred to speak of 'flourishing', emphasising their continued separateness.[50]

The Soviet Constitution of 1977 retained the federal structure, while incorporating the principle of 'democratic centralism' into the state as advocated by Lenin in 1916. On the adoption of the Constitution, Brezhnev said that certain 'very few' comrades had argued that there was now a single Soviet nation and that the republics could therefore be liquidated. But they were confusing the 'socio-political unity of the Soviet people' with the disappearance of national distinctions, and it would be wrong artificially to force the process of *sblizhenie*.[51] In the course of the discussion on the draft Constitution, proposals were made to enhance the rights of the Union Republics, but the only one incorporated into the final version was the suggestion of Moscow University Law Faculty to define the Union Republic as 'a sovereign Soviet socialist State' (article 76).[52] This would appear to contradict the reference to the 'sovereignty of the USSR' (article 75). The Constitution also gave the union republics power to participate in federal policy-making (article 77) and granted them representation on the Presidium of the Supreme Soviet and the Council of Ministers of the USSR (articles 120 and 129, confirming a situation existing since the late 1960s).[53]

In the late 1970s, Russian nationalist sentiment became increasingly strong in sections of the party apparatus, the Komsomol and in some cultural fields. Sometimes this was linked with anti-Semitism, masquerading as anti-Zionism. From 1978, anniversary messages from the Central Committee to the republics regularly referred to the 'great Russian people'.[54] The Russian nationalist campaign reached its height in 1980 with the 600th anniversary of the Russian defeat of the Tatars at Kulikovo Field, celebrated at a time when the invasion of Afghanistan was already having unfavourable effects on some Central Asians. At the 26th Congress in 1981, Brezhnev's last, he praised the 'disinterested assistance of the Russian people' to the national minorities and called for the republican parties to do more for the cultural and language needs of the 'non-indigenous' population, presumably referring particularly to the Russians. He denounced chauvinism, nationalism, anti-Semitism and Zionism, and spoke of 'unity' and 'all-round *sblizhenie*', but not *sliyanie*.[55]

While the Brezhnev leadership defended socialist federalism and postponed *sliyanie*, academics retained some freedom to take different positions on the national question. A. E. Mordinov, a Yakutsk philosopher, claimed in 1971 that *sliyanie* was a process already occurring under socialism. He claimed that Lenin understood *sliyanie* to mean 'complete unity, and nothing else'. Mordinov was talking of political, socio-economic and ideological *sliyanie*, rather than a racial–demographic process of the disappearance of national distinctions. He claimed that *sliyanie* had been wrongly associated with the view of Makar Nagulnov in Mikhail Sholokhov's *Virgin Soil Upturned*, of a future in which all people will have the same darkish colour of skin. Mordinov was implying that national differences would not disappear; and he quoted Lenin's writings against Russian chauvinism in defence of minority cultures and languages.[56] V. P. Sherstobitov in 1972 rejected Mordinov's interpretation of Lenin and emphasised the latter's centralism; he implied that all national differences would ultimately disappear. Like Mordinov, Sherstobitov claimed that 'elements of *sliyanie*' already existed, but it seems that the term 'assimilation' would be more appropriate to the examples he gave of minor nationalities adopting the Russian language.[57] A collection co-edited by Sherstobitov in 1975, however, hardly mentions *sliyanie*, stressing 'flourishing', *sblizhenie* and 'spiritual unity'.[58]

A scholar whose writing on the national question appeared to reflect the ideas of the Brezhnev leadership is Mikhail I. Kulichenko, head of the Section for the Theory of Nations and Nationality Relations of the Institute of Marxism–Leninism. He has rejected Mordinov's view that *sliyanie* meant only 'complete unity', and cited Engels and Lenin to show that under full world communism ethnic differences between nations will wither away and a single world language emerge. He accused Mordinov and others of implying that nations were eternal.[59] In a work of 1972, Kulichenko defended national statehood in the period leading from the phase of developed socialism up to 'complete unity'. National statehood helped encourage national pride in the building of socialism and loyalty to the USSR.[60] 'Complete unity' would come only when communism had basically been achieved. It would involve economic and political equality, a reduction in the importance of national statehood and the mutual enrichment of cultures. Russian would be the language of communication between the nationalities, but the national languages would continue to develop. Only after 'complete unity' would the movement towards *sliyanie* begin; although he added (somewhat confusingly) that elements of *sliyanie* already existed under socialism, in the sense of the increasing homogeneity of social, economic and political life.[61]

Kulichenko wrote in 1976 that it was generally accepted that transformations of nationality relations would take place very slowly. This, however, was to ignore the rapid changes in the development of some of the backward peoples of the USSR; and it was difficult to predict how the world victory of socialism would affect Soviet nationality relations. The fate of each nation, in the meantime, was not 'passively to await the inevitable *sliyanie*' but to develop its own possibilities.[62] Ethnic differences would persist after the disappearance of national states, but nations could not continue to exist after the social factors that had created them had evaporated. Instead of nations, new forms of community would evolve under communism.[63]

In two of his works of 1981 Kulichenko emphasised the importance of the federal system, which had been protected by the 1977 Constitution. He made no reference to the declining significance of national statehood;[64] it was necessary to strengthen both the federal bodies and the organs of national statehood. Such a statement might seem to have little meaning. In fact, his emphasis was on strengthening the centre, as economic imperatives dictated central decision-making on the implementation of technical progress and the conservation of natural resources. Kulichenko attacked Semenov for wishing to create a unitary state, asserting that a federal system would be justified for a long time to come.[65] He referred to the April 1979 Central Committee decree on ideological work, which called for respect for the dignity and culture of the minorities. He rejected the idea that the Soviet people was being transformed into a single nation; it was composed of many nations, although what was common to them was more important than what divided them.[66]

At a round-table organised by the journal *Istoriya SSSR* in December 1979, Kulichenko suggested that the role of the 'narrowly national, specifically national' was gradually diminishing. This provoked a sharp response from G. O. Zimanas, chief editor of the Lithuanian *Komunistas*. Kulichenko, he said, had not made himself clear. If he was referring to language, he was wrong, because national languages were flourishing under socialism. Zimanas asked scholars to stop talking about *sliyanie*, since it was not mentioned in any Central Committee document.[67]

Perhaps Zimanas' request had some effect. While rejecting the 'eternity of nations', Kulichenko suggested in 1981 that the concept of *sliyanie* might be soft-pedalled. Confusion had arisen from the fact that some writers were using the word incorrectly, to refer to particular cases of assimilation occurring under developed socialism. He pointed out: 'there are still not a few people on whom the very concept "*sliyanie* of nations" often acts as an irritant, provoking negative phenomena in consciousness and behaviour'.[68] Kulichenko added that *sliyanie* had not been mentioned at the 24th Congress, and in 1973 and 1977 Brezhnev had rejected the idea that *sliyanie* was in progress. Noting that K. P. Buslov had claimed that *sliyanie* of nations was occurring in a socio-political but not ethnic sense, Kulichenko suggested that the term should be reserved for the disappearance of ethnic distinctions. *Sliyanie* was inappropriate for the present, when national statehood and national cultures were being preserved.[69] It should be added that P. N. Fedoseev, Vice-President of the Academy of Sciences, held a similar position to Buslov's. In a 1980 article in *Kommunist*, Fedoseev stated that when Lenin had used *sliyanie* with reference to the socialist stage of development, he had used it in a political sense: 'not the removal of national distinctions, but a tighter unity, a fraternal union of socialist nations'.[70]

9.6 FROM BREZHNEV TO GORBACHEV

During the last years of the Brezhnev era, a growing ideological emphasis on the Russian people was accompanied by a major attempt to strengthen the role of the Russian language, and by the increasing weight of Russians in the apex of the party. In its first issue for 1982, *Istoriya SSSR* carried an article entitled 'The Role of the Russian Socialist Nation in the Development and Strengthening of the Internationalist Unity of the Soviet People'. This was a paean of praise to the Russian people, 'and first of all the Russian working class', for their aid to the other Soviet peoples. In keeping with Brezhnev's line, the article made no reference to the future *sliyanie*, in which the Russian nation would disappear together with all others.[71] Challenges to the Brezhnev line began not after his death, but around the time that Andropov rejoined the Central Committee Secretariat in May 1982 and was given responsibilities in the field of ideology. Already the May issue of *Problemy mira i sotsializma* included an article by D. A. Kunaev, Politburo member and Kazakh First Secretary, citing Lenin on *sliyanie*.[72]

At a conference in Riga in June 1982, R. I. Kosolapov, chief editor of *Kommunist* and a Central Committee member, launched a strong attack on those who wished to abandon the concept of *sliyanie* and who had even made it difficult for others to discuss it. Citing Lenin's view that *sliyanie* was an aim of socialism, Kosolapov said that some people, nevertheless, linked it with great-power chauvinism. He specifically attacked Kulichenko for soft-pedalling the concept in order not to upset people. But Kosolapov's view of *sliyanie* did not include the elimination of all ethnic distinctions. His view was similar to that of Mordinov in 1971 (see above); he cited the same passage from Sholokhov as Mordinov had, also claiming that it portrayed a false conception of *sliyanie*. Kosolapov ridiculed the idea that people in all continents would have the same skin, eyes, hair and even language. He went on: 'Racial–national–ethnic distinctions between large groups of the population . . . will be subject to essential changes, but are in principle indestructible. Only under this condition can one realistically think of the future *sliyanie* of nations'.[73] Kosolapov claimed that economic development was bringing the nations and classes of the USSR together, a theme repeated by other speakers such as Arutyunyan, who emphasised the growth of the production intelligentsia among the non-Russians. Referring to the 'vanguard role of the Russian workers', Kosolapov spoke of the dangers to social and national relations if substantial numbers of industrial workers were not recruited from all the major Soviet nationalities. He pointed to the ideological benefits that would result from the proposed redeployment of surplus labour from Central Asia and the Caucasus to the labour-deficit areas of the RSFSR.[74]

Kosolapov appears in Riga to have been alone in his attitude to *sliyanie*; certainly B. N. Ponomarev, candidate Politburo member and Central Committee Secretary, avoided the term.[75] Nevertheless, a leading article in Kosolapov's journal in August 1982, discussing national relations, referred to the 'future *sliyanie* of nations', while asserting that nobody wished to accelerate it artificially.[76] The speech by Andropov, by then General Secretary, on the sixtieth anniversary of the USSR in December 1982 seemed at first to mark the full rehabilitation of the concept of *sliyanie*.

Andropov said: 'Our final goal is clear. It is, to use V. I. Lenin's words, "not only the *sblizhenie* of nations, but also their *sliyanie*". The party well understands that the path to this goal is long. Here it is impossible in any event either to run ahead or to allow any holding back of processes that have already matured'. Nationality problems would survive 'while nations exist, while there are national distinctions. And they will exist for a long time, much longer than class distinctions'.[77] Andropov's implication was that national differences would ultimately disappear; it would seem, then, perhaps paradoxically, that Andropov did not subscribe to

Kosolapov's understanding of *sliyanie*, but was closer to Kulichenko's.

Progress had led to growing national consciousness, said Andropov, but this should not lead to national arrogance, conceit or disrespect to other nationalities. The continued existence of these was due not only to throwbacks from capitalism but also to mistakes of the present. All the nationalities in a republic should receive their due representation in party and state bodies. While praising the Russian people (in a low key), Andropov called for tact and attention to be paid to questions of language, historical monuments, historiography and the allocation of cadres, in order to promote internationalism.[78] Addressing the Presidium of the Supreme Soviet in January 1983, Andropov urged that more attention be given to the specific needs of all the nationalities, 'especially the small peoples'.[79]

Thus Andropov combined *sliyanie* with expressions of concern for national rights. K. U. Chernenko, Politburo member and Central Committee Secretary with responsibility for ideology, made a passing reference to *sliyanie* in December 1982.[80] After this, it appears that no Politburo member or republican leader mentioned it. Why the word was introduced and then abandoned remains a mystery. Martha Olcott is right to see Andropov's sixtieth anniversary speech as an assertion of his authority in nationality affairs.[81] It seems likely that both Andropov and Chernenko, whatever their other differences, were united in reasserting the importance of ideology, in reaction to the cynicism of the latter Brezhnev years. Whether either of them wished to use *sliyanie* as an ideological weapon against those who promoted 'eternal Russia', and whether they backed down in the face of opposition, are matters for speculation at present. At the June 1983 Central Committee Plenum on ideology, Andropov and Chernenko both used *sblizhenie*. Chernenko spoke of the need to study the specific needs of the nationalities, if ideological work was to be effective.[82] As General Secretary, Chernenko appears to have made little impact on the national question; in his speech to the April 1984 Central Committee Plenum on the preparation of the new party programme, he referred to the 'gradual but undeviating *sblizhenie*' of nations.[83]

While the leaders avoided the term, specialists continued to discuss *sliyanie*. A. M. Khalilov of Daghestan University and E. V. Tadevosyan of the Ministry of Foreign Affaris, in separate articles, insisted that *sliyanie* was for the future, not the present. Khalilov argued that national statehood was being strengthened. In most union republics the titular nationality was increasing its share of the population, and where it was not, the fall was not significant. He ignored the situation in

Estonia and Latvia where the share of the titular nationality has been steadily falling. Tadevosyan saw a future 'nationless' humanity, but noted in the meantime the low rate of party membership among the Kirghiz, Moldavians, Uzbeks and Turkmenians.[84]

Further support for a future *sliyanie* came from Academician Yu. V. Bromlei, director of the Academy's Insititue of Ethnography. He identified some processes of *sliyanie* in the present, the fusion of ethnic groups to form nations; and some ethnic assimilation, involving mixed marriages or dispersed nationalities such as the Jews. But he saw the main ethnic process in the USSR as being 'inter-ethnic integration'. This was the *sblizhenie* of nations in economic, social, political–ideological and ethno-cultural contexts, and it laid the basis for *sliyanie* in the distant future.[85] The chief editor of the Azerbaijan *Kommunist*, A. F. Dashdamirov, emphasised that *sliyanie* was a long way away, and would come only under mature communism. The present was a time of internationalisation, of the flourishing and *sblizhenie* of national cultures.[86] Finally, a book by Kulichenko which appeared in English in 1984 has at least five references to 'merging' as being a phenomenon of the future, two in which it is stated to be a phenomenon of today and two in which it is denied that it is part of the CPSU's current policy.[87]

The historian G. T. Tavadov discussed in late 1984 the contradiction between the flourishing and *sblizhenie* of nations, which would only be overcome with *sliyanie*. This logical contradiction was reflected in a number of political contradictions, including the contradiction between each nationality and the Soviet people as a whole. Tavadov's view was that, in the past, the priority had been to develop the backward nations and promote national statehood. Now that backwardness had been overcome, however, it was necessary to assert the prior economic interests of the USSR over the individual nationalities. This is the policy which seems to have been implemented since the late 1970s. The other contradictions identified by Tavadov were between individual republics, between the titular and non-titular nationalities within a republic, and contradictions within multinational collectives.[88]

The definitive statement of party ideology in relation to the national question came in the new edition of the CPSU Programme, approved at the 27th Party Congress in February–March 1986. This was an opportunity for M. S. Gorbachev, General Secretary since March 1985, to make his mark. Perhaps the most significant change was the omission of any reference to the 'great Russian people'. In other respects, the Programme continued the trends of the previous few years. It attacked both nationalism and chauvinism and repeated the Brezhnev line that while the national problem remaining from the past had been solved, new tasks continued to arise. It spoke of the 'further flourishing' and 'undeviating *sblizhenie*' of the nations, warning that *sblizhenie* could be neither accelerated nor held back. It contained no threats to the federal system, but promised 'the further raising of the role' of the republics in solving all-union tasks. There was no mention of *sliyanie*: *sblizhenie* would bring 'in the distant historical perspective, the complete unity of nations'. It will be recalled that this 'complete unity' referred to also in the 1961 Programme, was seen by Kulichenko as a stage to be reached only after the achievement of communism, and it would develop into *sliyanie*. The new Programme, it should be pointed out, deals with the 'improvement of socialism and the gradual transition to communism', and *sliyanie* would seem to be consigned to an even more remote future. At the same time, the need for non-Russians to master Russian is emphasised.[89]

Gorbachev made no mention of *sliyanie* in his report to the 27th Congress. He spoke against 'attempts to shut oneself off from the objective process of the mutual influence and *sblizhenie* of national cultures'.[90] The decision to avoid excessive praise for the Russians, and maintain the embargo on *sliyanie* in party documents, may reflect Gorbachev's experience in handling nationality problems; the Stavropol territory, where he spent most of his career, includes the Karachai–Cherkess autonomous region with its non-Slav population.

It may be too early to point to changes in the policies pursued towards the nationalities since 1982. Throughout the period of Andropov's dominance there were attacks on some literary and dissident manifestations of Russian nationalism which had been allowed while Brezhnev was in power. At the same time, the Russian language has continued to be promoted (particularly in the school reform) as a tool to be used along with the native language. Virtually all the new appointments to the Politburo and Secretariat made under Andropov and Gorbachev up to March 1986 inclusive (there were none under Chernenko) have been of Russians. The only exceptions were N. N. Slyunkov, Belorussian First Secretary, elected a candidate Politburo member under Gorbachev; and more significantly, Heydar Aliev, First Deputy Prime Minister, and E. A. Shevardnadze, Foreign Minister, both with full Politburo status, chosen under Andropov and Gorbachev respectively. The Politburo elected at the 27th Party Congress, then, continued to be dominated by Russians, who made up eight of the twelve full members and six of the seven candidate members. The Secretariat was composed of ten Russians and a Belorussian. In some union republics, especially in

Central Asia, anti-corruption purges during Gorbachev's first year in office represented attempts to re-assert central control by making changes in the local leadership.

9.7 CONCLUSION

It appears that it would be wrong to speak of a single ideology, a single Marxism–Leninism, having dominated the USSR since its formation. Rather there have been a number of ideologies, all known as Marxism–Leninism, containing different combinations of Marxism, Leninism and Russian nationalism. (For non-Russians, Marxism–Leninism might instead include elements of their own nationalism). It also appears that, as might be expected, ideology has been more important at some times than at others in the making of policy.

Lenin's attitude to the nationality question was influenced primarily by the ideas of Marx and Engels, but in his final years it was tempered by an increasing sensitivity to the needs of the non-Russians. In the 1920s and 1930s, the policies of encouraging the flourishing of national cultures and *korenizatsiya* probably arose largely from the influence of Leninist ideology. The reassertion of Russian primacy under Stalin was associated with the idea of 'socialism in one country' and the need to build on the loyalty of the one ethnic group which could hold the Soviet Union together. De-Stalinization led to the political and cultural revival of the nationalities; but this was then threatened by Khrushchev's desire to move forward to a nation-less communist society and by his promotion of the Russian language.

Brezhnev, lacking Khrushchev's ideological enthusiasm, soft-pedalled on the fusion of nationalities. In the 1970s, however, for reasons that were demographic, economic and military as well as ideological, he launched a drive to promote the Russian language. He increasingly relied on Russian cadres and sought support particularly from the Russian people. Discrimination in favour of the non-Russians and their republics was reduced. By the end of the Brezhnev era, Russian nationalism was becoming an important part of the ruling ideology in some official circles. This threatened to antagonise national minorities, as well as tending to legitimise undesirable traditions such as Russian Orthodoxy.

Andropov and Chernenko both attacked Russian nationalism and cited Lenin's view that the ultimate aim of the party was the fusion of all nationalities. This, however, would be a very long process. From 1982, scholars discussed this fusion in theoretical terms more frequently, while generally denying that it was a process which the party was immediately pursuing. It was not mentioned in the 1986 Party Programme. There is no evidence that this ideological rehabilitation of *sliyanie* had any effect on policy; as under Brezhnev, the Russian language continued to be promoted.

NOTES

Abbreviations: 1st – Istoriya SSSR; Kom – Kommunist (Moscow); *PC – Problems of Communism; PMiS – Problemy mira i sotsializma; SGiP – Sovetskoe gosudarstvo i pravo; SS – Soviet Studies; VF – Voprosy filosofii; VI – Voprosy istorii.*

I am grateful for financial support from the Social Science Research Fund of the University College of Wales, Aberystwyth.

1. K. Marx and F. Engels, *Werke* (39 vols., Berlin: Dietz, 1956–68), vol. IV, p. 479.
2. M. Lowy, 'Marx and Engels: cosmopolites. The future of nations under communism (1845–1848)', *Critique*, no. 14 (1981), pp. 5–12, at pp. 11–12.
3. For example, Marx, Engels, *Werke*, vol. V, p. 80.
4. M. I. Kulichenko, *Nations and Social Progress*, trans. G. Glagoleva (Moscow: Progress, 1984), p. 138.
5. V. I. Lenin, *Polnoe sobranie sochinenii*, 5th edn. (55 vols., Moscow: Politizdat, 1958–65), vol. XLVIII, pp. 233–6.
6. Lenin, vol. XXIV, p. 131.
7. Lenin, vol. XXIV, p. 237. His emphasis.
8. Lenin, vol. XXVII, p. 256.
9. Lenin, vol. XXVII, p. 457.
10. Lenin, vol. XXX, pp. 21, 22 (including quotation), 44, 120 (twice), 121, 129.
11. Lenin, vol. XXXVI, p. 76.
12. Lenin, vol. XXXVIII, pp. 94, 111.
13. Lenin, vol. XXX, pp. 38–9.
14. E. H. Carr, *The Bolshevik Revolution 1917–1923*, vol. I (Harmondsworth: Penguin, 1966), p. 272.
15. Lenin, vol. XXXV, p. 223.
16. Lenin, vol. XXXVIII, p. 94–5, 111 (quotation).
17. Lenin, vol. XXXVIII, pp. 181–4.
18. *V. I. Lenin, KPSS o sovetskom mnogonatsional'nom gosudarstve* (Moscow: Politizdat, 1981, hereafter *Lenin, KPSS*), pp. 15–96, includes examples of this, frequently referring to the impact on the peoples of Asia and Africa.
19. Lenin, vol. XLI, p. 77.
20. *KPSS v rezolyutsiyakh i resheniyakh s"ezdov, konferentsii i plenumov TsK*, vol. II, *1917–1922* (Moscow: Politizdat, 1983), p. 79.

21. *Lenin, KPSS*, p. 104.
22. *Lenin, KPSS*, pp. 84–6.
23. Carr, *Bolshevik Revolution*, pp. 259–413; Moshe Lewin, *Lenin's Last Struggle* (London: Pluto, 1975), esp. pp. 43–89.
24. Lenin, vol. XLV, pp. 356–62.
25. I. Kreindler, 'The changing status of Russian in the Soviet Union', *International Journal of the Sociology of Language*, no. 33 (1982), pp. 7–39, at pp. 9–10.
26. J. E. Mace, 'Famine and nationalism in Soviet Ukraine', *PC*, vol. XXXIII no. 3 (May–June 1984), pp. 37–50, at pp. 41–43.
27. Sh. R. Rashidov, *Bratskoe sotrudnichestvo narodov SSSR na etape zrelogo sotsializma* (Tashkent: Izd. TsK KP Uzbekistana, 1983), p. 10.
28. Walker Connor, *The National Question in Marxist–Leninist Theory and Strategy* (Princeton University Press, 1984), pp. 394–7; *Lenin, KPSS*, pp. 147–8.
29. M. S. Agursky, 'The Soviet legitimacy crisis and its international implications', in M. A. Kaplan (ed.), *The Many Faces of Communism* (New York: Free Press, 1978), pp. 153–66.
30. A. Bennigsen and C. Lemercier-Quelquejay, *Islam in the Soviet Union* (New York: Praeger, 1967), pp. 84–161; M. Rywkin, *Moscow's Muslim Challenge: Soviet Central Asia* (London: Hurst, 1982), pp. 34–44.
31. Mace, 'Famine', pp. 37–40, 43–9.
32. J. B. Dunlop, *The Faces of Contemporary Russian Nationalism* (Princeton University Press, 1983), pp. 9–14; F. C. Barghoorn, *Soviet Russian Nationalism* (New York: Oxford University Press, 1956), pp. 34–42; Kreindler, 'Changing status', pp. 10–11.
33. A. M. Nekrich, *The Punished Peoples: The Deportation and Fate of Soviet Minorities at the End of the Second World War*, trans. G. Saunders (New York: Norton, 1978).
34. Barghoorn, *Soviet Russian Nationalism*, p. 27.
35. H. Carrère d'Encausse, *Decline of an Empire: The Soviet Socialist Republics in Revolt*, trans. M. Sokolinsky and H. A. La Farge (New York: Newsweek Books, 1979), pp. 33–6; Dunlop, *Faces*, pp. 15–25, 135–6; Barghoorn, *Soviet Russian Nationalism*, pp. 199–220.
36. Carrère d'Encausse, *Decline*, pp. 36–45.
37. *Lenin, KPSS*, pp. 165–9.
38. T. Rakowska-Harmstone, 'The dialectics of nationalism in the USSR', *PC*, vol. XXIII no. 3 (May–June 1974), pp. 1–22, at pp. 18–19.
39. *Lenin, KPSS*, pp. 183–4.
40. 'Torzhestvo leninskoi natsional'noi politiki', *Kom*, 1969, no. 13, p. 11.
41. P. G. Semenov, 'Programma KPSS o razvitii sovetskikh natsional'no-gosudarstvennykh otnoshenii', *SGiP*, 1961, no. 12, as cited in G. Hodnett, 'The debate over Soviet federalism', *SS*, vol. XVIII no. 4 (April 1967), pp. 458–81, at p. 474.
42. P. G. Semenov, 'Suverenitet sovetskikh natsii. (Iz istorii razvitiya)', *VI*, 1965, no. 12, pp. 22–33, at pp. 28–32, 23.
43. P. M. Rogachev and M. A. Sverdlin, 'O ponyatii "natsiya"', *VI*, 1966, no. 1, pp. 33–48, at pp. 48, 37.
44. M. S. Dzhunusov, 'Natsiya kak sotsial'no-etnicheskaya obshchnost'

lyudei', *VI*, 1966, no. 4, pp. 16–30, at p. 30.
45. G. Hodnett, 'What's in a nation?', *PC*, vol. XVI no. 5 (September–October 1967), pp. 2–15, at p. 4.
46. J. Critchlow, 'Nationalism in Uzbekistan in the Brezhnev era', in G. W. Simmonds (ed.), *Nationalism in the USSR and Eastern Europe in the Era of Brezhnev and Kosygin* (University of Detroit Press, 1977), p. 312.
47. *Lenin, KPSS*, pp. 268–70.
48. A. B. Evans Jr., 'Developed socialism in Soviet ideology', *SS*, vol. XXX no. 3 (July 1977), pp. 409–28, at p. 421.
49. *Lenin*, KPSS, pp. 321 (main quotation), 319, 332.
50. M. Rykwin, 'Code words and catchwords of Breznev's nationality policy', *Survey*, vol. XXIV no. 3 (Summer 1979), pp. 83–90, pp. 84–5.
51. L. I. Brezhnev, 'O proekte Konstitutsii (Osnovnogo Zakona) Soyuza Sovetskikh Sotsialisticheskikh Respublik i itogakh ego vsenarodnogo obsuzhdeniya', *Kom*, 1977, no. 15, pp. 7–19, at pp. 10–11.
52. E. Schneider, 'The discussion of the new all-union Constitution in the USSR', *SS*, vol. XXXI no. 4 (October 1979), pp. 523–41, at pp. 531–2.
53. Rakowska-Harmstone, 'Dialectics', p. 18.
54. *Lenin, KPSS*, pp. 447–522. See also A. L. Yanov, *The Russian New Right: Right Wing Ideologies in the Contemporary USSR*, trans. S. P. Dunn (Berkeley, Cal.: Inst. of International Studies, University of California, 1978), and my 'The party and Russian nationalism: From Brezhnev to Gorbachev', in P. J. Potichnyj (ed.), *USSR: Party and Society*, forthcoming.
55. *Literaturnaya gazeta*, 25 February 1981.
56. A. E. Mordinov, 'Aktual'nye problemy razvitiya mezhnatsional'nykh otnoshenii v SSSR', *VF*, 1971, no. 6, pp. 23–33, at pp. 26, 28, 31–2.
57. V. P. Sherstobitov, 'Obrazovanie SSSR i istoricheskie sud'by narodov nashei strany', *Ist*, 1972, no. 3, pp. 20–41, at pp. 36–7.
58. M. P. Kim and V. P. Sherstobitov (eds) *Sovetskii narod – novaya istoricheskaya obshchnost' lyudei. Stanovlenie i razvitie* (Moscow: Nauka, 1975).
59. M. I. Kulichenko, 'Aktual'nye problemy teorii i metodologii razvitiya natsii i natsional'nykh otnoshenii v SSSR', in Kulichenko (ed.), *Aktual'nye problemy natsional'nykh otnoshenii v svete Konstitutsii SSSR* (Moscow: Nauka, 1981), p. 49; idem, *Natsional'nye otnosheniya v SSSR i tendentsii ikh razvitiya* (Moscow: Mysl', 1972), pp. 551–4; idem, *Ukreplenie internatsional'nogo edinstva sovetskogo obshchestva* (Kiev: Politizdat Ukrainy, 1976), pp. 364–5, 369–70.
60. Kulichenko, *Natsional'nye otnosheniya*, p. 547.
61. Ibid., pp. 551–2.
62. Kulichenko, *Ukreplenie*, pp. 362–3.
63. Ibid., pp. 370–7.
64. M. I. Kulichenko, *Rastsvet i sblizhenie natsii v SSSR. Problemy teorii i metodologii* (Moscow: Mysl', 1981), and 'Aktual'nye problemy', pp. 25–54.
65. Idem, *Rastsvet*, pp. 354–61.
66. Idem, 'Aktual'nye problemy', pp. 38–43.
67. 'Stanovlenie i razvitie novoi istoricheskoi obshchnosti – sovetskogo naroda', *Ist*, 1980, no. 6, pp. 23–83, at pp. 41–2, 60–2.
68. Kulichenko, 'Aktual'nye problemy', p. 48.

69. Ibid., pp. 48–53.
70. P. N. Fedoseev, 'Teoreticheskie problemy razvitiya i sblizheniya natsii', *Kom*, 1980, no. 1, pp. 57–70, at p. 59.
71. M. N. Rosenko, 'Rol' russkoi sotsialisticheskoi natsii v razvitii i ukreplenii internatsional'nogo edinstva sovetskogo naroda', *Ist*, 1982, no. 1, pp. 50–61.
72. D. A. Kunaev, 'Leninskie printsipy ravenstva i edinstva natsii', *PMiS*, 1982, no. 5, pp. 3–9, at p. 5.
73. R. I. Kosolapov, 'Klassovye i natsional'nye otnosheniya na etape razvitogo sotsializma', *Sotsiologicheskie issledovaniya*, 1982, no. 4, pp. 8–21, at pp. 9–15. On the Riga Conference, see M. B. Olcott, 'Yuri Andropov and the "national question"', *SS*, vol. XXXVII no. 1 (January 1985), pp. 103–17, at pp. 109–11.
74. Kosolapov, 'Klassovye', and Yu. V. Arutyunyan, 'Korennye izmeneniya v sotsial'nom sostave sovetskikh natsii', *Sotsiologicheskie issledovaniya*, 1982, no. 4, pp. 21–7, at pp. 24–5.
75. B. N. Ponomarev, 'Leninskaya natsional'naya politika KPSS i ee mezhdunarodnoe znachenie', *PMiS*, 1982, no. 9, pp. 3–9.
76. 'My – sovetskii narod', *Kom*, 1982, no. 12, pp. 3–12, at p. 11.
77. Yu. V. Andropov, 'Shest'desyat let SSSR', *Partiinaya zhizn'*, 1983, no. 1, pp. 3–15, at pp. 5–9.
78. Ibid.
79. R. Solchanyk, 'Andropov and the Supreme Soviet on the national question', *Radio Liberty Research Bulletin*, RL 27/83 (13 January 1983), p. 2.
80. K. U. Chernenko, 'Shest'desyat let bratskoi druzhby narodov', *PMiS*, 1982, no. 12, pp. 6–14, at p. 11.
81. Olcott, 'Yuri Andropov', p. 103.
82. *Pravda*, 15 and 16 June 1983.
83. 'Vystuplenie tovarishcha K. U. Chernenko na zasedanii TsK KPSS po podgotovke novoi redaktsii Programmy KPSS', *Kom*, 1984, no. 7, pp. 4–8, at p. 7.
84. A. M. Khalilov, 'Puti sovershenstvovaniya sovetskoi natsional'noi gosudarstvennosti', *SGiP*, 1982, no. 12, pp. 23–31., at pp. 27–8; E. V. Tadevosyan, 'Sovetskii narod – sotsial'naya osnova sovetskogo mnogonatsional'nogo obshchenarodnogo gosudarstva', ibid, pp. 13–22, at pp. 17, 21.
85. Yu. V. Bromlei, 'Etnicheskie protsessy v SSSR', *Kom*, 1983, no. 5, pp. 56–64.
86. A. F. Dashdamirov, 'Dialektika natsional'nogo i internatsional'nogo v sfere kul'tury', *VF*, 1983, no. 8, pp. 31–43, at pp. 41–3.
87. Kulichenko, *Nations*, pp. 124, 125, 127, 174, 188 for *sliyanie* in the future; pp. 165, 166 for it today; pp. 192, 194 for it not being current policy.
88. G. T. Tavadov, 'K kharakteristike sovremennogo etapa natsional'nykh otnoshenii v SSSR', *Nauchnyi kommunizm*, 1984, no. 5, pp. 33–9, at pp. 36–8.
89. *Pravda*, 7 March 1986.
90. Ibid., 26 February 1986.

10 The Long and Winding Road: Trajectories to Peace and Socialism in Contemporary Soviet Ideology

STEPHEN SHENFIELD

10.1 INTRODUCTION

'Peace' and 'socialism' are the twin core values of Soviet ideology.[1] World socialism was for Lenin the absolute value, and efficacy in advancing it the yardstick of all policy. Among relative values, subsidiary to socialism, in the Bolshevik outlook, peace soon came to occupy first place. Following early disillusionment with the strategy of revolutionary war, it was established as axiomatic that avoiding involvement in large-scale war was essential to the security of the Soviet state and to the cause of which that state was the bastion. This goal motivated both the search for collective security in the 1930s and the Nazi–Soviet Pact of 1939–41. The experience of the Nazi invasion, of course, confirmed its vital importance.

The status of peace as a value has been further enhanced in the nuclear age, in line with growing Soviet recognition of the likely catastrophic consequences of a nuclear war[2] and the perceived high probability of escalation once war breaks out. The necessity of pursuing the struggle between socialism and capitalism in ways that excluded world war has been enshrined since 1956 in the doctrine of peaceful coexistence.

The higher the status of peace is raised, the more salient becomes the problem of its relationship with its twin value, socialism. To what extent does pursuit of one come into conflict with pursuit of the other? Over what trajectory, by means of what priorities, can both a secure peace and world socialism eventually be attained? The attempts of contemporary Soviet ideology to deal with these questions is the subject of this chapter.

It will be useful to start with a general discussion of the role played by ideology in Soviet foreign policy (this is undertaken in Section 10.2). We shall then examine in Section 10.3 the official ideology of the road to peace and socialism, as it took form, with relatively minor variations, during the period of detente in the 1970s. According to this ideology, the struggle for peace and the struggle for socialism are, over the longer term, not only compatible but mutually reinforcing, while short-term tensions between the two are manageable. The reversion to cold war in the 1980s has, however, put the orthodoxy of the 1970s under great strain. In the mainstream of Soviet commentary, the orthodoxy has been adapted in various ways in order to reaffirm its long-term validity. (This will be examined in Section 10.4). In Section 10.5 we will look at some more radical responses to the new situation, which cast doubt on the prospects for simultaneous attainment of peace and socialism. Finally, in Section 10.6 we shall tentatively assess the political significance of the ideological material reviewed.

10.2 THE ROLE PLAYED BY IDEOLOGY IN SOVIET FOREIGN POLICY

It is widely agreed that there is a relationship between Soviet ideology and Soviet foreign policy. Disagreements relate to the nature of the relationship – its direction, strength and degree of directness – and to varying conceptions of 'ideology' as a monolithic system or a flexible medium of debate. The divergent interpretations of well-informed observers, whether Western analysts, Soviet citizens speaking off the record or émigrés, suggest that there are no simple answers to these problems.

Ideology may be regarded at one extreme as a 'guide to action', or at the other extreme as mere *post hoc* rationalisation of policy which is really motivated by such unadmitted considerations as traditional Russian national goals or the self-interest of the élite. Analysis of the ideological framework which members of the Soviet foreign policy élite are obliged to use in public shows that it both gives considerable scope for manoeuvre and imposes definite limits on the positions that can be defended within it. The testimony of defectors reveals both a cynically instrumental approach to ideology on the part of Soviet leaders and top officials and the deep impact that ideology has on their assumptions and perceptions.[3] We may therefore accept Judson Mitchell's balanced description of the process of revising ideology under the influence of changing circumstances as 'neither wholly opportunistic nor totally grounded in philosophical assumptions'.[4]

It seems likely that the interplay of institutional interests within the Soviet system also contributes to such an intermediate status for ideology. Some institutions – for instance, Institutes and Faculties of Philosophy – have a material stake in the recognition of ideological elaboration as a vitally important activity. Many other institutions have no such stake, and may react to ideology as to an extraneous impediment to the practical tasks with which they are charged. It appears that the Ministry of Foreign Affairs, oriented towards the conduct of inter-state relations of the traditional kind, tends towards a de-ideologised 'pragmatism', while the International Department of the party Central Committee takes a more 'ideological' approach.[5]

It must be borne in mind that 'ideology' covers a vast range of subject matter and appears in many different forms. The role played by ideology varies according to topic and form. Differences in presentation between inner-party, academic and mass-propaganda sources may simply reflect their different functions.

There have been quite a few substantial analyses of Soviet academic discourse in the field of international relations by western researchers. Some analysts consider that such discourse, correctly interpreted, is a reliable indicator of real policy deliberations, while others are more sceptical concerning the closeness of the link between the two. Hough argues that the mechanisms of patronage of prominent Soviet scholars by policy-makers bring about a 'functional equivalence' between academic and practical policy debates, so that 'the debates that we observe are somewhat like the shadows on the wall of Plato's cave', a more or less hazy reflection of policy debates at the highest level.[6]

Propaganda sources are particularly difficult to assess. Material designed to influence a target audience in a desired direction cannot be assumed to reflect the views either of its author or of élite groups, though neither can it be assumed to bear no relation to real views. Thus, the genre known as 'unmasking polemic' may exaggerate perceptions of the military threat from the West in order to enhance popular discipline, but this does not exclude the likelihood that a threat from the West, in a less extreme form, is indeed perceived. Moreover, even insincere propaganda has an influence on the social atmosphere in which policy formulation takes place, and so is not without political significance.

A particularly controversial question among Western analysts is that of the possible existence of Soviet source material which, even if ostensibly internally directed, is really designed to 'disinform' western opinion concerning the nature of Soviet policy. Some reject the idea out of hand, while others go so far as to regard all open sources as suspect.[7] To the extent that the use of sources for disinformation would interfere with their primary internal functions, doubt is cast on the plausibility at least of the most far-reaching claims of this kind.

10.3 THE 1970S: VARIANTS OF THE ORTHODOX TRAJECTORY TO PEACE AND SOCIALISM

In the Soviet view, peaceful coexistence is 'a unity of cooperation and struggle'. The relative stress put on the two elements varies around the even-handed formulation of Nikol'sky and Grishin:

> Peaceful coexistence . . . has a dual nature. It is . . . a system of . . . cooperation between, and . . . a special form of class struggle between, states with different social systems. The unity of these two aspects consists in the fact that both struggle and cooperation proceed . ... by peaceful means.[8]

Of seven components of peaceful coexistence identified by Milovidov and Zhdanov, four are cooperative (political, economic, scientific–technical and cultural cooperation) and three conflictual (political struggle, economic rivalry and ideological conflict).[9]

In the struggle between the two systems, the interests of socialism coincide with those of peace, for socialism contains no social forces with a stake in war. Therefore (in this simplest version of the ideology) the world victory of socialism will be 'the full and final guarantee of peace among peoples'. Capitalism, on the other hand, has a tendency to generate war, although it contains some countervailing forces such as sober-minded politicians and capitalists interested in East–West trade. Shakhnazarov lists four types of war danger arising from capitalism:

1. Wars against the national-liberation movement in the Third World to protect investments and sources of raw material;
2. The possible recurrence of inter-imperialist war among the USA, Japan, France, West Germany etc. for division and redivision of the world;
3. The profit interests of the Military–Industrial Complex, 'ready for

any extremity, including the risk of nuclear war'; and
4. The striving of monopoly capital to save capitalism at any price.[10]

Fortunately, 'the correlation of forces in the world changes to the advantage of socialism, though at varying rates and not without reverse phenomena at certain periods'.[11] Peace becomes more secure in the course of this process, both because the social basis of war (capitalism) is abolished in more and more countries and because the strength of the forces of peace relative to that of the forces of war increases on the international arena. For example, new socialist, socialist-oriented and non-aligned states throw their support behind the peace policy of the socialist community.

Soviet ideologists in the 1970s conceived of the advance of peace and socialism in the world in five stages, of which the third had been reached. Before the Second World War, the influence of socialism was still too weak to avert war, which was at that time rightly regarded as inevitable. The change in the correlation of forces after the Second World War is held to have opened up real perspectives of preventing war. The new situation was codified from 1956 in the doctrine of peaceful coexistence. The achievement by the USSR of approximate strategic parity with the USA created the objective conditions for the next advance, the turn to détente in the 1970s, which 'bears witness to the fact that the ruling circles of capitalist countries have begun to recognise the impossibility of deciding the outcome of the struggle to their advantage by military means'.[12] Further progress towards peace could be expected in connection with the next major shift in the balance of forces towards socialism, and with completion of the transition to world socialism the war danger would finally disappear forever.

Thus, Shakhnazarov, writing in the late 1970s, forecasts the gradual strengthening of détente over the next fifty years, with the war danger lessening from year to year. 'Within the existing correlation of forces . . . there is not yet the possibility of fully excluding aggression and the local wars associated with it, but there is already the possibility of sharply limiting the sphere of arbitrary action of imperialist reaction'.[13] The next twenty five to thirty years would be the most dangerous period. Within fifty years a decisive shift would be likely, with the establishment of socialism in Western Europe and other parts of the world.[14]

The potential for peace of this penultimate stage appears to be a matter for dispute. Nikol'sky and Grishin hold that war can be 'excluded from the life of society with capitalism still remaining in part of the world'.[15] A more common position is that this must await the elimination of capitalism. However secure détente may seem, argue Milovidov and Zhdanov, 'the existence of imperialism, the presence of an objective basis alien to peace, preserves the possibility of a return to tension and even to war'.[16]

If the advance of socialism strengthens peace, the strengthening of peace, in turn, facilitates the advance of socialism. 'Détente creates the purest conditions, those most free of artificial obstacles, for the development of social processes.' Détente enables the socialist countries to reduce their military burden, and (some add) to develop democracy more easily and overcome 'deformations' caused by international tension. Anti-communism becomes a less effective ideological weapon against working-class struggle in the capitalist countries. Détente in general eases imperialist pressure on the revolutionary movement, reducing the danger of 'export of counter-revolution'.[17] 'Recent decades prove that the revolutionary forces have achieved their greatest results . . . under conditions of détente', argues Filatov. Thus, the 1970s saw the victory of the national-liberation movement in Indochina, Angola, Mozambique, Ethiopia and other countries, the fall of fascist regimes in Greece, Portugal and Spain, the breaking of the blockade of Cuba and the international recognition of East Germany.[18] This does not mean that détente benefits *only* socialism: it is an objective necessity for the survival of all humanity, and socialism advances under conditions of confrontation as well, although more slowly.

In the simplest version of the 1970s orthodoxy, the mutually reinforcing nature of the struggles for peace and for socialism rules out conflict between the two values. However, in the more complex and realistic variant elaborated by Shakhnazarov, certain tensions between peace and socialism are explored, although these are argued to be manageable in the context of the long-term coincidence of peace and socialism.

First of all, Shakhnazarov acknowledges that 'solidarity [with revolutionary forces] may call for participation in political and military actions fraught with a certain risk' of war. 'There are no general formulas which can solve such problems'. On the one hand, *excessive* risks must certainly be avoided: 'careful analysis would probably show that in certain cases the sharpness of the international situation was not sufficiently taken into account'. On the other hand, *some* risks must be taken, in the long-term interest of peace itself, requiring the attainment of world socialism:

> the optimal relation between the two goals [of peaceful coexistence and social progress] is the most complex problem of the nuclear age. It

is clear that the prevention of total war is a precondition of any progress. It is equally clear that without such progress humanity would be doomed to stagnation and unable to escape the dangers of the nuclear age.

> Imagine a man who has fallen into a quagmire . . . Any sharp movement may prove fatal to him. [But] he is in danger of perishing, not indeed with great delay, if he does not try to pull himself on to firm land. He has no choice but to move forward, maintaining the utmost caution.

Thus, 'it is just as harmful to bewitch oneself with the nuclear peril as it is to ignore its reality'.[19]

Secondly, Shakhnazarov admits that the sharpness of the inevitable ideological conflict between the two systems is a factor working against peace, for which 'compensation' must be found in economic interdependence and East–West cooperation in the solution of global problems.[20]

Thirdly, Shakhnazarov is concerned with the continuing danger of war *among* socialist countries. Such wars are not exceptional phenomena: they reflect a definite tendency, though not a fatal regularity. They bear witness to 'the immaturity of socialist social relations and consciousness' and to the need for further efforts by the socialist countries to learn new modes of conducting their relations. 'The future of humanity decisively depends on the successful development of this process'.[21] It follows from this that the world victory of socialism does not, after all, entail the full exclusion of war from the life of society, which requires the attainment by world socialism of 'a sufficiently high level of maturity in all spheres of social life'.[22]

10.4 THE 1980s: ADAPTING THE ORTHODOX TRAJECTORY TO THE NEW COLD WAR

The orthodoxy of the 1970s was built on the conviction that history guarantees irreversible progress towards a more secure peace. The turn to détente had been the product of 'new realities', of the shift in the global correlation of forces in general and of the attainment of strategic parity by the USSR in particular. Indeed, it was 'the surest criterion of the current correlation of forces'.[23] Therefore, the return to East–West confrontation at the turn of the 1980s appears deeply anomalous within the framework of the existing orthodoxy, frontally challenging its capacity to explain events. It becomes necessary to assert that American ruling circles have a grossly deficient perception of reality. Alexei Arbatov poses the puzzle as follows:

> Return to [the Cold War], it would have seemed, had been securely barred by the events of the 1960s and 1970s – the failure of US aggression in Vietnam, the radical change in the global correlation of forces . . . the successes of détente . . . It was as if all this did not exist for the new American leadership, as if they had knocked a 'window' through history and missed these events . . .
>
> If the positive changes in American policy [in the 1970s] were conditioned by objective circumstances . . . then what has become of these circumstances [now]? Why does the Reagan Administration find it possible not to take account of them, and in general to deny their existence? . . . [So] which was a passing chance development, and which was objectively inevitable and long-term in American policy: the transition to détente . . . or the return to confrontation?[24]

Zhurkin resorts to a similar metaphor when he complains that 'the Reagan Administration conducts its bellicose escapades as if it occupies a vacuum'.[25] The USA, and the world, are off the tracks of Soviet-conceived 'history'.

The strength of the 1970s orthodoxy may account in part for the slowness with which Soviet analysts of American politics came to appreciate the seriousness and durability of the new hard line of the Reagan Administration. Writing in 1980, in the aftermath of Reagan's election as President, Trofimenko could see no difference between the two candidates:

> The foreign policy line of the new Administration still has to be worked out. It is characteristic, however, that both candidates began their electoral campaign by trying to outdo one another in bellicosity, but finished it by . . . trying to prove that he was a more sober-minded . . . politician than his opponent. This was an adaptation to the [pro-peace] mood of the electors . . .[So] we would hope that the new Administration . . . will take a constructive approach to American–Soviet relations, including the problem of SALT.[26]

'The new masters of the White House', predicted Pechatnov, 'will undoubtedly discover that in practice they have to measure up not to their pre-election rhetoric but to the objective realities of the contemporary world'.[27] A year later, Zhurkin found the confrontational strategy of the Reagan Administration 'increasingly clear', but nevertheless made the forecast that it 'will have to face up to the realities . . . whether it wishes to do so or not'.[28]

As the Reagan administration continued to avoid 'facing up to reality', some Soviet commentators preferred to attribute this to superficial cultural and psychological factors, rather than to deep 'historical' reasons. If Reagan and his colleagues took an absolutist approach to politics, this was because they were deficient in foreign-policy experience and in general culture.[29] One could hope that 'the continuing policy process' would 'strengthen realistic principles' within the administration. At worst, the USSR need only wait until a new and more reasonable President came along.[30]

One means of easing, if not eliminating, the problem of accounting for the contrast between the détente of the 1970s and the confrontation of the 1980s is, of course, the retrospective re-evaluation of the progress made in the 1970s. Soviet analysts, like Western ones, have concluded that détente was not as firmly established as it appeared to be at the time. As in the West, some analysts argue, as Yakovlev does, that the other side was never seriously committed to détente: 'détente was a tactical expedient for the US; the ruling circles did not regard it as a long-term policy'.[31] Other analysts make less sweeping re-evaluations that enable détente still to be viewed as a big step forward. 'Events of the past few years have demonstrated how strong the enemies of détente remain'.[32] Traditional American foreign-policy dogmas 'have proven more stable than the realistic policy trends'.[33] Georgii Arbatov concludes that objective changes are not in themselves enough to bring about corresponding irreversible subjective changes:

> The American power elite has never been enchanted by detente, [which is] not [its] most typical or habitual attitude . . . Objective realities can sometimes . . . compel people . . . to change their attitudes. But this does not mean that such changes come easily or that they are irreversible. The old, the habitual . . . tends to come back to the fore at the slightest provocation.[34]

If 'the adaptation of the US ruling class to the new world situation proceeds so painfully and contradictorily',[35] the future of East–West relations in coming decades lies at the mercy of the vagaries in mood of the US élite, which cannot be predicted with any confidence by Soviet ideology, although it is assumed that in the long term (if war is avoided) the painful process will be successfully completed. The straightforward trajectory to peace and socialism of orthodox 1970s doctrine has been revised to include what may be a fairly prolonged period of unpredictable zigzags, coinciding with the 'zone of approximate strategic parity' entered around 1970.

At least two variants of the zigzag trajectory to be expected during this transitional period have been suggested by Soviet commentators. One theory is that there is 'a cyclical character to the evolution of Soviet–American relations, an alternation between periods of détente and confrontation', reflecting 'the confrontation between different groups within the US ruling class'.[36] If, as has been hypothesised, each phase of the cycle lasts about ten years, a period of détente can be expected in the 1990s and renewed confrontation at the beginning of the next century. As what is here assumed is a regularity internal to American politics, it is implied that nothing the USSR does can make much difference, one way or the other.

A theory with more activist implications is that advanced by Yakovlev, who accuses of 'complacency' those who regard the turn of the US from détente 'as a chance moment in history, a moment of an irrational nature, and attibute it to the personal qualities of President Reagan'.[37] For Yakovlev, the new offensive strategy of imperialism is a purposeful attempt to recover lost economic, political and military–strategic positions:

> There is a certain objective basis for the socio-political anxiety . . . increasingly felt by Washington's ruling circles over the past 10–15 years. The nervousness of the American plutocracy . . . has real roots . . . The quickening pace of historical progress step by step narrows the potential and space for manoeuvre of imperialism.

However, the current militaristic reaction of imperialism to its decline will not succeed in its aims, for

> adaptation to the real world development is inevitable . . . a historical imperative for capitalist society . . . Sooner or later a new détente will replace confrontation with the regularity of a historical tendency smoothing over an arbitrary zigzag . . . But that can happen only if the forces of socialism, democracy and progress continue resolutely to counteract the capitalist system, which still has considerable reserves for economic and political manoeuvre and development.[38]

The implication is that the attainment of a reliable détente *is*, after all, a function of the global correlation of forces, but that the correlation reached in the 1970s is, contrary to what then appeared to be the case, inadequate. Only the further advance of socialism can bring the roads to peace and to socialism back together.

10.5 THE 1980s: REVISIONIST RESPONSES TO THE NEW COLD WAR

So far, we have considered attempts to preserve the orthodox 1970s trajectory to peace and socialism, or at least its long-term trend-line, while allowing for the temporary failure of détente. There are, however, Soviet commentators whose writing appears to depart substantially from the orthodoxy, loosening the tight interconnection between the values of peace and socialism. We call such authors 'peace revisionists' and 'war revisionists'. The peace revisionists hold that peace can and must be secured prior to further large-scale advance towards socialism, while the war revisionists tend implicitly to move towards the position that war is once again becoming inevitable.

The central idea of peace revisionism is that the Marxian doctrine of the primacy of productive activity and the class struggles associated with it in moulding the course of events is no longer adequate in the nuclear age. If the cultural and political 'superstructure' still rests upon the 'base' of material production, the latter itself now rests on a 'sub-base' of the conditions of survival. Tomashevsky and Lukov argue:

> in his time, Engels . . . stressed 'the simple fact that people must first of all eat, drink, have shelter and clothing before they are in a position to occupy themselves with politics, science, art, religion, etc.' Today, one might add to this that before eating, drinking, having shelter and clothing, people must first of all secure the preservation of the human race . . . The solution of all other questions – economic, social, political, ideological etc. – depends on this. Einstein expressed this thought in his own way: 'Man must first secure his own survival; only then may he pose to himself the question of the kind of existence he prefers'.

Thus, 'elimination of the danger of [nuclear] war is a prerequisite of further successes of socialism and communism, of social progress as a whole'.[39] This ordering of tasks over time stands in stark contrast to that, say, of Yakovlev, for whom the further success of socialism is a prerequisite even of the reduction, let alone the elimination, of the war danger.

The relationship between the time perspectives of the struggle for peace and the struggle for socialism is arguably the point at issue in an apparently pedantic discussion of Burlatsky's concept of 'the planning of peace', by which is meant an agreed programme of joint East–West measures aimed at the prevention of nuclear war.[40] Shakhnazarov criticises this concept as 'inaccurate', preferring that of 'organised peace'.[41] A reviewer of Shakhnazarov's book offers the following clarification of the matter:

> I think . . . that this counterposition [of 'planned peace' to 'organised peace'] is based on a misunderstanding. When one speaks of the planning of world peace, one has in mind first, the relatively foreseeable future, and second, not the whole of social development but the evolution of the system of international relations . . .
>
> As for 'organised peace' . . . here one has in mind the distant future, when a radical change will occur in the conditions of the whole of social development on Earth.[42]

Yet this distinction, which sets elimination of the war danger as the overriding immediate task and relegates radical social change to the distant future, can hardly be acceptable to ideologists like Shakhnazarov, for whom the struggles for peace and for socialism are interdependent and to be pursued jointly.

This interpretation is supported by Burlatsky's espousal of the concept of world peace as 'an absolute value, as distinct from relative values having significance for particular states, nations and social groups'.[43] Socialism is by implication here included as a mere relative value, not only subordinate to but incommensurable with peace. Shakhnazarov, in his writing, seems determined to deny peace such an exalted status:

> the problem of peace can be regarded . . . from different points of view. The solution will be one thing if at the centre of view is set simply the requirement that humanity survive, and quite another if one considers survival insufficient and takes into account requirements of a higher social nature.[44]

While Shakhnazarov's ideal leader is a careful strategist, weighing gains to socialism against possible risks to peace, Burlatsky's is the 'responsible statesman', a rather de-ideologised figure who is concerned first and foremost with consolidating peace and 'leaves questions relating to the nature of social systems to scholars'.[45]

In the orthodox view, as we have shown, the strengthening of peace relies on continuing movement of the correlation of forces in favour of socialism. Inasmuch as peace revisionists see the struggle for socialism in a much longer time perspective than the struggle for peace, they must identify other catalysts of the demilitarisation of East–West relations. One such catalyst is a growing awareness of the common interest of the human race in survival, reflecting after a time lag the emergence of the new 'sub-base' of social life.

In the past, Marxists regarded talk of the unity of interests of humanity as 'impractical idealism' or 'political romanticism', infinitely removed from social reality, riven by class and other antagonisms. But now 'the threat of general annihilation [has] cast doubt on the idea of the divisibility of the fates of different nations . . . in the event of war, [and] given rise to a "global" consciousness speaking "in the name of humanity'". The social significance of humanistic appeals is 'essentially changed': 'it is as if they have been brought down to Earth, more and more compellingly seen as practical and urgent'.[46] World politics can no longer be analysed in the categories of class, state and national interests alone; a realistic foreign policy must take account of the new objective category of all-human interests. The basis of peaceful coexistence shifts from 'temporary, partial coincidence of interests' to 'the objective long-term common interest' of humanity in preventing nuclear war.[47]

The unified consciousness of common interests develops in conflict and interaction with the pre-existing divided consciousness of opposed interests:

> the working-out of the new world-perception of human unity . . . proceeds in the presence of [continuing] social, class, ideological, political, national and state . . . contradictions and conflicts . . . All these contradictions are not abolished by awareness of the nuclear threat, but they cannot but be modified by it.[48]

> This 'unification' of the fate of the human race has been imposed as if from the outside, with retention of the deepest class and political antagonisms. So recognition of this 'unity' . . . is attained in an extremely contradictory and complex way. It first conquers those spheres of culture furthest removed from direct political reality: art, literature, the 'classless' exact sciences.

A crucial issue from the Soviet perspective is whether the rise of all-human consciousness affects also the western élite. According to Zhilin, there is indeed taking place 'a shift in the awareness of the ruling class in capitalist countries' towards recognising and giving priority to the prevention of nuclear war as their dominant long-term interest.[50]

In order to argue that peace can be ensured on the basis of the prolonged coexistence of the two systems, it is necessary to contest the orthodox position that militarism is an inevitable aspect of the 'essence' of contemporary capitalism (imperialism). A vigorous defence of the contention that a 'non-militarised model' of capitalism is quite possible, and in fact exists in 'a significant group of countries', is provided by Ivanov. Far from militarism being, or over time becoming, 'an objectively necessary link in the functioning of the capitalist economy', he argues, it is a 'secondary', 'parasitic', even 'alien' phenomenon in an economy which does not need 'to throw part of its capital into the water.' As for the defensive reaction of capitalism to the advance of socialism in the world, it 'may take various forms, not necessarily military ones'.[51]

In holding out the hope that 'compromises' and 'an extremely agonising search to combine conflicting aims and interests' might make it possible to 'enter into an era of peaceful relations [and] cooperation',[52] the peace revisionists rely on the assumption that capitalism is still capable of defending its positions by non-military means. Here they confront the more influential and harsher view that, 'having lost the historical initiative . . . imperialism is no longer in a position to oppose the socialist world with anything other than armed force, the threat of nuclear conflict'.[53]

The war-revisionist response to the return to Cold War most radically undermines the 1970s orthodoxy by placing in doubt the conception that the further advance to socialism is, at least over the longer term, naturally accompanied by the strengthening of peaceful coexistence. An editorial in *Voprosy filosofii* (*Questions of Philosophy*) speaks of 'the growing aggressiveness' of the capitalists 'as the process of social transformations advances, as the correlation of forces on the international arena changes', and of how 'the opposition of the old and the new [systems] . . . more and more clearly takes on the form of a general split'.[54] Some writers go further and conclude that capitalist ruling circles, or the dominant reactionary grouping within them, are such 'nuclear maniacs' that they will choose nuclear war, in full awareness of the consequences, rather than gracefully accept their own demise:

> swallowed up in the abyss of its general crisis, capitalism becomes especially dangerous. In ancient times, slave-holders and feudal lords ordered that their wives, servants and slaves be buried with them when they died. In our times, capitalism, in leaving the historical scene, is ready to take with it all life on Earth.[55]

> The most extreme . . . of the American hawks are prepared . . . to throw us back to the Stone Age, if this will help them save themselves from socialism. In their undeclared opinion, Neanderthal cavemen are better than Communists.[56]

Krivitsky argues that any ruling class facing defeat will blow up the world if it can. Would the European aristocrats not have used nuclear weapons to prevent the French Revolution? Would Hitler from his Berlin bunker not have 'blotted out the light with malicious joy'? The modern capitalist class can hardly be expected to act differently: 'there is no price which capitalism is not prepared to pay for its eternal dominion. Either its overlordship – or let everything fall into the abyss!' It is therefore 'an enormous misfortune that nucelar weapons have fallen into the hands' of imperialism.[57]

Although no Soviet writer openly states that war is inevitable, and although it can logically be argued that negative trends do not exclude the possibility that the forces of peace may manage to avert war until the safety of world socialism is reached, the idea that nuclear holocaust is the most likely end-point of social development does seem implicit in war-revisionist theories. Readers of *Literaturnaya Gazeta* (*Literary Gazette*), expressing in their letters to the magazine their fears that 'humanity is irresistably sliding down the slope to the Third World War' and evoking the advice of the magazine's commentator not to 'boundlessly dramatise the situation', were surely drawing the natural conclusion from such gloomy material.[58] Timofeyev finds it necessary to refute the 'mechanical' thesis that the capitalist crisis must lead to war, under the guise of a critique of Western ultra-leftist theorists.[59]

Both the struggle for peace and the struggle for socialism are essential to Soviet ideology: they must somehow be reconciled. 'Were the processes of development of the social revolution and of the establishment of a new [peaceful] world order . . . to contradict one another', observes Shakhnazarov, 'then humanity would be faced with an insoluble problem'.[60] This is the problem of war revisionism.

10.6 ASSESSMENT

In Sections 3–5 we have focused on the nature of the ideas to be found in Soviet publications concerning the road to peace and socialism. We have shown how the coherent orthodoxy of the 1970s has, under the stress of the collapse of détente, fractured into several alternative variants within the fixed framework of Soviet ideology, some minimal adaptations of the 1970s orthodoxy (zigzag and cycle theories) and others quite radical revisions of it (peace revisionism and war revisionism). It now remains to assess the political weight and significance of the ideas surveyed.

To preclude possible misunderstandings, we start with a series of provisos. First, although we have for convenience spoken of the 'views' or 'positions' of particular Soviet authors, this refers only to the ideas contained in their published work. The division between 'official' and 'unofficial' worlds in the USSR is such that published views may bear little relation to people's 'real views' (if any) as thought or revealed to intimates.[61] Views expressed orally in internal policy deliberations, which probably have greater political impact than either published or private views, may well differ from both. Published ideas reveal tensions within Soviet ideology, but they are unreliable (though suggestive) guides to the motives and alignments of individual political actors.

Published sources have a certain importance as accessible products of hidden political processes, and also as influences on Soviet public consciousness. But we should not exaggerate their significance, bearing in mind that what remains hidden from us is incomparably more significant than what is accessible to us. Thus, the system of tendencies proposed by us should be regarded not as a new factional analysis of Soviet élite politics, or even as a set of well-defined schools of political thought, but as a heuristic aid to organising the content of a body of ideological texts. There may be other ways of organising the material which are no less illuminating. The pattern would also be changed, perhaps radically, if ideas relating to additional important issues were integrated into the analysis.

To the extent that the political weight of different tendencies can be judged on the basis of the status in the political system of the authors expressing them, there can be little doubt of the continuing dominance of 'orthodox' variants of the road to peace and socialism. While peace-revisionist authors tend to be researchers at international affairs institutes (for example, Mitrokhin, Melikyan) and war-revisionist authors publicists (for example, Genri, Krivitsky), orthodox authors include prominent officials of the Central Committee apparatus (for example, Shakhnazarov, Yakovlev).[62] On the other hand, this contrast should not be overdrawn. The peace-revisionist Burlatsky has been an influential Central Committee consultant in the past,[63] and Zhilin (whose ideas may more tentatively be linked with peace revisionism) heads the group of consultants to the International Department of the Central Committee. Again, one of the authors whose war-revisionist ideas we have cited, Kosolapov, was until recently editor of the party theoretical journal *Kommunist*. Moreover, an author of modest status is not likely, in the Soviet system, to be able to express unorthodox ideas in print unless he enjoys some protection at a higher level. All this suggests that there may be disagreements, or at least uncertainty, concerning this area of ideology at a very high level of the party-state hierarchy.

Some special problems in assessing the real political significance both of peace revisionism and of war revisionism must be considered. As peace revisionism is, from the point of view of western interests, by far the most attractive of the variants surveyed, it might be suspected of serving the purpose of 'disinforming' western opinion about Soviet views. The significance of war revisionism might be discounted on the grounds that it is just war-scare propaganda, not believed by the power élite, but used by them to inspire greater loyalty and discipline in the Soviet people or otherwise to manipulate the public mood.

While it is reasonable to be wary of Soviet propaganda specially directed at a western audience and to check it against internal sources, the conspiratorial assumptions needed to envisage what appears to be arcane internal ideological controversy as a disinformation game strain plausibility. Little if any effort is made by the Soviet authorities to make peace-revisionist theory known in the West. Much that is published in Soviet sources seems repulsive to their relatively few western readers, and would presumably be avoided if disinformation of the West really were a high-priority consideration. Finally, even if the desire to create a good impression in the West does sometimes help unorthodox ideas find their way into print, this is quite consistent with their having some internal impact as well.

The characterisation of war revisionism as war-scare propaganda is more convincing. Its vehicle is not abstract scholarship, but sensational journalism. However, though the purpose of internal discipline may be served by scaring people in moderate measure, scaring them out of their wits, or proving to them that the prospects for peace are hopeless, is surely counterproductive. Perhaps this is why war-scare propaganda is balanced by other propaganda with a more hopeful message. An explanation solely in terms of manipulation has its difficulties. Moreover, according to the testimony of the high-level defector Arkady Shevchenko, war-revisionist ideas are not alien to the mentality of the Soviet leadership: they do believe that reactionary forces *might* launch a nuclear attack on the Soviet Union in a desperate attempt to save capitalism.[64]

A final indicator of the current political weight of different conceptions of the road to peace and socialism is provided by the treatment of the theme at the 27th Party Congress in March 1986. The new Party Programme adopted by the Congress[65] is ambiguous in this area. Capitalism 'is still strong and dangerous', implying that it should become less dangerous as it grows weaker. On the other hand, the remark that 'imperialism does not wish to reckon with the political realities of the contemporary world' is unaccompanied by any assurance that it will have to learn to reckon with them. Quite the contrary: 'the more powerfully the course of historical development undermines the positions of imperialism, the more hostile to the interests of the peoples becomes the policy of its most reactionary forces'. This may or may not be consistent with the 1970s orthodoxy, depending on whether the policy of imperialism as a whole can be expected to remain under the domination of its most reactionary forces. But on this point there is no clue, although the characterisation of imperialism as 'parasitic, decaying and dying capitalism', incapable of overcoming its contradictions by reform, does not bode well for the demilitarisation of relations between the systems.

It is, to be sure, reaffirmed that world war is not inevitable: 'never has there been such terrible danger hanging over humanity. But never have there been such real possibilities of preserving and strengthening peace'. The theoretical basis of this declaration, however, seems rather thin, and the optimism consequently a little forced. In the theoretical section on 'the struggle between the forces of progress and reaction in the contemporary world' (First Part, Section II), the word 'détente' is not mentioned once.[66]

Gorbachev's report to the Congress is less evasive and even more pessimistic than the Party Programme. Militarism is explicitly declared to be of 'the very socio-economic essence of imperialism'.[67] Although continuation of the unrealistic policy of imperialism is not inevitable, a turn to realism becomes progressively less likely as capitalism goes more deeply into decline:

> the ruling circles do not wish soberly to assess world realities . . . All this is an indicator of the wearing-out of the internal 'immune systems' [of capitalism], of its social decrepitude, which reduces the probability of big changes in the policy of the ruling forces and heightens the irrationality of their policy.

This prognosis is more closely related to war revisionism than to the 1970s orthodoxy. Gorbachev retreats into equivocation – 'it is very difficult to forecast the future of [East–West] relations' – and finally has to resort to a declaration of will:

will the ruling centres of capital be able to step on to the path of sober, constructive assessment of events? Easiest would be to answer – maybe yes, and maybe no. But history does not give us the right to such a forecast. We cannot take 'no' as an answer to the question – is humanity to be or not to be? We say – social progress, the life of civilisation must and will continue. (*Prolonged applause*).

The road to peace and socialism will be followed, come what may. But it is no longer clear whether the road which humanity is on leads in that direction at all. We suspect that the confusion in this vital area of Soviet ideology will not be easily resolved.

NOTES

1. 'Socialism' in this paper refers to the new social formation as a whole, including 'communism' as its highest phase. Omission of quotation marks from terms taken from Soviet usage does not imply any recognition of the validity of such usage.
2. See Raymond L. Garthoff, *Détente and Confrontation: American–Soviet Relations from Nixon to Reagan* (Washington D.C.: Brookings Institution, 1985), pp. 768–85; S. D. Shenfield, 'Soviet thinking about the unthinkable', *Bulletin of the Atomic Scientists*, vol. 41 no. 2 (Feb. 1985), pp,. 23–5.
3. Perhaps the most revealing testimony is that of Arkady N. Shevchenko, *Breaking with Moscow* (London: Jonathan Cape, 1985), e.g. pp. 104–5, 180, 190, 280–1.
4. R. Judson Mitchell, *Ideology of a Superpower: Contemporary Soviet Doctrine on International Relations* (Stanford, Cal.: Hoover Institution Press, 1982), p. 5.
5. Shevchenko, *Breaking with Moscow*, p. 190.
6. Jerry F. Hough, *The Struggle for the Third World: Soviet Debates and American Options* (Washington D.C.: The Brookings Institution, 1986), pp. 267–8. Other useful studies of Soviet international relations scholarship, containing discussion of problems of interpretation, are: William Zimmerman, *Soviet Perspectives on International Relations 1956–1967* (Princeton University Press, 1969) and Neil Malcolm, *Soviet Political Scientists and American Politics* (London: Macmillan, 1984). For analyses of the Soviet ideology of détente in the 1970s, see Peter M. E. Volten, *Brezhnev's Peace Program: a Study of Soviet Domestic Political Process and Power* (Boulder, Colorado: Westview Press, 1982) and Garthoff, *Détente and Confrontation*, pp. 36–53.
7. See 'A Debate Between Raymond Garthoff and Richard Pipes on Soviet Nuclear Strategy', in P. E. Haley et al. (eds), *Nuclear Strategy, Arms Control, and the Future* (Boulder, Colorado: Westview Press, 1985), pp. 169–79.
8. N. M. Nikol'sky and A. V. Grishin, *Nauchno-tekhnicheskii progress i mezhdunarodyne otnosheniya* (Moscow, 1978), pp. 71–3.
9. A. S. Milovidov and Ye. A. Zhdanov, 'Sotsial'no-filosofskie problemy

voiny i mira', *Voprosy filosofii*, 1980, no. 10, p. 32.
10. G. Shakhnazarov, *Sotsializm i budushchee* (Moscow, 1983), pp. 346–50.
11. Ibid., p. 316.
12. Ibid., p. 317.
13. Ibid., p. 318.
14. Ibid., p. 396.
15. Nikol'sky and Grishin, *Nauchno-tekhnicheskii progress*, pp. 234–7.
16. Milovidov and Zhdanov, 'Sotsial'no-filosofskie problemy'. See also, for example, V. P. Filatov, 'Vneshnyaya politika KPSS i mirovoi revolyutsionnyi protsess', in *Problemy kommunisticheskogo dvizheniya. Ezhegodnik* (Moscow: Institut Obshchestvennykh Nauk, 1982), p. 19.
17. Shakhnazarov, *Sotsializm i budushchee*, pp. 331–2; Milovidov and Zhdanov, 'Sotsial'no-filosofskie problemy'.
18. Filatov, 'Vneshnyaya politika'.
19. Shakhnazarov, *Sotsializm i budushchee*, pp. 309–10, 319; G. Shakhnazarov, 'Logika politicheskogo myshleniya v yadernuyu eru', *Voprosy filosofii*, 1984, no. 5, p. 68.
20. Shakhnazarov, *Sotsializm i budushchee*, pp. 334–5.
21. Ibid., pp. 143, 322.
22. G. Shakhnazarov, 'Ideya mirovogo poryadka v sovremennykh kontseptsiyakh mira', *Problemy mira i sotsial'nogo progressa v sovremennoi filosofii* (Moscow, 1983), p. 73.
23. Shakhnazarov, *Sotsializm i budushchee*, p. 317.
24. A. Arbatov, *Voenno-strategicheskii paritet i politika SShA* (Moscow, 1984), pp. 148–50.
25. V. V. Zhurkin, 'Respublikanskaya administratsiya: formirovanie voenno-politicheskoi strategii', *SShA*, 1981, no. 11, p. 4.
26. G. A. Trofimenko, 'Strategicheskie metaniya Vashingtona', *SShA*, 1980, no. 12, p. 52.
27. V. O. Pechatnov, 'Chto pokazali vybory', *SShA*, 1980, no. 12, p. 47.
28. Zhurkin, 'Respublikanskaya', pp. 4, 16.
29. A. Bovin, *The Observer*, 24 April 1983.
30. G. Arbatov, *The Dream World of American Policy* (Moscow: Novosti, 1982).
31. A. Yakovlev, 'Rakovaya opukhol' imperskikh ambitsii v yadernyi vek', *Mirovaya ekonomika i mezhdunarodnye otnosheniya*, 1984, no. 1, p. 3.
32. A. Arbatov, *Voenno-strategicheskii paritet*, p. 305.
33. G. A. Trofimenko, 'Osnovnye postulaty vneshnei politiki SShA i sud'by razryadki', *SShA*, 1981, no. 7, p. 3.
34. G. A. Arbatov and W. Oltmans, *Cold War or Détente? The Soviet Viewpoint* (London: Zed Books, 1983), p. 5.
35. Trofimenko, 'Osnovnye postulaty'.
36. A. Bovin, '50 let – chto dal'she?', *Izvestiya*, 16 November 1983; conversation with researchers of the Institute for the Study of the USA and Canada.
37. A. Yakovlev, 'Zakusivshie udila', *Izvestiya*, 7 October 1983.
38. A. Yakovlev, 'Confrontation is anomaly in international relations', *Twentieth Century and Peace*, 1985, no. 2, p. 24.
39. D. Tomashevsky and V. Lukov, 'Interesy chelovechestva i mirovaya politika', *Mirovaya ekonomika i mezhdunarodnye otnosheniya*, 1985, no. 4,

p. 17; see also O. Bykov, 'Revolyutsionnaya teoriya izbavleniya chelovechestva ot voin', ibid., 1983, no. 4, p. 3.
40. See F. Burlatsky, *Planning of World Peace: Utopia or Reality?* (Moscow: Novosti, 1970).
41. Shakhnazarov, *Sotsializm i budushchee*, p. 445n.
42. I. Mikhailov, 'Mir v 2017-m', *Literaturnaya gazeta*, 7 November 1984.
43. F. Burlatsky, 'Filosofiya mira', *Obshchestvennye nauki*, 1986, no. 1, p. 56; see also Burlatsky, *Planning*, pp. 1–2.
44. Shakhnazarov, *Sotsializm i budushchee*, p. 319.
45. F. Burlatsky, 'Otvetstvennost' rukovoditelei', *Literaturnaya gazeta*, 5 October 1983.
46. L. Mitrokhin, 'Khristianstvo i bor'ba za mir', *Voprosy filosofii*, 1984, no. 11, p. 79; Tomashevsky and Lukov, 'Interesy chelovechestva'.
47. Tomashevsky and Lukov, 'Interesy chelovechestva'.
48. O. N. Melikyan, 'Reshayushchii vybor', *Rabochii klass i sovremennyi mir*, 1983, no. 6, p. 11.
49. Mitrokin, 'Khristianstvo'.
50. Yu. A. Zhilin, 'Bezopasnost' v yadernyi vek', *Rabochii klass i sovremennyi mir*, 1984, no. 2, p. 9.
51. I. D. Ivanov, 'Amerikanskie korporatsii i militarizm', *SShA*, 1986, no. 2, p. 14. For another discussion, see *SShA*, 1984, no. 3, p. 18.
52. V. M. Gavrilov and S. V. Patrushev, 'Bor'ba protiv gonki vooruzhenii kak faktor razvitiya', *Latinskaya Amerika*, 1984, no. 2, p. 5.
53. V. V. Kortunov, *Strategiya mira protiv yadernogo bezumiya* (Moscow, 1984), p. 136.
54. 'Peredovaya', *Voprosy filosofii*, 1984, no. 1, pp. 13–14.
55. Interview with R. Kosolapov, *Literaturnaya gazeta*, 1 February 1984.
56. E. Genri, 'Kto za vozvrat v kamennyi vek?', *Literaturnaya gazeta*, 4 July 1984.
57. A. Krivitsky, 'Teni Dantona ada', *Literaturnaya gazeta*, 7 March 1984.
58. F. Burlatsky, '1984-i god: Chto on gotovit chelovechestvu?', *Literaturnaya gazeta*, 4 January 1984.
59. T. T. Timofeev, 'Imperializm, antivoennye dvizheniya i ideologicheskaya bor'ba', *Rabochii klass i sovremennyi mir*, 1984, no. 1, p. 18.
60. Reference in note 22.
61. Thus, one might suspect the 'reality' of the published foreign-policy controversies between Shakhnazarov and Burlatsky in view of their close links as political scientists. (They are respectively Chairman and Deputy Chairman of the Soviet Political Sciences Association). Shakhnazarov, as a Central Committee official, writes under tighter constraints than Burlatsky as a publicist.
62. Although Yakovlev served as Ambassador in Canada and was for a time Director of the Institute of World Economy and International Relations, his background lies in the Propaganda Department of the Central Committee, to which he has now returned as Head.
63. At present he is Head of the Philosophy Faculty of the Academy of Social Sciences under the Central Committee and political observer for *Literaturnaya Gazeta* (*Literary Gazette*).
64. Shevchenko, *Breaking with Moscow*, p. 288.

65. 'Programma Kommunisticheskoi partii Sovetskogo Soyuza', *Literaturnaya gazeta*, 12 March 1986, pp. 4, 8.
66. The Soviet proposals for détente and international security are set out in Section III of the Third Part, 'Relations with capitalist countries. Struggle for a firm peace and disarmament'.
67. *Literaturnaya gazeta*, 26 February 1986, pp. 2, 3.

11 Ideology and the Policy Process

ALEX PRAVDA

Does ideology matter in the Soviet Union? This is a question that naturally comes to mind when reviewing the preceding chapters. In a basic sense, ideology clearly matters inasmuch as it figures importantly in Soviet political life.[1] The Soviet party continues to devote considerable resources to keeping ideology visible and conveying its content to a mass domestic and international audience. But visibility is not what most have in mind when asking whether ideology matters. What is really meant is: does it make a difference, and if so, how great a difference? Who believes in what elements of the ideology and, perhaps most pertinent, what role does it play in politics? The central concern of most posing such questions is the effect of ideology on the making of Soviet policy at home and abroad.

Western assessments of the relationship between ideology and policy have varied considerably with changing images of the nature of the Soviet system. Prominent within the first generation of post-war studies of the USSR, associated with a totalitarian image of the system, was an 'essentialist' view of Soviet policy which saw ideology as the key to policy intentions and conduct. Dissecting the content of ideology to reveal discrepancies between Marxian, Leninist, Stalinist and post-Stalinist elements was considered well worth the effort, because the doctrinal mix revealed the real objectives that motivated Soviet policy. At home the ideology determined policy direction, abroad it provided a 'masterplan' for global revolutionary expansion. In the essentialist view ideology also shaped strategy, and Bolshevik precepts guided the actions of Soviet leaders.[2]

The changing political environment in the Soviet Union in the first decade following Stalin's death produced a shift in academic analysis of the role of ideology. From occupying centre stage in major scenarios of Soviet politics and policy, ideology found itself relegated to the sidelines.

Extensive ideological revision and the openness of political debate under Khrushchev encouraged scholars to play down the role of ideology. The debacle of the new third Party Programme, the apogee of Khrushchev's efforts to revitalise ideology, confirmed its decline. The pragmatism shown by his successors prompted analysts to extend to the Soviet Union some of the 'end of ideology' generalisations then prevalent in western academic discussion. Ideology no longer bore on politics except as an unsuccessful attempt to inspire the masses and an unconvincing justification of policy. The debate on Soviet ideology in the mid and late 1960s, discussed by Stephen White in Chapter 1, reflected this view.

A growing 'mechanistic' focus on opinion and interest groups further marginalised ideology as a factor in Soviet policy.[3] Seminal studies of both domestic and foreign policy-making, rather than analysing developments in ideology, concentrated on distilling different currents of opinion from specialist debates.[4] Ideology hardly figures in the best of the recent literature on Soviet policy; indeed, some authors avoid the concept altogether, preferring instead terms such as 'official thought'.[5] Even erstwhile essentialists have shifted their deterministic explanations of Soviet foreign policy from ideology to Russian nationalism.[6] Only a few scholars, and then almost exclusively in the international relations field, consider ideology a really significant policy factor.[7] Yet their assessments of the relationship between ideology and policy typically fail to match the precision of 'mechanistic' policy analysis.[8] The nature of the relationship lends itself to impressionistic assessments, rather than precise statements. This, together with the taint of essentialism and the general trend of scholarship, has led to the general neglect of ideology as a window on Soviet politics and policy. This volume has sought to make a start in opening that window. The preceding chapters show that examining the nature, uses and changing content of Soviet ideology does throw light on both politics and policy in the USSR. My aim is not so much to add to the rich empirical material on ideology and policy these chapters contain; rather, I wish to sketch the general patterns of interaction to which this material points and within which it may be sited. This involves first setting out the structure of relations between ideology and policy.

11.1 THE STRUCTURE OF RELATIONS BETWEEN IDEOLOGY AND POLICY

The preceding chapters have avoided dragging the reader into the swamp of definition which most writers on ideology bemoan yet seem unable to avoid. Attempts to produce definitions to comprehend the entire 'cluster complex'[9] of ideology often result in the kind of confusion of meanings that Meyer mentions in chapter 3. The approach adopted in this volume seeks to avoid such confusion by conceiving ideology as a set of systematic theoretical principles projecting and justifying a socio-political order.[10] Following these conceptual lines, White identifies Soviet ideology with Marxist–Leninist doctrine.

In order to explore how ideology relates to policy it is useful to distinguish between three components of ideology: the normative, the analytical and the strategic.[11] The normative component of Soviet ideology comprises fundamental Marxist–Leninist values that define and underpin the socialist order and its consummatory goal of communism. These include belief in and commitment to materialism, the collective, the socialisation of the means of production, social equality, classlessness, and a law-governed historical process leading to the global victory of socialism and communism. Thus the normative dimension encompasses most of what are often called 'philosophical assumptions'. Some of these assumptions are to be found in our analytical component. This comprises the epistomology and methodological techniques – notably dialectics, dialectical and historical materialism – that Marxism–Leninism lays down. These provide an analytical framework of reference as well as an analytical tool box for understanding how society works and history develops and encourage a focus on the operation of underlying social and economic forces, contradictions and conflicts. It is with the aid of this analytical equipment that Marxist–Leninists notionally elaborate the strategies by which to achieve their normative goals.

The strategic component of the ideology outlines the path towards communism at home and abroad, and stipulates intermediate stages and goals as well as how to reach them. The strategic component, therefore, is akin to but not synonymous with an action programme, a term often used to describe the prescriptive applied part of Soviet ideology.[12] It also contains an ideological evaluation of achievements. Essentially, then, strategic ideology prescribes broad policies and offers theoretical justification for them. However, not all theoretically couched statements which explain and justify policies belong in the strategic ideology category. To adopt such an all-inclusive definition, as does Seliger for what he calls operative ideology, is to preclude any comparison between ideology prescriptions and policy. Seliger, in his stimulating study, only compares operative with what he terms fundamental ideology.[13] It is difficult, admittedly, to define precisely which policy principles qualify as elements of the strategic ideology. As a rough guide they must (i) hold an established position in authoritative documents or statements; (ii) refer to policy trends rather than discrete measures; and (iii), most importantly, relate to the normative and analytical dimensions. Examples of strategic ideological elements are the phasing of socialist development and the theory of peaceful coexistence.

All three components of the ideology relate indirectly to the Soviet policy process and policy outputs via the beliefs, assumptions and attitudes of the policy élite, what, following George, we call their operative principles.[14] This élite does not have an absolute monopoly on mediating between ideology and policy. Specialists outside decision-making bodies contribute increasingly to policy-related debates which, as the chapters by Buckley and Shenfield show, play an important part in ideological development. But it is still overwhelmingly through influence on decision makers that ideology affects policy. It is also by way of élite operative principles that policy feedback influences the development of ideology, particularly its strategic component. Given the complex nature of this interactive relationship, I shall consider one set of linkages at a time: how ideology relates to élite operative principles; how the ideological constituents of élite principles bear on the policy debates and decisions; and, lastly, what connections exist between policy performance, élite perspectives and ideological change.

11.2 IDEOLOGY AND ÉLITE OPERATIVE PRINCIPLES

Getting at élite beliefs and outlooks is difficult even in open political systems where inside accounts and interview material shed some light on policy thinking.[15] In the Soviet context, the near absence of such evidence makes generalising about élite principles extremely hazardous. One response to this situation is to deduce principles from policy action and compare these with formal doctrine. Such comparisons often lead to categorical conclusions that Soviet ideology plays no part in élite principles.[16] While this approach can yield some interesting insights, it can also lead to methodological pitfalls. Many who use the comparative technique wrongly assume a zero-sum relationship between the doctrinal and non-doctrinal elements comprising élite principles. They also commonly counterpose ideology to concepts such as national interest and reach the predictable conclusion that the latter invariably prevail. The help guard against these and similar pitfalls, it is useful to conceive of doctrine not as conflicting but rather as interacting with core values, political experience and what Bialer calls 'cultural heritage' to shape élite principles.[17]

National security in the international arena and political survival on the domestic front are core values, pre-ideological inasmuch as every ruling élite puts them before all other others in defining national and public interest. Ideology cannot supplant these core values; it may influence how the élite thinks they should best be upheld, that is, what interests it should pursue. Ideology does not conflict with the national and public interest; along with the influences of tradition, cultural heritage and political experience it can play a part in defining those interests. Doctrine is therefore one of a configuration of interacting elements that shape the policy values, beliefs and attitudes of the Soviet élite.

I shall try to shed some light on the role of doctrine in this configuration, first by sketching some of the ideological components that seem to figure in élite principles, secondly by looking at various ways in which these components impinge on policy making. In making even these very preliminary approaches to the question, I remain keenly aware of the problems posed by evidence. Official documents, speeches and articles by members of the élite can tell us something about their predispositions and policy preferences; they can give us some idea of the relative emphasis politicians place on ideological terms when publicly presenting policy arguments. Opinions differ as to whether such statements, and their doctrinal content, bear any resemblance to private discussions within élite policy circles. Still, according to one specialist with considerable first-hand experience of dealing with Soviet officials, the terms used in public discourse are 'set in the same mold' as those employed in private debate.[18] Used carefully, therefore, published material can form the basis for what admittedly remain impressionistic generalisations about élite principles.

In discussing the influence of ideology on élite principles, it is useful to distinguish once again between normative, analytical and strategic components. Basic beliefs and assumptions are the most difficult to get at, yet perhaps are also the most likely to be influenced by ideology, or more precisely, its normative component.[19] After all, this constitutes the basis for political education in the party, provides a foundation for élite self-legitimation as well as a basis for its right to rule. It is hardly surprising that the Soviet élite have absorbed some basic ideological values. Among those widely shared are the progressive nature of socialism as a system that history will ultimately vindicate; identification of the Soviet Union with socialism, social justice and the good of mankind; and an image of the Soviet Union as a force with a mission identified with world peace and the ultimate achievement of communism.[20] Elite attachment to such basic ideological norms is an emotional or cathetic one.[21] As deeply embedded articles of faith, these fundamental beliefs may be largely immune to testing against reality. But even if we assume that the Soviet élite are not cynical about the validity of such values and goals, it is difficult to escape the impression that they have growing doubts as to their practicability. The frequent amendment of strategic prescriptions to bridge the gap between the desirable and the feasible may not destroy deeply buried values, but it does create a second set of derived goals and commitments. Closer to the surface of policy thinking, these operative goals present significantly different versions of subterranean commitments. The socialism uppermost in the élite's corporate policy mind is dominated by notions of economic and particularly technological modernity, rather than by ones of social equality and political democracy.

If we turn from the normative to the analytical dimension of élite principles, we also find a weakening of what may be seen as ideological influence. Most observers, however, do mention Marxism–Leninism as a factor still affecting the cognitive framework of decision makers. Particularly in the foreign policy field, ideology forms part of the prism through which the Soviet élite view the world, assess policy options and reach decisions.[22] Ideological influence on the approaches Soviet decisison-makers tend to adopt towards policy appraisal is evident in at least three respects:

1. A tendency to focus on underlying social and economic conflicts as the driving force of both domestic and international developments. While thinking on the linear decline of capitalism has been somewhat qualified in recent years, analyses still highlight labour–capital conflicts as central to its development. The working class continues to be seen as the major social force for socialist change. In the international arena, the stress on ideological conflict has become increasingly tempered and is a pale shadow of the Manichean original. Yet Soviet leaders still tend to look at the world in terms of a divide along socialist–imperialist lines. Closely connected with this perception is the image of the United States as the leading imperialist power, driven by a united military–industrial complex inherently opposed to the Soviet Union and eager to attack its interests. While much US foreign policy behaviour may in fact bear out this analysis even to the neutral observer, doctrinal lenses filter out evidence that counters the stereotype.

2. A sensitivity to factors highlighted in the analytical component of Marxism–Leninism. Thus, Soviet leaders tend to pay particular atten-

tion and assign substantive as well as symbolic significance to economic and technological aspects of development. To be sure, economic issues figure prominently on most public political agendas, yet hardly so heavily and so consistently as in the USSR. Soviet politicians have long been preoccupied with the scientific–technical revolution and international economic comparisons. Though extremely proud of having achieved military parity with the U.S., doctrinal tradition heightens élite concerns about the persistent economic inferiority of the USSR.

3. A propensity to see purposive planning in all developments and a corresponding difficulty in accepting uncoordinated events at face value. This is part of a lingering general conviction that history is a law-governed process. Many specific laws propounded by Marxism–Leninism have of course been amended, discarded or simply ignored (as Dyker shows in the economic context). Yet politicians continue to ask theorists to search for the right laws; even a problem-oriented leader like Gorbachev is concerned with identifying 'the key tendencies'.[23] This makes the Soviet élite somewhat more holistic in their approach, more concerned than their Western counterparts with overall connections; the continuing focus on the 'correlation of forces' in the world is a case in point.

All this is not to imply that ideology dominates the way the élite approach issues or diagnose policy problems. The above ideological traits usually colour and coexist with, rather than exclude, other approaches. Their focus on lines of international ideological conflict, for instance, has not prevented Soviet leaders from seeing the strategic advantages of cross-cutting alliances. Nor does their interest in overall patterns of events and policy connections mean Soviet leaders are wedded to a synoptic theological approach to decision-making. Indeed the long-standing emphasis within the leadership on consultation and consensus favours an incrementalist style.[24] The technical education and line experience typical of the policy élite makes likely the spread of an incrementalist and problem-fixing approach.[25]

An important factor also working for a broadening of analytical approaches is a growing realisation that Marxist–Leninist analytical tools must be supplemented by other approaches. Given the failure of doctrinal 'laws' to account for, let alone predict, domestic and international developments, many have turned to Western social science theories of decision-making, management and administration.[26] If anything, such interest is growing, with high-ranking officials admitting privately to Westerners that Marxism–Leninism simply has no bearing on a whole range of current policy issues, arms control being an important case in point. Publicly, the same point is made in more general, yet no less forceful, terms. Vehement in his criticism of attempts to substitute inadequate ideological slogans for proper analysis of complex problems, Gorbachev seems particularly anxious to encourage analytical eclecticism.[27]

A similar process of measuring ideology against practical requirements has undermined the influence of doctrinal prescriptions regarding policy means. By international standards, the Soviet élite still retain a strong belief in the efficacy of education, propaganda and moral stimuli in getting people to work for the collective good. They continue to emphasise group, rather than individual, motivation. At the same time, though, Soviet leaders appear to have just as great an operative confidence in mobilisation, discipline and material reward, means that are more closely linked to tradition than doctrine (even if here as elsewhere the two are difficult to disentangle).

In foreign policy strategy, theoretical pride of place is still given to economic strength and political and ideological influence as the gauge of Soviet power. Soviet leaders remain notionally committed to peaceful furtherance of socialism and opposed to any military export of revolution. Yet the contrast between the inefficacy of economic and political instruments and the relative success of military means in extending Soviet global reach must have had a major impact on operative thinking. As far as tactics are concerned, whether in routine situations or the handling of crises, the ideological connection seems tenuous at the best. While one can point to some links between Leninist precepts and patterns of Soviet behaviour, political experience and traditions provide more persuasive explanations.[28]

An additional and important factor qualifying the influence of ideology on operative strategic principles is the sheer variety of policy prescriptions that general ideological commitments produce. To start with, it strains credibility to claim that the basic tenets and principles of Marxism–Leninism mean the same to all members of the élite, since the corpus of Marxist–Leninist doctrine provides more than sufficient material for a wide spectrum of interpretation. Members of the élite make use of different ideological elements, and the elasticity of certain central doctrines, to support varying policy stances. And those stances are largely shaped by an array of non-doctrinal factors, including political generation. It is often said that Khrushchev was the last Soviet leader to hold the basic doctrinal values as articles of faith and that

Suslov was among the last of the true 'ideologues'. While the intensity of attachment to Marxist–Leninist values may well have declined over the last thirty years, it is likely that Gorbachev believes in the fundamental superiority of socialism and the ultimate attainment of communism, although his doctrinal time-table differs considerably from that of Khrushchev.[29] In terms of specific policy strategy, however, age seems less important than political experience, organisational role and institutional affiliation.[30] Thus officials in Central Committee departments concerned with foreign policy apparently take more interest in the ideological dimensions of foreign policy than do their Ministry of Foreign Affairs counterparts. Because their operative ideology is shaped more by agency standpoint and vested interest than doctrinal values, the fact that certain officials take an ideological view is a poor predictor of their policy perspective. While a doctrinal emphasis is often linked with a traditional and 'hard' policy stance, ideological arguments can also be adduced in favour of a 'soft' strategy. In 1968, for instance, the 'ideologues' Suslov and Ponomarev used ideological arguments, relating to repercussions for the international communist movement, to make the case against invading Czechoslovakia.[31] Such is the low discriminatory power of ideology for most politicians' operative policy strategy that analysts typically distinguish between traditionalists/conservatives on the one hand and non-traditionalists/modernisers on the other.[32]

All this is compatible with ideology providing the Soviet élite with some shared values as well as colouring sections of their framework of analysis. As far as strategic prescriptions are concerned, however, ideology operates as a medium of discourse and thus as a marginal rather than determining influence. To gain some insight into the kind of influences that operative doctrine exercises on policy decisions, we now turn to the role of ideology in the policy cycle.

11.3 IDEOLOGY AND THE POLICY CYCLE

As the role of ideology varies through the phases of the policy cycle, it is best examined sequentially under the following headings: policy debate and agenda building; decision-making and policy output, clearly the phase central to our concerns; and policy feedback, which helps shape doctrinal development and thus completes the ideology–policy cycle. These headings are by no means exhaustive; a thorough examination would involve breaking them down further into initiation, formulation, controversy, consultation and decision as well as considering the implementation stage. They are adequate, though, for the more modest purpose of conveying some idea of the major patterns of influence and interaction.

Policy debate and agenda building

Agenda building can be seen as a two-stage process. A large number of policy issues first emerge in the course of academic and professional discussions which produce a wide-ranging specialist agenda (see the chapters by Buckley, Duncan and Shenfield). If adopted by sufficiently influential members of the policy élite, some of these specialist issues, and even a few of the analyses, may find their way onto the political agenda.

Ideology enters into the shaping of the specialist agenda in two ways. First, Marxism–Leninism provides some of the values, assumptions and analytical techniques that specialists bring to bear on policy problems. Ideological elements tend to bulk less large in the operative principles of academics than those of the policy élite. To start with, recruitment into specialist ranks produces a far broader range of opinion. Professionals may well believe in basic socialist ideals, yet they do not have the same need as politicians to cling to doctrine for reasons of self-legitimation or corporate identity. Moreover, their training and access to non-Marxist–Leninist literature encourages a questioning approach to doctrine. It is in the academic community that the decline in the intellectual attraction and influence of Marxism–Leninsim has perhaps been most evident. At the same time, sophisticated academics sometimes still subscribe to rather crude doctrinal ideas. For even the ritualistic use by specialists of doctrinal concepts can make an impact on their analytical thinking. Such concepts may often serve as politically expedient vehicles for essentially non-doctrinal ideas, but here, as elsewhere, form often fashions content.[33]

Indeed, it is through operating as a vehicle, or more precisely a framework, for professional discussions, rather than providing values and analytical tools, that Soviet ideology exercises influence over specialist agenda building. Marxism–Leninism defines the rules of the game and sets the parameters of debate. While such parameters are often broadly defined and doctrinal elasticity allows considerable latitude for creative thinking, ideological limits still circumscribe and hamper expert policy thinking. They do so most commonly by excluding from legitimate consideration various avenues of analysis and options that could provide an effective solution to the problem being discussed.[34] As Buckley shows in the context of women's issues (chapter 8), as ideological parameters shift, so specialists use the new space to push policy analysis forward. Such advances, however slight, can gain their own momentum. For under certain circumstances specialist analyses may feed into the political agenda; the policies thus produced can help to move the ideological framework further, thus completing the cycle.

The precise nature of the relationship between the specialist and the political policy agenda remains unclear. Western analysts seem to agree that specialist debates may significantly affect the general climate of policy thinking but have very limited *direct* influence on the formulation of specific policy options.[35] Politicians may sympathise with several of the views in a particular specialist discussion; which view they support actively, however, and which makes its mark on the political agenda hinges in small part on ideology. True, at least on the domestic front, doctrine militates strongly against some of the radical revisionist analyses that emerge occasionally in academic discussions. Political sponsorship depends in part on the overall orientation of leading politicians and thus, as we have already noted, tends to be defined less in terms of doctrine than attitudes towards change. And those attitudes with regard to specific policy options often hinge on the policy environment, leadership alignments, bureaucratic and organisational interests. So, in debates on the political as well as on the specialist agenda, ideology may set the broad parameters of debate, but it scarcely shapes the choice of particular policy options.

Decision-making and policy output

As we move from agenda building to decision, we enter the darkest regions of the black box of policy making. Granted only very occasional glimpses of the processes involved, we have to rely on inductive and probabilistic reasoning. Operative ideology – those elements of doctrine that have entered élite operational principles – interacts with the other components of those principles to shape preferences and assign weights to the costs and benefits of various policy options.

To disentangle the ideological strands from the skein of influences acting on decision makers, analysts typically use two techniques. One involves deriving the influence of ideology from the observed fit between doctrine and policy output. The greater the congruence between the two, the stronger the impact of ideology. This technique works best in the rare instances when both doctrine and policy are unambiguous;[36] it has been applied most persuasively to show ideological insignificance where policy measures clearly breach doctrinal provision. More useful over a wider range of cases is an associational approach using the notion of adequacy. Here ideological influence is estimated on the basis of assessing the adequacy of doctrinal factors in accounting for policy output. To be sure, the obscurity of the black box means that our assessments still rely on impressionistic and probablistic judgements about the relationship of policy inputs and output.

To supplement and help strengthen estimates of the presence and especially the power of ideology in the black box, we should also take account of the likely sources of its influence, the ways in which doctrinal functions bear on particular policy situations. Ideology can come into the decision-making picture by way of two basic routes which we shall call the substantive and the instrumental.

Substantive influence on policy decisions flows directly from the effect of the ideological components of élite operative principles on policy preferences. This kind of influence tends to operate fairly consistently in the same issue area in a variety of political settings. Instrumental influence acts as a less steady if more common source of ideological policy effect. Here ideology plays a role, not because it is thought directly to faciliate the substantive solution of the problem, but by dint of its usefulness for related political purposes. These include wielding doctrine as a weapon in élite politicking, and using ideology as a means of policing opinion, whether within the party *aktiv* or among professional groups. By far the most important instrumental use of ideology is to legitimate policy and thus help maintain and strengthen the popular legitimacy of the party leadership and the Soviet regime at home and their reputation abroad. It is useful to distinguish analytically between substantive and instrumental influence and role to avoid the kind of misplaced generalisation often made about the decline (or growth) of doctrine as a whole, which is in fact based on the assessment of changes in the use of ideology as an instrument of policy. Empirically, of course, these analytically distinct types of influences often combine; the greater the overlap between them, the larger the part ideology may be assumed to have played in shaping a particular policy decision.

A thorough-going examination of the range of ideological influence on policy would involve examining these types of influence and applying the techniques we have noted to a representative sample of policy issues and decisions. As this task lies beyond the capacities of a chapter-length survey, the following section reviews a selection of cases chosen specifically to illustrate the range of ideological influence. The cases are discussed under self-explanatory headings denoting the level and kind of ideological influence and role involved.

Determinant influence. Though this category formed the basis for essentialist arguments well into the 1960s, nearly all the convincing examples of ideology actually determining policy fall within the early post-revolutionary period. As Gill notes in chapter 4, ideology played a central policy-making role only as long as real ideological debate lasted. From the early 1930s, and arguably much earlier in some areas, dogmatised ideology became an instrument of control, rather than a source of policy thinking. As a policing mechanism, ideology dominated most professional activity. For the last thirty years, ideologically couched limits have become far broader and more elastic, albeit fitfully so, and exercise only indirect influence over the content of policy on the social, let alone the natural, sciences. Even in the area of literature, ideological formulae such as socialist realism loom over and influence the form, rather than determine the content of policy.[37] Similarly, Marxism–Leninism clearly affects the focus, scope and style of censorship, yet it hardly determines its policy thrust or explains its existence.[38]

The policy areas in which ideology appears most dominant are typically ones where doctrine played an important historical part in initiating changes which have subsequently been shaped and perpetuated by tradition and institutional interest rather than ideology. So closely do doctrinal and institutional power influences coincide that it is extremely difficult to make a convincing case for ideological determination. This is hardly surprising since clear-cut instances of doctrinal determination of policy are to be found where ideological parties come to power seeking to change the status quo; the alternating economic and financial policies of successive British Labour and Conservative governments are a case in point.[39] In the Soviet Union even new leaders, who distance themselves from their predecessors in policy terms, try to point up basic structural and ideological continuity. Ideology may well help to perpetuate traditional features of the system such as the centrally planned economy and job security and to hamper their antonyms, marketisation and private ownership, but vested interest and fear of change, powerful forces in Soviet politics, are probably equally or more important here. Such cases thus illustrate predispositional, rather than determinant ideological influence.

Predispositional influence. A good deal of evidence can be found for Soviet ideology operating to predispose decision makers for or against particular policy options by affecting their appraisal of the different sets of costs and benefits involved. The fact that the following examples show that ideology contributes to a variety of policies should not be taken as an argument that doctrine exercises a powerful and all-pervasive policy influence. For the most part, even in these cases selected to illustrate doctrinal influence, ideology has little impellant force and its effect depends on an absence of countervailing forces. Only in exceptional cases, such as job security which we discuss below, does ideology possess quite considerable force, and even then it is exercised against change, always a relatively easy task in the Soviet Union.

The foreign policy field, where ideology generally plays a marginal role, provides some interesting examples of substantive influence, albeit of a weakly predispositional kind. Doctrinally-based perceptions of the ideological divide between socialism and capitalism have long affected Soviet notions of the rules of the international game and continue to complicate understanding between the USSR and the US, whose own ideology, as Meyer notes in chapter 3, compounds the problem. The case of détente provides a recent illustration of the policy ramifications of differing ideological perceptions. For Soviet leaders the concept of détente was restricted only to some aspects of East–West relations; in the developing world, the ideological struggle went on and Moscow acted in that spirit.[40] The Americans, by contrast, assumed that détente had comprehensive coverage and therefore reacted far more strongly to Afghanistan and general Soviet Third World ventures than decision makers in Moscow had anticipated.

Soviet policy in the Third World also provides an example of doctrinal assumptions helping to predispose leaders to make a major policy departure. Ideologically founded optimism in the 'natural' progress of former colonies to socialism encouraged Khrushchev actively to support the cause of 'socialist progress' in developing states. Not that ideological beliefs directly precipitated specific ventures; as in the case of Soviet involvement in India, specific moves by Moscow were largely responses to changes in regional power alignments.[41] Here, as in all instances of predispositional influence, ideology did not trigger particular moves, but rather, in conjuction with other considerations, affected the longer-term direction of policy development. In a recent attempt to assess the factors shaping Soviet aid and support for Third World countries, Papp found that ideology – a bias towards states of 'socialist orientation' – provides no better an explanation of the pattern of distribution than does military and strategical reasoning.[42] In the overwhelming majority of foreign policy decisions, such reasoning, combined with political and diplomatic considerations, relegates ideology to a very marginal or wholly negligible role.

On the domestic front, there seems to be evidence of somewhat more widespread and stronger predispositional ideological influence, particularly in the agricultural, labour and welfare policy areas. Agriculture provides a *locus classicus* for ideological influence. The doctrinal prejudice against the peasantry, mentioned by Gill in chapter 4, certainly contributed to forced collectivisation and to the subsequent treatment of the countryside.[43] Higher ideological status helps to account, along with considerations of economic and political control, for the precedence given to state over collective farms. Doctrinal doubts lie behind the grudging policy on private plots, notwithstanding their proven economic advantages. Long hesitation about the link (*zveno*) system on collective farms has owed more, however, as Dyker persuasively argues,[44] to apprehension about its implications for traditional regime controls than to doctrinal concern.

It is in the labour and welfare policy areas that ideological values and commitments have exercised the strongest predispositional influence. However chequered the regime's record on social equality, incomes policy has kept pay differentials relatively narrow by international standards.[45] The current link drawn between 'social justice' and 'political stability' suggests that instrumental as well as substantive doctrinal influence lies behind moves to reduce conspicuous material inequalities and privileges.[46] An ideological commitment to full employment has been a major reason for the reluctance of successive Soviet leaderships to tackle the economic problems linked with absolute job security. Nor have they undone the huge network of economically counterproductive subsidies that underpins the welfare system.

The ideological constraint on Soviet leaders changing welfare policy rests on both substantive and instrumental influence. It is reasonable to assume that most Soviet leaders have seen welfare as an integral part of what Dyker in chapter 6 calls the Soviet socialist tradition. Decision-makers are also aware of the key importance of the welfare tradition in sustaining their own and the regime's popular legitimacy. There are indications that the more technocratically minded of the current leadership want to qualify the absolute right to a chosen job and educate workers to accept transfers more readily. They may find it possible to alter some of the customs of the welfare system. The combined force of tradition, institutionalised practice and ideology, however, will make it difficult to change the welfare principle. In the area of welfare, as in others where predispositional influence, albeit of a weaker kind, obtains, ideology shapes the overall orientation rather than the specific features of policy.

Environmental influence. This category covers ideological effects on the climate, tenor and style, rather than the overall content and direction of policy. Environmental effects can have an important cumulative policy influence, yet their inherently diffuse nature makes this impact particularly difficult to assess.

The influence of ideology on political language is the most obvious and pervasive kind of environmental effect. Even though their dominance of political vocabulary is waning, doctrinal terms continue to permeate public political discourse. They still provide a code of communication for the policy community. Urban explores the semiotic dimension of ideology in chapter 7. The use of ideological terms and concepts can affect the tenor of policy where ideology is used for regulatory purposes. On the domestic front, the most obvious examples come from the area of literature where, as we have already noted, doctrinal formulas often have more effect on the climate of relations between writers and the regime than on the actual content of literary production.

Ideological impact on the tenor of policy is also evident in Soviet relations with socialist states. Even if security and issues of regional power and national pride have always been at the heart of the Sino-Soviet dispute, the salience of ideological issues raised the stakes and thus deepened the conflict. Through the years, the use of doctrinal terms has at times made positions more inflexible and reconciliation more difficult, even if ideology does not currently present a real obstacle to *rapprochement*.[47]

Similarly, ideology has affected the form rather than the substance of Soviet policy towards Eastern Europe. It could be argued that East European policy straddles the predispositional/environmental categories. After all, doctrine played some part in predisposing Stalin to try and create Soviet-type states in Eastern Europe, rather than simply establishing firm control over the region. The scope and throughness of the campaigns for socialisation surely owed something to ideology. And doctrine continues to help sustain the impression among Soviet leaders that they can maintain a special kind of relationship with the socialist states. For the most part, of course, doctrine serves to justify Soviet control; Marxism–Leninism has done little, if anything, to shape critical decisions regarding the region. Thus the predominant influence of ideology is of a strongly environmental kind.

The prominent role played by ideology as an instrument of control has given all doctrinal developments in Eastern Europe, and indeed in all Soviet-type states, a particularly important political dimension. Doctrinal developments in those states are often taken by Moscow as one of the gauges of compliance. One of the factors that prompted Moscow to support the replacement of Ulbricht as East German party leader in 1971, for instance, was his apparent attempt to steal a doctrinal lead on the Soviet Union by making claims about having achieved the stage of developed socialism.[48] During the Czechoslovak crisis, ideological heterodoxies of a far more heinous kind formed part of the evidence which the Politburo considered when assessing developments. Yet throughout the Soviet monitoring process and élite debates on policy alternatives, issues relating to political appointments and security remained uppermost. Most important of all is the fact that doctrinal concerns seem scarcely to have figured in the final decision to intervene.[49]

Rather than proceed to review the mass of policy decisions where even the environmental and atmospheric effects of ideology evaporate and doctrine makes no perceptible difference, it may be useful at this point to suggest some general propositions relating to the policy salience and influence of Soviet ideology.

1. Ideology tends to affect the direction of policy rather than discrete policy decisions. Doctrine is far more likely to figure in routine than in crisis decisions where pressures of time and events beyond the decision makers' control favour a problem-fixing approach.
2. Analytical ideological elements are most influential where, as on many foreign policy questions, decision-makers have neither detailed knowledge of the issues nor strong institutional interests riding on particular options. Here doctrinal stereotypes commonly affect general policy approaches, yet rarely shape decisions, as these are effectively taken by a small group of foreign policy specialists.[50]
3. Ideological norms make most impact on policy – in practice this means a strong predispositional effect – where substantive and instrumental influences combine and doctrine acts with tradition as a constraint on change. Where these conditions do not obtain, ideological influence rarely exceeds a weak predispositional effect.
4. Where ideology operates as a policing or control mechanism, doctrine affects form and style rather than the content of policy.
5. The patterns summarised above suggest that ideology is more salient in domestic than foreign policy. On the domestic front, redistributive policies are more susceptible to ideological influence than those of a distributive or regulative kind.

Policy feedback and ideological change

In this last phase of the cycle the flow of influence is reversed and policy performance exercises a major influence on ideological development. Instead of dismissing this dimension of policy–ideology interaction merely as evidence of ideological insignificance, the contributors to this volume have rightly viewed doctrinal change as a window on policy thinking.

Doctrinal development is particularly important to the vitality of Soviet ideology. As a self-proclaimed scientific doctrine, Marxism–Leninism lays special emphasis on the need to keep abreast of changing realities. Updating ideology is clearly important for practical political reasons. To be of any use to policy-makers, the ideology must provide analytical concepts and tools that actually help to resolve the problems they face. To have any credibility with the general public, and thus help legitimate the regime, ideology must explain and if possible justify policy performance. At the same time, it must also maintain reasonable internal coherence: consistency between its normative, analytical and strategic components. In a sense, therefore, the requirements and principles of ideological development resemble those underlying accountancy. Indeed the following definition of a an accountant fits Soviet (and other) ideology-makers remarkably well: a person who 'enables a demoralised modern society to live with itself by reassuring it that its models and data can pass for "truth"'.[51] Although not particularly successful in achieving these objectives, Soviet ideological accountancy has nevertheless been fairly active in developing doctrine.

Doctrinal development has drawn increasingly in recent years on the kind of specialist debates discussed in the chapters by White, Evans, Duncan, Buckley and Shenfield. The impressive variety of doctrinal interpretations and modifications that these specialists have produced may be seen as forming a pool of proto-ideology, ideas available for incorporation into official doctrine. Whether these innovations are allowed to join the ideological mainstream depends not so much on their theoretical relevance as on political utility and timeliness. Some concepts and theories emerge before the political time is right and either simply languish or attract official disapproval. Butenko's theories about contradictions and conflicts of interest under socialism (see chapter 1) are one recent instance of politically premature ideological innovation. Here, as in other cases, the way ideas are packaged is as important as their content. Thus, many of Butenko's basic concerns, expressed in a more acceptable form, appear in the analyses of Novosibirsk sociologists and economists, notably Zaslavskaya. Their substance, including the recognition of contradictions between the forces of production and production relations, have apparently gained Gorbachev's approval.[52]

The attraction of these ideas, as of doctrinally innovative arguments in general, lies not just in the substantive insights they offer into the policy problems at hand, but also in their instrumental utility. The Novosibirsk arguments provide a doctrinally founded case for policies to improve productivity. That key terms used in these and cognate arguments have found their way into official speeches may signal Gorbachev's approval. Whether these ideas become an established part of the ideology depends, though, on how Gorbachev fares politically and how acceptable they are to strategic groups. For, to use White's apt terms, ideology is the product of a process of negotiation and renegotiation between political interests. Ideological changes can therefore shed light on ascendant political tendencies. The use of key phrases relating to doctrinal debates can help us place a politician in the policy spectrum. This is the way in which some analysts have identified Gorbachev's position on economic change,[53] and the technique Shenfield uses in chapter 10 to locate the General Secretary's stance on questions of peace and war.

Apart from helping to identify the policy orientation of individual leaders and groups, ideological developments also shed light on general trends in policy thinking. Doctrinal modifications or innovations usually emerge as a response to policy or general environmental developments that depart from ideological prescriptions. However, major long-term doctrinal changes, such as the elaboration of developed socialism, may initially be responses but then evolve in parallel to policy change. Thus, as Evans notes in chapter 5, these longer-term shifts in ideology can reveal a good deal about the general perspectives of the political leadership.

Developments in Soviet Third World policy and doctrine may help to illustrate the relationship between policy performance and ideological change. As we have already noted, under Khrushchev policy shifts preceded and were justified by changes in theoretical views of Third World development. The very mixed results of Khrushchev's expansive support for all forces that claimed to oppose imperialism brought about a reappraisal of doctrine and policy. At the strategic level, doctrine elevated the importance of vanguard Marxist–Leninist parties, which also became the focus of Soviet policy support in the 1970s. However, given the failure of some of these parties to consolidate power, faith in communist vanguards is now giving way to support for a broader spectrum of political forces. At the analytical level, the practical difficulties encountered by Soviet policy and 'socialist progress' in the Third World have been accompanied by growing qualifications to traditional historical determinism. Doctrine now gives more weight to cultural factors, the intractability of backwardness, and the attractiveness of capitalism.[54] This shift links up with a wider reappraisal of the staying power of capitalism and the interdependence of the global economy.

The changes in Soviet doctrine on developing states have not provided clear signals of impending Soviet policy moves in the Third World. More often policy shifts have led to theoretical reappraisals. Still, in the words of a recent study, doctrinal reassessments have served 'to delineate the major phases in the evolution of Soviet strategy towards the Third World'.[55] In this policy area, as in many others, changes in ideology have helped shape the framework and climate within which policy is appraised and new options formulated. Rather than enabling us to project Soviet moves, doctrinal developments both reflect established policy thinking and often point to emerging policy predispositions. Thus current doctrinal uncertainty and sobriety about prospects for socialism in the developing states correlates closely with Gorbachev's low-key references to Soviet Third World policy.[56]

If we turn from the Third World to the general policy front, current ideological shifts also provide a window on policy thinking and development. Under Gorbachev the most evident changes in ideology have affected doctrinal perspective and style. The revised version of the Party Programme differs in a number of ways from the Khrushchevian original which Evans discusses in chapter 5. It is worth underscoring the important shift from a teleological to a more technical ideological perspective. Instead of focusing on the consummatory goal of communism, the revised programme centres on 'improving' or 'perfecting' the here-and-now of socialism by accelerating social and economic development.[57] Evidently the leadership has decided that stressing even intermediate doctrinal goals is an ineffective ideological accounting device which undermines, rather than strengthens, legitimacy. The attempts made under Brezhnev to create the impression of progress by introducing new stages of socialism have largely been abandoned. Developed socialism, the doctrinal centre-piece of the Brezhnev era, hardly figures in the new programme and received no more than passing mention in Gorbachev's 27th Congress speech. In that report, Gorbachev made a point of lambasting the general tendency of using ideological slogans as substitutes for progress and covers for 'sluggishness'.[58]

To a great extent, of course, such ideological points are used as a way of discrediting the whole Brezhnevite era and those Brezhnevites who stand in the way of change. Still, the criticism of ideological sloganeering is not merely a convenient political ploy. It forms part of a new political style notable for the replacement of ideological slogans by a direct approach to policy problems.

The ramifications of this new style extend beyond the realm of public relations into that of ideological method and policy analysis. Gorbachev appears to be seriously concerned to remove some of the doctrinal constraints on specialist discussion of policy problems; he cited money–commodity relations as an example of an issue where dogmatic prejudice had hampered progress.[59] Rather than being preoccupied with forcing policy thinking into Procrustean beds of established doctrine, theorists should use Marxist–Leninist approaches in combination with other techniques where these shed light on policy problems. This surely was the point of regaling congress delegates with Lenin's remark that not even seventy Marxs could hope to comprehend all the complexities of capitalism.[60] The message was spelled out in a subsequent central committee decree on the role of *Kommunist*, the party's main ideological journal. This directs *Kommunist* to deal with difficult problems more openly and imaginatively by opening its pages to a wide range of social science approaches and views.[41] That the debate on contradictions under socialism, suspended under Chernenko, has now re-emerged is a token of this more tolerant approach.[62]

A more open, less doctrinaire attitude to ideology also emerges in some foreign and domestic policy areas. Certainly the style in which the Gorbachev leadership has conducted its foreign policy reflects a more flexible and open approach. Some observers have noted a movement away from the more traditional ideological stress on bipolarism and towards a less doctrinaire multipolar view of the world.[63] Increased overtures to Western Europe, Japan and China might be seen in this light, though continued preoccupation with arms control and summitry suggests that US relations remain central to Soviet concerns.

The policy record on the domestic front is also mixed. Some initiatives betoken a less ideological approach. For example, the encouragement of small-scale private entrepreneurship in the context of housing construction, agricultural plots, horticultural allotments and small family work groups on farms indicates that Gorbachev is more concerned with improving incentives and economic returns than with observing traditional ideological niceties. So too does his support for schemes to reduce overmanning and tighten the relationship between pay and performance. At the same time, a doctrinal concern emerges in the stress Gorbachev places on the collective basis of private enterpreneurship, the importance of social justice, and the need to control unearned income. Current ambiguity on the central issue of economic reform is due perhaps in part to a continuing commitment in principle to the central planning system, albeit one with greater organisational devolution.[64] The major campaigns against corruption and alcoholism may not clearly signal any ideological intent. But, if anything, their preoccupation with establishing firm control over the élite and society and instilling discipline smacks of a traditional doctrinal emphasis on a puritan ethic. Like his mentor Andropov, Gorbachev, while aiming to improve material incentives, seeks to strengthen the sense of moral purpose in Soviet society; hence the strong emphasis placed on the spiritual superiority of socialism and the need to guard against the incursions of bourgeois mentality.

Indeed, basic ideological values figure far more prominently in Gorbachev's report to the 27th Congress than they do in the equivalent report delivered by Brezhnev in 1981. Gorbachev may have devoted remarkably little attention to the new programme, yet he spent far more time than his predecessor in extolling the basic virtues of socialism and listing the evils of capitalism. Fundamental doctrinal values such as collectivism, party leadership, participation and peace are being asserted more forcefully, it could be argued, than at any time since Khrushchev. Even the largely non-doctrinal sounding slogan 'the acceleration of social–economic progress' is being used to as a vehicle for ambitious ideological goals including self-government and the highest social labour productivity in the world. Despite the criticism of traditional sloganeering, 'acceleration' is seen as 'the key to all our problems' and the concept hailed as one of 'the greatest achievements of contemporary Marxist–Leninist thought'.[65] Not that parallels with Khrushchev should be carried too far. Gorbachev's philosophy and political style may have a populist strand, but the thrust of his ideological programme strongly echoes the prevailing technocratic tendencies in the 1970s. There is somewhat more stress on social factors, including social justice, collectivism and participation. Yet technology, organisational efficiency, professional expertise and the intensive modernisation they can generate are all integral to the concept of 'acceleration' as they were to the 'technocratic socialism' of the late Brezhnev period.[66] As far as motivating the Soviet people to achieve such dynamism is concerned, Gorbachev seems to place a particular emphasis on material rewards; otherwise he favours the conventional blend of moral stimuli (socialist consciousness) and traditional values such as patriotism and nationalism.

If Gorbachev succeeds in pushing through 'acceleration' based on his somewhat populist version of technocratic socialism, ideology may become a more powerful force in the Soviet system. If, as seems more likely, his efforts bring about an acceleration of drift, ideology will continue to be a medium of discourse and a currency for creative political accountancy. In any case, ideology will continue to change, and its shifting sandbanks[67] will continue to define the contours, direction and flow of Soviet policy and politics over the years to come.

NOTES

1. See J. P. Scanlan, *Marxism in the USSR. A Critical Survey of Current Soviet Thought* (Ithaca, N.Y.: Cornell University Press, 1985), pp. 12–13.
2. A classic study is N. Leites, *The Operational Code of the Soviet Politburo* (New York: McGraw-Hill, 1951).
3. The essentialist/mechanistic/cybernetic typology of approaches to the study of Soviet foreign policy – also applicable to the domestic sphere – is discussed in W. Zimmerman, 'Choice in the Post-War World (1): Containment and the Soviet Union' in C. Gati (ed.), *Caging the Bear: Containment and the Cold War* (Indianapolis and New York: Bobbs-Merrill, 1974), pp. 85–108; and by R. N. Cutler, *Soviet Debates on the Conduct of Policy Toward Western Europe: Four Case Studies 1971–75* (PhD thesis, University of Michigan, 1982), pp. 3–6.
4. For instance, H. G. Skilling and F. Griffiths (eds), *Interest Groups in Soviet Politics* (Princeton University Press, 1971); and W. Zimmerman, *Soviet Perspectives on International Relations 1956–68* (Princeton University Press, 1969).
5. B. Parrott, *Politics and Technology in the Soviet Union* (Cambridge, Mass.: MIT Press 1983), p. 4.; also see T. Gustafson, *Reform in Soviet Politics: the Lessons of Recent Policies on Land and Water* (Cambridge University Press, 1981).
6. This is exemplified by Z. Brzezinski; see his 'The Soviet Union: Her Aims, Problems, and Challenges to the West', in R. F. Laird and E. P. Hoffmann (eds), *Soviet Foreign Policy in a Changing World* (New York: Aldine Publishing Company, 1986), pp. 3–15.
7. For instance see R. F. Staar, *USSR: Foreign Policies after Detente* (Stanford: Hoover Institution Press, 1985); R. Judson Mitchell, *Ideology of a Superpower: Contemporary Soviet Doctrine on International Relations* (Stanford: Hoover Institution Press, 1982); and C. Linden, *The Soviet Party-State: The Politics of Ideocratic Despotism* (New York: Praeger, 1983). Interesting discussions of the relationship between ideology and Soviet foreign policy include L. Labedz, 'Ideology and Soviet Foreign Policy', in C. Bertram (ed.), *Prospects of Soviet Power in the 1980s* (London:

Macmillan, 1980), pp. 22–30; and H. Adomeit, 'Ideology in the Soviet View of International Affairs', in Bertram, *Prospects of Soviet Power*, pp. 103–10.

8. For methodological criticism of H. Adomeit, *Soviet Risk-Taking and Crisis Behaviour. A Theoretical and Empirical Analysis* (London: Allen and Unwin, 1982), one of the more sophisticated studies stressing ideology, see J. Snyder, 'Richness, Rigor and Relevance in the Study of Soviet Foreign Policy', *International Security*, Winter 1984/85, pp. 89–108, at p. 102.
9. G. Sartori, 'Politics, Ideology, and Belief Systems', *American Political Science Review*, vol. 63 (1969), pp. 398–410, at p. 398.
10. Cf. D. Bell, 'Ideology and Soviet Politics', *Slavic Review*, vol. 24 no. 4 (December 1965), pp. 398–410, at p. 595; and Z. Brzezinski and S. P. Huntington, *Political Power: US/USSR* (New York: Viking Press, 1964), p. 19.
11. This division is based on the very helpful scheme proposed by Alex George in 'Ideology and International Relations: A Conceptual Analysis', a revised (May 1985) version of a paper presented to the conference on Ideology and Its Influence on International Politics, Leonard Davis Institute for International Relations, The Hebrew University of Jerusalem, 7–9 January 1985; see especially pp. 2–3. My understanding of the relationship between ideology and foreign policy has greatly benefited from George's writings as well as from George Breslauer's presentation on ideology and Soviet foreign policy at the seminar on the Comparative Study of Communist Societies, University of California, Berkeley, 7 February 1986.
12. Brzezinski and Huntington, *Political Power*, p. 21.
13. See M. Seliger, *Politics and Ideology* (London: Allen and Unwin, 1976), esp. pp. 120, 175.
14. George, 'Ideology and International Relations', pp. 18–20. For an earlier and fuller description of what he then called the operational code, see A. L. George, 'The "Operational Code": A Neglected Approach to the Study of Political Leaders and Decision-Making', in E. P. Hoffmann and F. J. Fleron (eds), *The Conduct of Soviet Foreign Policy* (London: Butterworths, 1971), pp. 165–98.
15. See, for instance, R. Putnam, 'Studying Elite Political Culture: the case of Ideology', *American Political Science Review*, vol. 65 (September 1971), pp. 651–81.
16. For a recent statement of this view, see A. Nove in evidence submitted to the Foreign Affairs Committee, quoted in *UK–Soviet Relations*. Second Report from the Foreign Affairs Committee of the House of Commons, vol. I (London: Her Majesty's Stationery Office, 1986), p. xii.
17. S. Bialer distinguishes between doctrine, historical experience and cultural heritage; see his *The Soviet Paradox: External Expansion, Internal Decline* (New York: Knopf, 1986), pp. 262–4. For a lucid discussion of 'irreducible' values, ideology and national interest, see George, 'Ideology and International Relations', pp. 14–16.
18. Raymond L. Garthoff, *Détente and Confrontation: American–Soviet Relations from Nixon to Reagan* (Washington DC: Brookings Institution, 1985), p. 50; contrast Meyer, 'Assessing the Ideological Commitment of a Regime', in J.L. Nogee (ed.), *Soviet Politics: Russia after Brezhnev* (New York: Praeger, 1985), pp. 107–21, at p. 111. For discussion of the political

significance of media material, see L. Dzirkals, T. Gustafson and R. Johnson, *The Media and Intra-Elite Communication in the USSR* (Santa Monica: Rand, 1982).

19. George, 'Ideology and International Relations', p. 20.
20. Garthoff, *Détente*. p. 20; Judson Mitchell, *Ideology of a Super Power*, pp. 100–1 ff.; and C. Jonsson, 'Foreign Policy Ideas and Groupings in the Soviet Union', in R. F. Kanet (ed.), *Soviet Foreign Policy and East–West Relations* (Elmsford N.Y.: Pergamon, 1982), pp. 3–28, at p. 6. A. N. Shevchenko, *Breaking with Moscow* (London: Cape, 1985), talks of the basic faith of even the pragmatic Gromyko in the eventual victory of socialism (p. 154) and a shared sense of the general 'rightness' of the Soviet system (p. 180).
21. For discussions of cathetic and other forms of attachment, see P. Diesing, *Science and Ideology in the Policy Sciences* (New York: Aldine, 1982), p. 10.
22. R. Legvold, 'The Nature of Soviet Power', in Laird and Hoffmann, *Soviet Foreign Policy*, pp. 29–48, at p. 43; Garthoff, *Détente*, p. 20; Brzezinski and Huntington, *Political Power*, pp. 42, 56; and J. F. Triska and D. D. Finley, *Soviet Foreign Policy* (New York and London: Collier-Macmillan/Macmillan, 1968), pp. 115–6.
23. M. S. Gorbachev, 'Politicheskii doklad Tsentral'nogo Komiteta KPSS XXVII s"ezdu Kommunisticheskoi Partii Sovetskogo Soyuza', *Pravda*, 26 February 1986, pp. 2–10, at p. 2.
24. For a discussion of ideological style, see Putnam, 'Studying Elite Political Culture'. A discussion of Soviet consultative procedures may be found in E. Jones, 'Committee Decision-Making in the Soviet Union', *World Politics*, vol. 36 no. 2 (June 1984), pp. 165–88.
25. For educational background and likely effects, see R. Theen, 'Party and Bureaucracy', in E. P. Hoffmann and R. F. Laird (eds), *The Soviet Polity in the Modern Era* (New York: Aldine, 1984), pp. 131–66, at p. 135; and Triska and Finley, *Soviet Foreign Policy*, pp. 123–4.
26. See, for instance, R. F. Vidmer and J. C. Thompson, *Administrative Science and Politics in the USSR and the United States. Soviet Responses to American Management Techniques 1917–Present* (New York: Praeger, 1983).
27. Gorbachev, 'Politicheskii doklad', p. 2.
28. For a study that stresses the significance of ideology for strategy and tactics, see Adomeit, *Soviet Risk-Taking and Crisis Behavior*, esp. pp. 115–6, 120.
29. For a discussion of Gorbachev's background and likely outlook, see A. H. Brown, 'Gorbachev: New Man in the Kremlin', *Problems of Communism*, vol. 34 no. 3 (May - June 1985), pp. 1–23, esp. p. 23.
30. Cutler, *Soviet Debates*, pp. 251, 269; and M. R. Beissinger, 'In search of Generations in Soviet Politics', *World Politics*, vol. 32 no. 2 (June 1986), pp. 288–314, at pp. 288–90.
31. See K. Dawisha, *The Kremlin and the Prague Spring* (Berkeley: University of California Press, 1985), p. 260; and P. Tigrid, *Why Dubček Fell* (London Macdonald, 1971), pp. 96, 127–8.
32. See, for instance, Parrott, *Politics and Technology*, pp. 5–6; Jonsson, 'Foreign Policy Ideas', pp. 11–13; and E. P. Hoffmann and R. F. Laird, '*The Scientific–Technological Revolution' and Soviet Foreign Policy* (Elmsford N Y: Pergamon Press, 1982).

33. See J. DeBardeleben, *The Environment and Marxism–Leninism* (Boulder, Col.: Westview, 1985) p. 269; and J. F. Hough, *The Struggle for the Third World: Soviet Debates and American Options* (Washington DC: Brookings, 1986), p. 103.
34. De Bardeleben, *The Environment*, pp. 368–70.
35. See Hough, *The Struggle for the Third World*, pp. 262–4; Gustafson, *Reform in Soviet Politics*, p. 17; and N. Malcolm, *Soviet Political Scientists and American Politics* (London: Macmillan, 1984), pp. 163–4.
36. For problems of ideological 'indeterminacy' see D. D. Comey, 'Ideology and Soviet Policy', *Studies in Soviet Thought*, vol. 2 no. 4 (1962), pp. 301–20, at pp. 307–8.
37. See, for instance, M. Crouch and R. Porter, 'Ideology and Literary Policy' (mimeo. paper, Bristol University, April 1985); and K. Clark, 'The Mutability of the Canon: Socialist Realism and Aitmatov's *I dol'she veka dlitsia den*'', *Slavic Review*, vol. 43 no. 4 (Winter 1984), pp. 573–87.
38. Meyer is rightly unimpressed by censorship as testimony to the strength of ideology; see his chapter in this volume. Scanlan points out that the ideology has prevented public challenges to its general validity; see his *Marxism in the USSR*, p. 12.
39. For an examination of the ideological basis of taxation policy, see A. Robinson and G. Sandford, *Tax Policy-Making in the United Kingdom. A Study of Rationality, Ideology and Politics* (London: Heinemann, 1983), p. 40. See Garthoff, *Détente*, pp. 42 ff.; and Judson Mitchell, *Ideology of a Superpower*, pp. 55–67. Of course, ideology was only one of the elements contributing to misperceptions here just as misperception provides only a partial explanation for the course of détente in the late 1970s. For an analysis which stresses other factors, see G. Breslauer, 'Why Detente Failed: An Interpretation', in A. L. George et al., *Managing U.S.–Soviet Rivalry. Problems of Crisis Prevention* (Boulder, Col.: Westview, 1983), pp. 319–40.
40. See Breslauer, 'Why Detente Failed', pp. 319–40.
41. See R. H. Donaldson, 'Soviet Intervention in South Asia and the Indian Ocean', in R. Kanet (ed.), *Soviet Foreign Policy in the 1980s* (New York: Praeger, 1982), pp. 330–1.
42. D. S. Papp, *Soviet Perceptions of the Developing World in the 1980s. The Ideological Basis* (Lexington: D. C. Heath, 1985), esp. pp. 127ff.
43. See A. Nove, *The Economics of Feasible Socialism* (London: Allen and Unwin, 1983), pp. 115–6.
44. See chapter 6.
45. For a recent survey of the evidence on income distribution, see A. Bergson, 'Income Inequality under Soviet Socialism', *Journal of Economic Literature*, no. 22 (September 1984), pp. 1052–99, esp. p. 1070.
46. See 'Programma Kommunisticheskoi Partii Sovetskogo Soyuza. Novaya redaktsiya', *Pravda*, 7 March 1986, pp. 3–10, at p. 6. Also see P. Frank, 'Gorbachev's dilemma: social justice or political stability?', *The World Today*, vol. 42 no. 6 (June 1986), pp. 93–5.
47. See, for instance, Bialer, *The Soviet Paradox*, pp. 231, 244, 264. For an analysis that plays down the role of ideology, see D. S. Zagoria, 'Ideology and Chinese foreign policy', in G. Schwab (ed.), *Ideology and Foreign Policy* (New York: Cyrco, 1978), pp. 103–16.

48. See A. J. McAdams, *East Germany and Detente. Building Authoriy after the Wall* (Cambridge University Press, 1985), ch. 4, esp. pp. 112–15.
49. See Z. Mlynář, *Mraz přichází z kremlu* (Cologne: Index, 1979), pp. 202–13; J. Valenta, 'Soviet Decision-Making on Czechoslovakia, 1968', in J. Valenta and W. C. Potter (eds), *Soviet Decision-making for National Security* (London: Allen and Unwin, 1984), pp. 165–84. For a detailed and penetrating study of Soviet decision-making in 1968, see K. Dawisha, *The Kremlin and the Prague Spring*.
50. Cf. Triska and Finley, *Soviet Foreign Policy*, ch. 4, esp. pp. 119–22.
51. T. Gambling, quoted in G. Hofstede, *Culture's Consequences: International Differences in Work-Related Values* (Beverly Hills and London: Sage, 1980), p. 160.
52. For instance, see Gorbachev's questioning of traditional assumptions about the 'automatic' conformity of production relations and productive forces under socialism in his 'Politicheskii doklad', p. 5. For the Russian text of the 'Novosibirsk Report', see T. Zaslavskaya, 'Doklad o neobkhodimosti bolee uglublennogo izucheniya v SSSR sotsial'nogo mekhanizma razvitiya ekonomiki', RFE/RL, *Materialy samizdata* (Munich), issue no. 35, 1983 (26 August 1983). For a translation, see 'The Novosibirsk Report', *Survey*, vol. 28 no. 1 (Spring 1984), pp. 88–108 (also see the comment by P. Hanson on pp. 83–7).
53. T. Gustafson and D. Mann, 'Gorbachev's first year: building power and authority', *Problems of Communism*, vol. 35 no. 3 (May–June 1986), pp. 1–19, at p. 16.
54. This and the following paragraph is based on F. Fukuyama, 'The Rise and Fall of the Marxist–Leninist Vanguard Party', *Survey*, vol. 29 no. 2 (Summer 1985), pp. 116–35; E.K. Valkenier, 'Revolutionary Change in the Third World: Recent Soviet Reassessments', *World Politics*, vol. 38 no. 3 (April 1986), pp. 415–34; E. K. Valkenier, 'The USSR and the Third World: Economic Dilemmas', in Laird and Hoffmann (eds), *Soviet Foreign Policy*, pp. 731–57; and Hough, *The Struggle for the Thrid World*, esp. pp. 259–61.
55. Fukuyama, 'The Rise and Fall', p. 116.
56. Gorbachev, 'Politicheskii doklad', p.2.
57. See 'Programma', p. 3.
58. 'Politicheskii doklad', p. 10.
59. Ibid., p. 5.
60. Ibid., p. 2.
61. 'O zhurnale "Kommunist". Postanovlenie TsK KPSS', *Kommunist*, no. 12 (August) 1986, pp. 3–10, esp. pp. 5, 10.
62. See V. Kulikov, 'Protivorechiya ekonomicheskoi sistemy sotsializma kak istochnik ee razvitiya', *Voprosy ekonomiki*, no. 1, 1986, pp. 117–28; and N. Shekhet, 'Protivorechiya planomernosti i puti ikh razresheniya', *Voprosy ekonomiki*, no. 6, 1986, pp. 63–73. This discussion is continuing.
63. See the Meeting Report of a talk by J. F. Hough on 'Recent transformations in Soviet Ideology' at the Kennan Institute for Advanced Russian Studies, Washington DC, on 9 April 1986.
64. For a discussion of policy ambiguity under Gorbachev, see Gustafson and Mann, 'Gorbachev's first year', pp. 16–17.
65. 'S"ezd strategicheskikh reshenii', *Kommunist*, no. 5, 1986, pp. 6–7.

66. See E. Hoffmann and R. F. Laird, *Technocratic Socialism: The Soviet Union in the Advanced Industrial Era* (Durham N. C: Duke University Press, 1985), esp. p. 19.
67. The metaphor is Therborn's, cited in R. Taras, *Ideology in a Socialist State. Poland 1956–83* (Cambridge University Press, 1984), p. 255.

Index